*U*NDERSTANDING
Learning
Styles
in the
Second Language
Classroom

Other Prentice Hall Regents books by
JOY M. REID

Basic Writing *Second Edition*
The Process of Paragraph Writing *Second Edition*
The Process of Composition *Second Edition*
Teaching ESL Writing

UNDERSTANDING

Learning

Styles

in the

Second

Language

Classroom

Edited by

Joy M. Reid
University of Wyoming

PRENTICE HALL REGENTS
A VIACOM COMPANY
Upper Saddle River, NJ 07458

Library of Congress Cataloging-in-Publication Data
Understanding learning styles in the second language classroom /
   edited by Joy M. Reid.
      p. cm.
   Includes bibliographical references.
   ISBN 0-13-281636-9 (alk. paper)
   1. English language–Study and teaching–Foreign speakers.
   2. Second language acquisition. 3. Individualized instruction.
   4. Study skills. I. Reid, Joy M.
   PE1128.A2U52   1998
   428'.007–dc21   97–25281
                                                                CIP

Publisher: Mary Jane Peluso
Acquisitions Editor: Sheryl Olinsky
Development Editor: Janet Johnston

Electronic Production Editor/Interior Designer: Noël Vreeland Carter
Manufacturing Manager: Ray Keating
Art Director: Merle Krumper

Cover Designer: Merle Krumper
Electronic Art: Noël Vreeland Carter, Carey Davies
Art Production/Scanning: Steven D. Greydanus

Printed in the United States of America
10 9 8 7 6 5 4 3 2

0-13-281636-9

Prentice-Hall International (UK) Limited, *London*
Prentice-Hall of Australia Pty. Limited, *Sydney*
Prentice-Hall of Canada Inc. *Toronto*
Prentice-Hall Hispanoamericana, S.A., *Mexico*
Prentice-Hall of India Private Limited, *New Delhi*
Prentice-Hall of Japan, Inc. *Tokyo*
Pearson Education Asia Pte. Ltd., *Singapore*
Editora Prentice-Hall do Brasil, Ltda., *Rio de Janeiro*

Contents

Theory and Practice

Practice and Theory

Appendices

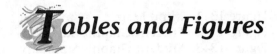

Tables and Figures

Tables

Figures

Preface

The terms "learner- (or student-) centered classroom" and "teacher-centered classroom" have been placed at opposite ends of a continuum in many current teacher preparation programs for ESL/EFL teachers. According to some definitions, in teacher-centered classrooms the teacher selects, teaches, and assigns material, and the students learn; in a learner-centered classroom the students are (more or less) decision-makers in the choice of tasks, materials, and learning. This anthology takes the middle road; the authors believe that in an effective classroom, everyone—teacher and students—learns, and that learning about learning (and teaching) styles is essential in order that all students have equal opportunities to use their strengths to learn.

Learning styles have been recognized widely in U.S. elementary school classrooms for more than a decade; teacher preparation programs in schools of education have included learning styles training in their curricula for nearly as long. In the 1990s, ESL teachers have begun to investigate the applications of learning styles in their multicultural classrooms. This anthology presents sixteen articles from ESL/EFL teacher-researchers whose work with learning styles has been substantial and who represent the breadth and variety in this area. We hope that this volume will allow teachers to "examine their best teaching techniques and strategies in light of human differences" (Christison 1996a, p. 10),* and, as did the editors of the *TESOL Journal* special issue on learning styles (1996), that this book will "help our students find out more about their uniqueness as language learners" (Ely and Pease-Alvarez 1996, p. 5) so that they can become fully empowered learners.

Definitions

Learning styles are internally based characteristics, often not perceived or consciously used by learners, for the intake and comprehension of new information. In general, students retain these preferred learning styles despite the teaching styles and classroom atmospheres they encounter, although the students may, over time, acquire additional styles. Research indicates that highly successful students often have multistyle preferences, and some research suggests that students adapt their learning styles with experimentation and practice.

In contrast, **learning strategies** are external skills often used consciously by students to improve their learning. Examples include metacognitive strategies such as self-monitoring and self-evaluation; cognitive strategies such as note-taking and inferencing; and social/affective strategies such as clarification questions and cooperative work. Rebecca Oxford's seminal book *Language Learning Strategies:*

---

* Citations for in-text references in this volume are listed in the References section at the back of the book.

What Every Teacher Should Know (1990) and her normed Strategy Inventory for Language Learning (SILL) provide teachers and students with practical and applicable strategy identification and training approaches.

Learning Style Terms

Table 1 is an overview of the learning styles discussed in this anthology, with a brief definition of each. More specific detail of each style will be given in the individual chapters. Notice that many of the terms are related in their definitions.

Table 1 Overview of Some Learning Styles

The Seven Multiple Intelligences

Verbal/Linguistic	ability with and sensitivity to oral and written words
Musical	sensitivity to rhythm, pitch, and melody
Logical/Mathematical	ability to use numbers effectively and to reason well
Spatial/Visual	sensitivity to form, space, color, line, and shape
Bodily/Kinesthetic	ability to use the body to express ideas and feelings
Interpersonal	ability to understand another person's moods and intentions
Intrapersonal	ability to understand oneself: one's own strengths and weaknesses

Perceptual Learning Styles

Visual	learns more effectively through the eyes (seeing)
Auditory	learns more effectively through the ear (hearing)
Tactile	learns more effectively through touch (hands-on)
Kinesthetic	learns more effectively through complete body experience
Group	learns more effectively through working with others
Individual	learns more effectively through working alone

Field Independent and Field Dependent (Sensitive) Learning Styles

Field Independent	learns more effectively sequentially, analyzing facts
Field Dependent	learns more effectively in context (holistically) and is sensitive to human relationships

Analytic and Global Learning Styles

Analytic	learns more effectively individually, sequentially, linearly
Global	learns more effectively through concrete experience and through interaction with other people

Reflective and Impulsive Learning Styles

Reflective	learns more effectively when given time to consider options
Impulsive	learns more effectively when able to respond immediately

Kolb Experiential Learning Model

Converger	learns more effectively when able to perceive abstractly and to process actively
Diverger	learns more effectively when able to perceive concretely and to process reflectively
Assimilator	learns more effectively when able to perceive abstractly and to process reflectively
Accommodator	learns more effectively when able to perceive concretely and to process actively

Myers-Briggs Type Indicator (MBTI)

Extraversion–Introversion

Extraverted	learns more effectively through concrete experience, contacts with and relationships with others
Introverted	learns more effectively in individual, independent learning situations

Sensing–Perception

Sensing	learns more effectively from reports of observable facts
Intuition	learns more effectively from meaningful experiences

Thinking–Feeling

Thinking	learns more effectively from impersonal and logical circumstances
Feeling	learns more effectively from personalized circumstances

Judging–Perceiving

Judging	learns more effectively by reflection, deduction, analysis, and processes that involve closure
Perceiving	learns more effectively through negotiation, feeling, and inductive processes that postpone closure

Right- and Left-Brained Learning Styles

Right-Brained	learns more effectively through visual, analytic, reflective, self-reliant learning
Left-Brained	learns more effectively through auditory, global, impulsive, interactive learning

For more complete information about these learning styles, see Reid (1995) and Christison (1996a)

Learning Style Issues

The most substantial problem for teachers interested in using a learning styles approach in their classrooms is that the "field" of learning styles is so fragmented. Researchers have regularly identified aspects of learning and created new terms and instruments, which is no doubt an indication of the complexity of the learning process. As others build on and modify that seminal research, the "field" becomes wider and less focused; consquently, the results of the research are more confusing for teachers and students to apply. Optimists hope that eventually much of the most valid and reliable learning style research will converge, making possible student "profiles" that are easily identifiable. It is probable, however, that even if student profiles became commonplace, the risks would be high. Students might be stereotyped, or students might pigeonhole themselves, thus limiting their learning potential and success. Profiles might change over time and in different learning situations, but not be identified, or students might be mis-profiled.

So teachers must approach learning styles with some caution; they are not a panacea. Rather, becoming aware of learning and teaching styles can better prepare teachers for the multicultural classroom (as well as for more homogenous classes, whose students' preferred styles will also almost certainly differ). In addition, raising student awareness to the advantages and disadvantages of learning styles instruments will make students not only more prepared for learning but also more analytic about learning styles.

Another problem facing teachers is the difficulty of being all things to all students. If, for example, we expect teachers to teach to the styles of every student in every learning situation, we will certainly be disappointed. One solution, to "match" teacher and student styles, seems impossible, not only because of the administrative nightmares involved but also because part of preparing students to be effective, life-long learners is to expose them to a variety of educational situations. Instead, we should be raising learning styles awareness in both teachers and students, asking teachers to develop teaching techniques that address the broad needs of most learners, and teaching students to experiment with extending their preferred styles.

A third controversy surrounding ESL/EFL students and classes is the issue of cultural learning style differences and differences in educational values (Nelson 1995). Specifically, teachers must become sensitive to the difference between identifying *typical* behavior and preferences and overgeneralizing trends into *stereotyping* students according to widely held sociocultural assumptions. After all, within a cultural group, variations among individuals are often as great as their commonalities. Nevertheless, tendencies in classroom behavior, which are culturally based, are often identifiable in groups of students. For example, Japanese EFL students have been described as group-oriented, focused on consensual decision-making, reserved, formal, and cautious; these characteristics are stressed even in Japanese pre-schools (Anderson 1995; Lewis 1991; Peak 1991). The characteristics valued by North Americans—self-reliance, frankness, informality, spontaneity, and talkativeness (Barlund 1975)—seem in direct contrast.

Yet we all know U.S. students who are reserved planners, who interact with difficulty in the classroom, or who prefer cooperation and harmony to conflict and confrontation. And we know Japanese students who are gregarious and self-confident, direct and decisive, who enjoy arguing more than consensus-building. To counter our human tendency to classify and stereotype, we teachers must see our students as individuals; we should use self-reporting instruments (surveys) as well as other data, such as having students write about or discuss their learning styles, interviewing each student, and observing student behavior in the classroom, to assist our students in identifying their learning styles. Further, we must view each learning style as occurring on a continuum: learners are *more* or *less* field dependent, visual, reflective, or tolerant of ambiguity.

We must also note that educational systems value different learning styles. In U.S. colleges and universities, successful students are often outspoken, independent individuals who think analytically, react objectively and accurately, use trial-and-error methods of learning, and take standardized tests well; these tests are, of course, reflections of the educational values. Effective students often participate in class (especially by asking and answering questions and by entering into verbal class discussion), and articulate, and support, individual opinions. As J. S. Condon (1984, p. 9) notes, "So many of the values Americans hold dear—equality, democracy, freedom, privacy, and even progress—are bound up with the American view of individualism."

Other cultures value different learning characteristics. Many Asian classroom teachers, for instance, find class "participation" discourteous. Individualism, sometimes labeled "creativity," which is prized highly by the U.S. educational system, contravenes the harmony and collective wisdom so highly valued by Asian educators. Korean educators, and so their students, value structured, formal lessons; Korean students are highly competitive and individual (Park 1995), but they do not "participate" in class individually because taking the teacher's time away from important information, and taking up their classmates' time with something they may not consider important, is rude. In contrast, many Hispanic educators may value cooperation far more than competition in the classroom. Consequently, predominantly Hispanic classes in the United States often function most successfully if the students are able to communicate with one another continually (even noisily at times) and to collaborate on work (perhaps even on tests) (Dunn and Griggs 1995). And in Navajo culture, observing, reflecting, cognitive rehearsal, and understanding precede performance (Ramasamy 1996).

Despite the many potential barriers to implementing knowledge of individual learning styles in the ESL/EFL classroom, raising student awareness of learning styles and strategies can illuminate learning. Moreover, students can comprehend (and are generally fascinated by) how learning processes occur, what choices they have in these processes, and how they can identify their learning strengths and weaknesses.

Learning Styles Instruments

Understanding learning patterns is a complex task, and the scope of the diagnostic tools used imposes limits on the teacher and the learner. That is, not all instruments are helpful, and some students may find some instruments more valuable than others. If we are to give our students the firmest foundation for identifying style preferences, for practicing and experimenting with style preferences, and for analyzing the results of using those preferences, we must look closely at the instruments we use.

First, assessment instruments must be interpreted in light of the reliability and the validity of the instrument. Has the instrument (survey, interview, observation form) been normed for the target population? Does it measure what it professes to measure? Have the results of the instrument been replicated in similar circumstances with a similar target audience? Or is the instrument targeted, for instance, at native speakers of English, or at ESL/EFL students with a different level of language proficiency, or at a different age group? Particularly for ESL/EFL students, has the instrument been carefully designed for access by second-language learners? After all, self-reporting instruments are language- and culture-specific: as learners complete the instrument, they interpret words through their cultural experiences. If an instrument has been created without adequate consideration of the audience and purpose, the results are not generalizable, even for the individual student. Even though students might find the information interesting, if the information is incorrect, it might distort students' views of learning and of learning styles.

At the very least, students and teacher should be clear about the strength of the assessment instrument. In this anthology, the instruments provided in the Appendices have been designed for ESL/EFL students at the intermediate level and above. Although some of the instruments may prove more valuable than others for individual students and teachers, each of them has provided information for many ESL/EFL classrooms. These instruments are available for informal use by teachers in their classrooms. For formal or large-scale research, however, the authors of the learning styles instruments should be contacted for permission to use the surveys. Contact information and biodata for the authors are listed in the Contributors section of this book; reader responses to and suggestions about the individual chapters should also be sent directly to the authors, who will appreciate and value the feedback.

Conclusion

Several fundamentals of learning styles are discussed in this volume:

- Every person has one or more learning styles, learning strengths, and learning weaknesses.
- Learning styles are a result of both nature and nurture.
- Learning styles exist on wide continuums.
- Learning styles are value-neutral.
- Often, students' strategies are linked to their learning styles.

In addition, chapter authors demonstrate how to implement their knowledge of learning styles in the ESL/EFL classroom.

A broad understanding of learning environments and learning styles will enable students to take control of their learning and to maximize their potential for learning. And a teacher who truly understands culture and learning styles, and who believes that all students can learn, will offer opportunities for success to all students (Guild 1994). The result will be educated students who are able to participate fully in society, both freely and responsibly.

Joy Reid

Understanding
Learning
Styles
in the
Second Language
Classroom

Chapter 1

An Introduction to Multiple Intelligence Theory and Second Language Learning

Mary Ann Christison
Snow College

Howard Gardner begins *Frames of Mind* (1983), his seminal work on Multiple Intelligences, in the following way:

> A young girl spends an hour with an examiner. She is asked a number of questions that probe her store of information (Who discovered America? What does the stomach do?), her vocabulary (What does *nonsense* mean? What does *belfry* mean?), her arithmetic skills (At eight cents each, how much will three candy bars cost?), her ability to remember a series of numbers (5, 1, 7, 4, 2, 3, 8), her capacity to grasp the similarity between two elements (elbow and knee, mountain and lake). She may also be asked to carry out certain other tasks—for example, solving a maze or arranging a group of pictures in such a way that they relate a complete story. Some time afterward, the examiner scores the responses and comes up with a single number—the girl's intelligence quotient, or IQ. This number (which the little girl may actually be told) is likely to exert appreciable effect upon her future, influencing the way in which her teachers think of her and determining her eligibility for certain privileges [p. 1].

Having been an educator for more than two decades, I have often witnessed this labeling that Gardner mentions. Many bright, intelligent children have been limited by IQ tests. Gardner created his theory of Multiple Intelligences (MI) in response to this state of affairs; he challenged the classical view of intelligence. Gardner believed that traditional methods for assessing the intellect were not sufficiently well honed to allow assessment of the wider range of intelligent behavior. In order to understand the importance of Multiple Intelligences as an important psychological theory, it is important to consider some facts about theory, research, and methodology in psychology that laid the groundwork for Gardner's theory of intelligence.

Background

Probably no aspect of contemporary psychology is more misunderstood by the general public than intelligence. We seem to be awed by our perception of intelligence in others. It has a profound effect on social status, educational opportunities, and career choices. Yet, despite all the importance attached to intelligence, most of us seem unable to define exactly what intelligence is. There is no objective agreed-upon referent.

Debates on various aspects of intelligence are often in the news. Consider the following story carried by the *Los Angeles Times.*

> Becky Swanston frequently taps out notes on a pure pitch xylophone for her daughter Kelly, age 9 1/2 months, and plays classical music for her "all the time." . . . Melenie Petropolous shows oversized flashcards to her son Tommy, age 3, with bits of information ranging from the names of different birds to the parts of a plant. . . . Karen Barer flashes cards with words, shapes and colors at her son Nicholas, who will be 3 in June and who can count to 10 and identify shapes and colors. . . . The three mothers are among the graduates of a $490, week-long course offered by a Philadelphia organization called the Better Baby Institute entitled "How to Multiple Your Baby's Intelligence" designed to teach parents how to make their infants, toddlers, and preschoolers smarter [*Los Angeles Times*, May 1, 1993].

This story, as you might guess, provoked impassioned debate among parents and citizens.

In addition, Marilyn Vos Savant is also in the news regularly. Vos Savant is the individual with the world's highest recorded score on an IQ test. She is often referred to as the most intelligent person in the world, and she writes a weekly syndicated column for many newspapers and magazines called "Ask Marilyn." If you ask the general public how they know that Marilyn is intelligent or what characteristics she exhibits that make her intelligent, they might not be able to tell you. But whatever intelligence means, Vos Savant is regarded for having lots of it. The general public seems very quick to adopt the theory that intelligence is what intelligence tests measure (Kail and Pellegrino 1985).

But the general public is not the only group with different opinions about intelligence. The debate among psychologists about a definition of intelligence emanates from the fact that psychologists themselves talk about intelligence in two different ways. The first is to use intelligence to refer to intelligent **acts**, such as writing a book or designing a new computer. The second way is to use intelligence to refer to mental **processes** that give rise to intelligent acts, such as the mental abilities that underlie intelligent acts (such as inferring, analyzing, reasoning, or deducing). One view says that, for example, Mozart was born with a specific talent to write his music, and the other extreme says that it was an accident of time and place, and that anyone could have written what Mozart wrote. Neither extreme view is very attractive. In fact, most psychologists take an intermediate view, stating that some finite set of multiple processes gives rise to a full range of intelligent human activities. Much of the work on mental processes has been to bridge the gap between these intelligent acts and processes.

In general, there are three different psychological perspectives on intelligence. The first is the psychometric tradition (Binet and Simon 1908; Cattell 1963). This tradition represents the branch of psychology that has been concerned primarily with developing tests to measure intelligence. The next view of intelligence is the information-processing perspective (Norman and Rumelhart 1975). It is an outgrowth of experimental psychology and provides descriptions of theories and mental activities that compose intelligence. The third traditional view of intelligence comes from cognitive developmental psychology and is associated with the work of Jean Piaget (1926, 1950, 1952), which investigated intellectual development. Several commonalties exist among these three perspectives. First, all three perspectives are concerned with knowledge, skills, and activities. In fact, all psychometric theories and tests of intelligence are based solely upon the products of reasoning and problem-solving tasks. Another commonality is that adaptability is considered an important component of intelligence. Measured intellectual skill depends on one's success in dealing with novel stimuli and tasks, not with familiar ones.

Each of the perspectives also has shortcomings. Most theories developed from a psychometric perspective do not focus on the processes of problem-solving or on how different cognitive factors and skills interact and interrelate (Guilford 1982). In the information-processing perspective, research involves a sampling of the knowledge and processes as reflected in a specific task that is almost always created to meet the needs of testing a theory or model. In other words, broad principles and theories of cognitive change are not recognized; moreover, there is a tendency to ignore differences among individuals and to focus instead on data from groups of individuals who have completed a specific task. The cognitive-developmental tradition focuses primarily on tasks that can be related to the emergence of a reasoning skill. By analyzing the components of different reasoning tasks, hypotheses are derived from the products, not the processes, of reasoning.

The Theory of Multiple Intelligences

In response to some of these shortcomings on intelligence theory, psychologists formulated eclectic theories of intelligence theories that cut across the traditional boundaries of the psychometric, cognitive, and developmental approaches (Gardner 1983; Sternberg 1977, 1984). Eclectic theories draw upon the assets of the distinct approaches to create a much broader perspective on intelligence (Kail and Pellegrino 1985, p. 159). One of these is Howard Gardner's theory of MI (Gardner 1983). In many ways, Gardner's theory is not far from the traditional view of intelligence in arguing that

> a human intellectual competence must entail a set of skills of problem solving—enabling the individual to resolve genuine problems or difficulties that he or she encounters and when appropriate, to create an effective product, and must also entail the potential for finding or creating problems—thereby laying the groundwork for the acquisition of new knowledge [1983, p. 62].

The scope of Gardner's work differs in the way he establishes seven distinct intelligences that can be developed over a lifetime. According to Gardner, intelligence is not a single construct, nor is it considered static. Gardner's MI theory is very important to ESL/EFL teachers because we work with such diverse learners. Through MI theory, we can nurture intelligences in many different ways. MI theory helps educators create an individualized learning environment. Table 1–1 is my thumbnail sketch of how Gardner conceived these intelligences.

Table 1–1. Gardner's Seven Intelligences

Verbal/Linguistic Intelligence

The ability to use words effectively, both orally and in writing. Sample skills are remembering information, convincing others to help, and talking about language itself.

Musical Intelligence

Sensitivity to rhythm, pitch, and melody. Sample skills are recognizing simple songs and being able to vary speed, tempo, and rhythm in simple melodies.

Logical/Mathematical Intelligence

The ability to use numbers effectively and reason well. Sample skills are understanding the basic properties of numbers, the principles of cause and effect, and the ability to predict.

Spatial/Visual Intelligence

Sensitivity to form, space, color, line, and shape. Sample skills include the ability to represent visual or spatial ideas graphically.

Bodily/Kinesthetic Intelligence

The ability to use the body to express ideas and feelings, and to solve problems. Sample skills are coordination, flexibility, speed, and balance.

Interpersonal Intelligence

The ability to understand another person's moods, feelings, motivations, and intentions. Sample skills are responding effectively to other people, problem solving, and resolving conflict.

Intrapersonal Intelligence

The ability to understand yourself, your strengths, weaknesses, moods, desires, and intentions. Sample skills are understanding how one is similar to or different from others, reminding oneself to do something, knowing about oneself as a language learner, and knowing how to handle one's feelings.[*]

Source: Christison 1996a, p. 11

Gardner (1983, p. 62) proposes "signs" that can be used to identify distinct intelligences.

1. *Isolation by brain damage.* Often injury to the brain results in the loss of a specific intellectual skill. Assuming that there are brain structures for each intelligence, brain lesions can impair one intelligence while leaving all the others intact.

---

[*] Gardner has since added an eighth intelligence called Naturalist. Naturalist intelligence is the ability to recognize species of plants or animals in one's environment.

2. *The existence of individuals with exceptional talent.* Some individuals are truly extraordinarily skilled in one intellectual domain but ordinarily skilled—or even retarded—in most other domains. Idiot savants, for example, are retarded persons who have one extraordinarily well developed talent, often in the areas of musical or numeric ability (Hill 1978). Such selective competence suggests autonomy of that particular competence.

3. *A distinct developmental history.* If an intelligence is autonomous, it should develop in a distinct manner and in much the same way in all people. Intelligence should have a time of beginning in early childhood and a time of peaking during one's lifetime. For example, most accomplished musicians show evidence of a well-developed musical intelligence at a young age. The developmental history is very different for Linguistic Intelligence; linguistic skills tend to peak much later in one's life.

4. *An evolutionary history.* Intellectual skills emerge as individuals age; they also have emerged as the human species has evolved. Each intelligence has its roots deeply embedded in the evolution of human beings. We find written notations in early cultures demonstrating the presence of linguistic intelligence. We also find early tool use showing bodily-kinesthetic intelligence.

5. *An identifiable set of core operations.* Each intelligence should have a distinct mental operation (or set of operations) that is the core of that intelligence. The intelligence may involve other mental operations, but they are secondary to the core process. For example, in musical intelligence, the core operations may be the ability to discriminate among different musical notes and among various rhythmic structures. An example of a secondary process would be that many composers are pianists and use the piano as they compose, but skill at the piano is only an adjunct skill for composers and is not at the core of musical composition.

6. *Experimental evidence.* Independence of intelligence can be demonstrated empirically. In one approach used in laboratory research, individuals perform two tasks simultaneously. In cases where the two tasks are difficult to perform concurrently—such as trying to write and listen to speech—the conclusion is that the two tasks require different skills. Independence of intelligences is implicated when such interference between tasks is minimal.

7. *Encoding in a symbol system.* Symbols such as words and pictures are fundamental to communication and thought in all human cultures. This universal human proclivity to use symbols leads to Gardner's final sign of an intelligence. Specifically, he suggests that "while it may be possible for an intelligence to proceed without its own special symbol system . . . a primary characteristic of human intelligence may well be its 'natural' gravitation toward embodiment in a symbolic system" (1983, p. 66) such as written language, mathematics symbols, and picturing.

8. *The existence of an intelligence may be supported by psychometric findings.* Gardner is no champion of standardized testing, but he does suggest that we can look at standardized tests for support of the theory of Multiple Intelligences. In the Wechsler Intelligence Scale, for example, children are

asked questions that require linguistic intelligence (such as vocabulary), logical-mathematical intelligence (e.g., arithmetic), and spatial intelligence (such as picture arrangement), and students test either high or low in each.

Gardner explains that the above are signs rather than exact criteria. Yet he believes that an intelligence should exhibit several (although perhaps not all) of those qualities. The signs act collectively as a screening device. Of the seven intelligences suggested by Gardner, verbal and mathematical skills are considered by many teachers to be central to intelligence—and indeed they do exhibit most of Gardner's signs—and musical and interpersonal intelligence may be seen as peripheral. Let's review the evidence that Gardner has marshaled for musical intelligence to demonstrate how he made his selections.

Support for Musical Intelligence

1. *Isolation by brain damage.* Gardner (1982) reviewed several fascinating case studies of brain-damaged patients in order to attest to the independence of musical intelligence. One case study involved the Russian composer Shebalin. Shebalin was afflicted with a brain injury, Wernicke's aphasia, the results of which left him verbally fluent with impaired comprehension. Nevertheless, Shebalin's ability to understand and compose music remained entirely intact.

2. *The existence of individuals with exceptional talent.* There have been many musical prodigies. Undoubtedly the best-known is Mozart, whose talent as both composer and performer was evident in early childhood. Less widely known are the idiot savants, whose mental retardation is often accompanied by inexplicable intelligence. Many idiot savants, for example, have the ability to play a musical tune correctly after hearing it only once, and do so without any formal musical training (Shuter-Dyson 1982).

3. *A distinct developmental history.* For most children living in Western cultures, musical ability develops little after the preschool years. Individuals learn more songs and sing them with greater precision and feeling, but there do not seem to be further qualitative changes of the Piagetian variety (Dowling 1982). Although children with musical talent demonstrate a different developmental pattern, they nevertheless demonstrate a pattern.

4. *An identifiable set of core operations.* Understanding music involves a set of core operations. The key components of music are **pitch,** the highness or lowness of sound; **rhythm,** the grouping of successive pitches; and **timbre,** the quality of a tone. All of these are essential factors in recognizing a piece of music.

5. *The existence of an intelligence may be supported by psychometric findings.* Although not mentioned by Gardner, some evidence from psychometric studies supports this view of musical intelligence. A number of tests of musical aptitude are available that assess perception of and memory of pitch and sensitivity to rhythm, and so on (Shuter-Dyson 1982). Musical aptitude is essentially uncorrelated with tests that measure general intelligence in individuals with IQ scores of roughly 90 or higher.

Understanding How MI Theory Applies to Teaching

MI has great potential for helping to revolutionize our concept of student language-learning capabilities in the ESL classroom. As language teachers, we know that our students learn differently. MI theory can help us develop language-learning materials to address these differences. Thomas Armstrong (1994) believes that before we can apply any model of learning in the classroom, we should apply it to ourselves as educators. Therefore, the first step in using MI theory is to determine our own Multiple Intelligence profile. If you have not taken an MI inventory recently, I encourage you to take the short inventory in Appendix 1 before you go further. The purpose of the Inventory is to connect your life's experiences to your concept of Multiple Intelligences.

MI theory offers ESL/EFL teachers a way to examine their best teaching techniques and strategies in light of human differences. The language-learning activities we choose as teachers are often directly related to the totality of our experiences, which, in turn, affect the Multiple Intelligence profiles of our students. Therefore, as we learn more about our own profile, we become more confident in the choices we make that affect our teaching. In order to understand how MI theory applies to TESL/TEFL, we must first identify the activities that we frequently use in our classes and categorize them. Which ones help develop verbal/linguistic intelligence? musical intelligence? logical/mathematical intelligence? Table 1–2 lists activities that address multiple intelligences in the classroom.

Table 1–2. Taxonomy of Language-Learning Activities for Multiple Intelligences

---

Linguistic Intelligence

lectures	student speeches
small and large group discussions	story-telling
books	debates
worksheets	journal keeping
word games	memorizing
listening to cassettes or talking books	using word processors
publishing (creating class newspapers or collections of writing)	

Logical/Mathematical Intelligence

scientific demonstrations	creating codes
logic problems and puzzles	story problems
science thinking	calculations
logical-sequential presentation of subject matter	

Spatial Intelligence

charts, maps, diagrams	visualization
videos, slides, movies	photography
art and other pictures	using mind maps
imaginative storytelling	painting or collage
graphic organizers	optical illusions
telescopes, microscopes	student drawings
visual awareness activities	

Bodily/Kinesthetic Intelligence

creative movement   hands-on activities
Mother-may-I?   field trips
cooking and other "mess" activities   mime
role plays

Musical Intelligence

playing recorded music   singing
playing live music (piano, guitar)   group singing
music appreciation   mood music
student-made instruments   Jazz Chants

Interpersonal Intelligence

cooperative groups   conflict mediation
peer teaching   board games
group brainstorming   pair work

Intrapersonal Intelligence

independent student work   reflective learning
individualized projects   journal keeping
options for homework   interest centers
inventories and checklists   self-esteem journals
personal journal keeping   goal setting
self-teaching/programmed instruction

The next step is to track what we are doing in our lesson planning and teaching. What activities do you do in your language classroom? How are you addressing multiple intelligences in your lesson planning? You might consider using a checklist (see Table 1–3) for at least a week.

Then analyze your teaching according to the different intelligences that you have used throughout the week. You can make a check mark or make brief notes in the boxes and tabulate your results. The analysis can be used to expand your teaching to include more and varied activities to address the different intelligences, and/or it can be used to come to a fuller awareness of your own teaching and how MI theory informs teaching and learning.

Table 1–3. TESL/TEFL Multiple Intelligences
Weekly Checklist

Course Title _____

From _____ *To* _____

	Monday	Tuesday	Wednesday	Thursday	Friday
Linguistic/Verbal					
Musical					
Logical					
Spatial/Visual					
Kinesthetic					
Interpersonal					
Intrapersonal					

Teaching Students About Multiple Intelligences

Recent research supports the idea that learners benefit from instructional approaches that help them reflect on their own learning (Marzano et al. 1988; Nunan, this volume). The more awareness students have of their own intelligences and how they work, the more they will know how to use that intelligence to access the necessary information and knowledge from a lesson (Christison 1996b). I suggest using MI inventories with students in order to help them connect their daily activities to MI theory. The sample inventory that appears in Appendix 2 was actually created by my students. It comprises statements my students wrote in response to the question "How do you use the seven intelligences in your daily lives?" Over time, I collected these statements and eventually created a survey from the most frequently appearing responses.

It has been my experience that the inventory is best used in sections, one intelligence at a time. Using the entire inventory is generally too much for language learners. If you feature one intelligence during the week, you can begin the week's lessons with the inventory. The students can work independently on one section of the list and then share with partners. The students always talk with animation during the sharing period; they are eager to learn from each other and to share their discoveries. As a follow-up to the inventory activity, you might ask students to create a bulletin board identifying the classroom activities for the week that support the intelligence being focused upon. This is yet another way of helping the students relate MI theory to their daily lives.

In Christison 1996a and 1997, I present a variety of activities that can be used to teach English language learners about MI theory. Perhaps one of the most popular ways comes from a suggestion offered by Armstrong (1994) called "The Intelligence Pizza." He begins by telling students that they are all smart and asks them to tell him some of the different ways they can be smart. As students respond, he writes their answers on the seven slices of "pizza" in a circle. Armstrong accepts all answers but includes only the seven "smarts" (as he refers to the intelligences). For my version of Armstrong's pizza, see Figure 1-1.

The "smarts" according to Armstrong are self-smart, word smart, logic smart, people smart, music smart, body smart, and picture smart. This approach uses language and concepts students understand plus visual reinforcement. Once students understand the different ways they can be "smart," they can take their own MI inventory and begin evaluating their own learning activities.

Figure 1–1. Teaching Students About the Seven Intelligences

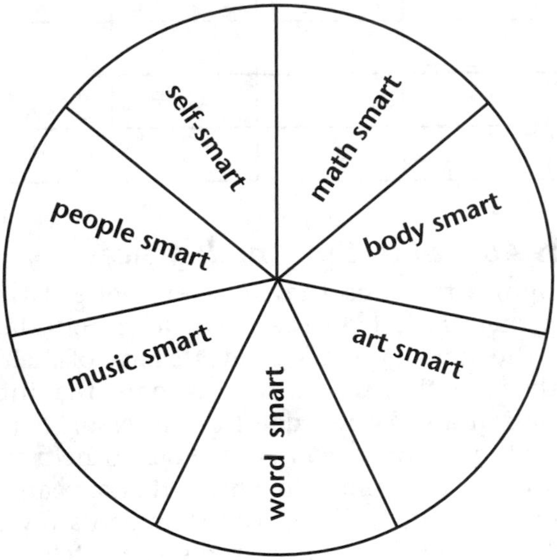

Creating Lesson Plans

Stages of Development in Lesson Planning

There are four stages to lessons that teach with multiple intelligences. The developmental sequence (Lazear 1991) is as follows:

Stage 1: *Awaken the Intelligence.* A particular intelligence can be activated or triggered through exercises and activities that make use of sensory bases (the five senses), intuition, or metacognition. For example, if you are teaching low-level ESL students how to use words to describe things, you might bring many different items to class. Ask your students to experience these words; they can touch something soft, rough, cold, or smooth, or taste something sweet, salty, sour, or spicy. An intelligence can be activated through activities that use the sensory bases.

Stage 2: *Amplify the Intelligence.* This part of the lesson focuses on improving and strengthening the intelligence. Like any skill, intelligences improve with use and practice. As a follow-up to the first part of the lesson, you might ask students to bring an object to class or to use something in their possession. Ask them to describe each object, using the five senses (sight, touch, taste, sound, and smell); see Table 1-4. In addition, ask the students to talk about the size and what it is used for (Bassano and Christison 1995a & b, pp. 31, 97).

Table 1–4. The Sensory Handout

Name of team _____

Team members _____

Sight	
Sound	
Feel	
Smell	
Size	
What it's used for	
Name of the object	

Stage 3: *Teach for/with the Intelligence.* Structure lessons for multiple intelligences, emphasizing and using different intelligences in the teaching/learning process. In this stage of the lesson, you might put your students into small groups. Give them a worksheet such as the one that appears in Table 1-5.

Stage 4: *Transfer of the Intelligence.* This stage is concerned with going beyond the classroom, with the integration of intelligence into daily living, such as solving problems and challenges in the real world. David Lazear (1994) suggests asking students some reflective questions about the lesson.

- What part of the lesson was the easiest?
- What did you learn about describing objects?
- What did you like the most in the lesson?
- What did you like about working with the group?
- What didn't you like about working with the group?
- Do you prefer to work with a group or alone?

Table 1–5. Multiple Intelligences Description Exercise
What am I describing?

Directions: Work with your group. Listen as the teacher reads the description of the object. Discuss what you hear with your group. Together, decide which object in the class is being described.

	Name of the object
Object 1	
Object 2	
Object 3	
Object 4	
Object 5	

Next, have each group describe an object in the classroom using the formula given in Stage 2. Then, collect the papers and read them, one at a time. Ask each group to work together to write down the name of the object in the classroom that you are describing.

According to Lazear, all of these stages need to be present in a lesson designed to emphasize the different ways of knowing, and he has developed model activities to illustrate what you can do at each of the four stages (1991, 1994). Christison (1996b, 1997) has applied Lazear's work and model activities to the ESL/EFL classroom. This particular lesson on describing objects has given students opportunities to develop their linguistic intelligence (for example, describing objects), logical intelligence (for example, determining which object is being described), visual/spatial intelligence (for example, determining how to describe things), interpersonal intelligence (for example, working in groups), and intrapersonal intelligence (for example, reflecting on one's involvement in the lesson).

Levels of Information Processing

Cognitive research in the last ten to fifteen years overwhelmingly supports the necessity and possibility of teaching students how to increase their skills of knowing, understanding, perceiving, and learning (Feurstein 1980; Gardner 1983). Lazear (1994) focuses on helping students continue to develop their intelligent behavior and their intellectual capacities throughout their lifetimes. To do this he suggests focusing on different levels of information processing. Research on metacognition (Costa 1984) documents four distinct levels of information processing, with each level becoming more metacognitively sophisticated than the previous one. Lazear suggests developing lessons around these different levels, thus helping students acquire "a full repertoire of intelligence tools and skills for dealing with the task of daily living beyond the classroom."

Level 1: *Tacit Intelligence.* This level involves helping students become aware of capacities and potentials that they generally take for granted. Every day they do intelligent things, but they take these acts for granted. Ask students to tell you what is involved in crossing a street, making a grocery list, or drawing a map to the school.

Level 2: *Aware Intelligence.* The aware level involves learning how each of the intelligences operates in one's own mind and body and evaluating one's own strengths and weaknesses. Ask students to complete an inventory and share the results with a classmate.

Level 3: *Strategic Intelligence.* The strategic level involves the conscious decision to employ the seven intelligences to enhance one's own learning, creativity, and problem-solving ability. Activities such as information-gap activities and cooperative problem-solving help students develop this intelligence.

Level 4: *Reflective Intelligence.* The reflective level involves integrating the seven ways of knowing into daily life. The seven intelligences broaden and deepen the knowledge base. Teachers might develop activities/ experiences such as asking students to keep an intelligence journal or having them create their own inventory.

Assessment

It is important to include assessment as well as language-learning activities when including MI theory in your lesson planning. What are your methods of assessment? Are your methods of assessment balanced for the different intelligences? Do you want them to be? What is the relationship between your language-learning activities and your methods of assessment? Armstrong (1994) suggests creating 49 assessment contexts. You might consider creating seven different generic assessments, one for each of the seven intelligences. For example, you might ask your students to read an article, a linguistic task. One method of assessment could include writing a response. In that case, you would have a linguistic task with a linguistic assessment. Or you might ask your students to read an article and

- draw a picture or a diagram that summarizes the article or describes one idea in the article (see Vann, this volume). In this case, you would be using a spatial assessment. If they then share it with a partner, students would be using interpersonal intelligence as a means of assessment.
- create a role-play and act it out—a bodily/kinesthetic assessment.
- write a short musical selection, combining different ideas from the article (musical assessment).
- analyze the article and extend the ideas to another domain, an excellent way to use logical/mathematical assessment.

It is not necessary to assess every activity in seven different ways, but it is important to offer several different options for assessment and allow students to choose from the two or three alternatives. When given this option, my students have come up with wonderful and creative ways to show what they know about the subject. For example, in an American Culture class I told the students they could take the traditional examination or they could figure out another way to show me what they knew about the information in the chapter. One group wrote a song; on the day of their presentation, a group member brought his guitar to class. First, the group sang the song for the class and then they taught the song to their classmates. Even though this activity happened more than a year ago, the students still remember the song, both the lyrics and the music.

Conclusion

Gardner's theory of Multiple Intelligences represents not only a sophisticated effort to bridge the gaps among the traditional approaches to intelligence but an adaptable framework for educational reform. George Miller (1983) wrote in evaluating Gardner's work, "For his attempt to integrate diverse approaches, Mr. Gardner deserves everyone's gratitude." English language teachers who work with learners from diverse linguistic backgrounds appreciate how well the theory applies to lessons and how it supports ESL students in the language-learning process.

D.H. Feldman (1980), Gardner (1993), and Walters and Gardner (1986) have developed and worked with the ideas of **crystallizing** and **paralyzing** experiences. These experiences are turning points in our lives; they cause us to develop intelligences. Crystallizing experiences move us closer to our goals, but paralyzing experiences have the opposite effect: they propel us to shut down an intelligence. As a language educator, I want my students to have crystallizing experiences. It seems logical that MI theory can help me do that. With the help of this theory, I can create activities that will be flexible, reflective, logical, and creative. I have tried in this chapter to introduce MI by showing its importance as a psychological theory of intelligence and also by showing its applicability to the language classroom. I hope the chapter has begun to open the door for you and that you will consider some of the ideas presented here in your lesson planning.

For Further Reading

Faculty of the New City School in St. Louis, Missouri. (1994). *Celebrating Multiple Intelligences: Teaching for Success*. St. Louis: The New City School.

> The authors of this book are all teachers, and the book is a collection of the best ideas and lesson plans that teachers in the New City School used during a five-year project using MI theory to design their curriculum. The book is very user-friendly. It is organized by intelligence and section (pre-primary, primary, and intermediate). Graphics are used so that the reader can peruse the pages by looking for lessons for a particular age level or for a particular intelligence.

Lazear, D. (1991). *Seven Ways of Teaching*. Palatine, IL: IRI/Skylight Training and Publishing.

> The author provides lesson plans and blackline masters for each of the seven intelligences. Although the lessons are not specifically for ESL, I have found them very easy to adapt. Lazear highlights four different stages in lesson planning and offers a vast array of visuals and graphic organizers to aid comprehension.

Chapter 2

Teachers as
Perceptual Learning Styles Researchers

Joy Reid
University of Wyoming

Manuel Vicente Mata Vicioso
Instituto de BUP " Franciso Tarrega," Villarreal de los Infantes,Castellón, Spain

Éva Gedeon, *ELTE English Department, Budapest, Hungary*

Katalin Takacs, *ELTE Center for English Teacher Training, Budapest, Hungary*

Zhanna Korotkikh, *Barnaul Pedagogical State Institute, Siberia, Russia*

Classroom teachers have always been researchers: they regularly reflect upon and interpret data such as test scores and student papers, lesson plans and student evaluations, class discussions and observations of student progress. Once they have gathered such information, they use those data to improve teaching and learning processes (Nunan 1990; Oxford 1997; Reid 1993; Richards 1996; Richards and Lockhart 1994; Wink 1993). Teachers assess the origins of the data, the purposes and consequences of their intentions, and, based on their interpretations, integrate their new knowledge into the classroom. This "acting upon" the information is the basis for "action research." Sometimes teachers share their action research with colleagues through conference presentations of published articles; more often, their research functions as individual professional development.

Since 1990, many teachers have become learning style researchers in their own classrooms (see Bruner and Majewski 1990; Christison and Bassano 1995; Dunn and Griggs 1995; Geisert and Dunn 1991; Kinsella 1995; Neely and Alm 1992; Oxford 1997; Tyacke 1996). Gathering background knowledge, administering various learning style surveys, and using those survey results, teacher-researchers raise student awareness about the existence of learning styles, refocus and expand their teaching styles, and help students experiment with "flexing" and extending their learning styles. In this chapter, the results of some teacher research with U. S. elementary and secondary school students are described. Then the chapter focuses on the use of one learning styles instrument, the Perceptual Learning Style Preference (PLSP)[*] survey, by English as a foreign language (EFL) teachers in four countries: Egypt, Spain, Hungary, and Russia (Siberia).

---

* For a copy of the PLSP survey, see Appendix 3.

Background

Teacher research has helped to describe the differences that exist between and among mainstream and minority group students in U. S. classrooms. Below are research scenarios from a few of the many formal studies of American students.

- Rita Dunn and a number of colleagues worked with a comprehensive model of learning "modalities" (styles), the Learning Styles Inventory (Dunn and Griggs 1988, 1995; Dunn, Dunn, and Price 1989; Dunn, Beaudry, and Klavas 1989). They found, for example, that "children taught with instructional resources that . . . matched their preferred modalities achieved statistically higher test scores" (Dunn, Beaudry, and Klavas 1989, p. 52); that except for gifted children, students in grades 3–8 learn better in small, well organized groups than either alone or with the teacher; and that males need more physical mobility than females in the classroom.

- Using the Gregorc Style Delineator, John Backes (1993) studied the differences in learning styles between Native American Chippewa (*Metis*) students in a Bureau of Indian Affairs/North Dakota Department of Instruction high school and non-Native American students in a Crookston, Minnesota, high school. He found significant differences between the two groups. While the non-Native American students preferred concrete/sequential learning (the inductive, linear patterns that dominate U. S. classrooms), the Native American students preferred deductive/holistic styles. They were open to sharing and community learning, indirect and reflective learning, and experiential learning.

- Jackie Hansen and Charles Stansfield (1981) administered the Group Embedded Figures Test (GEFT) to U. S. students studying Spanish as a second language to study the impact of field dependence/field independence on student success. They found that field-independent (that is, analytic) students do better on tests of grammatical accuracy, and that field-dependent (that is, global) students do not consistently perform better in communicative tasks, as might be expected.

- Shirley Griggs (1982, 1991) explored the roles and effectiveness of middle and high school counselors to make classrooms more humane and responsive to all students.

- R. L. S. Jacobs Sr. (1990) used several learning style instruments with African-American secondary school students and found that learning styles correlated with achievement levels. High achievers demonstrated a preference for structured classrooms and had multiple learning styles; average achievers preferred to learn through auditory, tactile, and kinesthetic modes; low achievers preferred "nonparental authority figures present while learning" (p. 262).

Like teachers in mainstream public school American classrooms, ESL teachers in U.S. schools have begun to research the learning styles of their students in order to improve the English language classroom learning environment (see Abraham 1985; Eliason 1995; Kroonenberg 1995; Oxford and Green 1995). A similar breadth of instruments and research scenarios follows, with the focus on data gathered by ESL teacher-researchers.

- Laura Rossi-Le (1995) found that among her adult immigrant community college ESL students, the older students and students with higher language proficiency showed a preference for visual learning. Higher proficiency English language students also preferred learning through interactive methods and direct experiences with language.

- In her study of Caucasian and Asian college students' environmental learning styles, Rita Dunn (1991) reported that Caucasians had a higher preference for warm temperatures, intake of food, and mobility in learning; they remembered less well aurally and visually.

- In a study of more than 500 ESL students in Australia, Ken Willing (1988) found that Arabic students preferred auditory and visual perceptual styles, and they learned best when they were performing activities that allowed them to be interactive and extroverted.

- To assess the field dependence/field independence of ESL students, Lynne Hansen-Strain (1989) administered the Group Embedded Figures Test (GEFT) to 884 ESL students (with 22 different first language backgrounds) at the English Language Institute at Brigham Young University–Hawaii. She found that the Asian groups (from Japan, Hong Kong, Korea, and "other Chinese") were substantially more field independent than the South Pacific groups (from Samoa, Tonga, Micronesia, the Philippines, and "other South Pacific").

- Torpong Goodson (1993) surveyed 227 East Asian students studying English at the University of Tennessee. In general, the students preferred visual and kinesthetic styles of learning. To be even more specific, the mainland Chinese and the Taiwanese students preferred visual learning, the Japanese students preferred kinesthetic learning, and the Korean students preferred tactile and visual learning. Moreover, Goodson found, most of the East Asian students indicated that they would not choose group learning.

- Patricia Carrell and Laura Monroe (1995) worked with post-admission university ESL and native English speaker students in first-year composition courses to investigate the possible relationships between the Myers-Briggs Type Indicator (MBTI) and composition skills and strategies. Carrell and Monroe found significant differences between the MBTI personality types of the ESL and the native English speaker students, and they reported that "the ESL sample was extremely homogenous, with 8 of 16 potential MBTI personality types not represented at all" (p. 152).

All of these ESL studies have taken place in English-speaking countries, in which students are studying English as a second language in an immersion situation. But what about students studying English as a foreign language (EFL) in their own countries? Many of the EFL classrooms are relatively homogeneous in terms of first language and culture; moreover, the students will not have been exposed to the learning styles of U. S. classrooms. Might that make a difference in their learning style preferences?

This chapter reports the research results of teachers who administered Reid's PLSP (Perceptual Learning Styles Preference Survey 1987) to their students in Egypt, Spain, Hungary, and Siberia. Several of the teachers gathered their information formally and analyzed their data for other teachers; some of the teachers collected the survey information informally. The results discussed in this chapter will therefore focus only on the general trends of the learning styles of students studying English in those countries.

History of the Perceptual Learning Style Preferences (PLSP) Survey

In 1984 Joy Reid developed and normed the PLSP survey. This questionnaire allowed ESL students to self-identify their preferred learning styles among six categories: visual, auditory, kinesthetic, tactile, group, and individual learning. Reid published (1987) the results of her large-scale study of nearly 1300 ESL students who completed the survey in intensive English language program classes across the United States. The data analysis showed that

- most ESL students studying English in the United States showed strong major learning style preferences for kinesthetic and tactile learning.
- most ESL students showed a negative learning style for group learning (that is, they preferred *not* to learn in that way).
- ESL students from different language/cultural backgrounds often differed significantly in their choices of major, minor, and negative learning styles.
- ESL students from specific major fields often preferred specific learning styles (for example, engineering students preferred tactile learning, and students in the hard sciences preferred visual learning).

Table 2-1 shows the general results of Reid's study for nine language backgrounds. The data in this study also indicate that ESL students whose stay in the United States is prolonged adapt their perceptual learning styles to the educational culture in which they are studying. That is, the longer ESL students stay in the United States, the more their learning style preferences resemble the preferences of native English speakers. Specifically, the ESL students became less tactile and more auditory. This finding suggests that students studying English as a foreign language (EFL)—that is, studying English in their native countries—who plan to attend school in the United States might benefit from learning about learning styles and from training in "flexing" or extending their learning styles in order to be more prepared for U.S. classrooms.

Table 2–1. Perceptual Learning Style Preference Results

Learning Style Preferences

Language (Number)	Major	Minor	Negative
Arabic (193)	Visual Auditory Kinesthetic Tactile	Group Individual	NONE
Spanish (130)	Kinesthetic Tactile	Visual Auditory Individual	Group
Japanese (130)	NONE	Visual Auditory Kinesthetic Tactile Individual	Group
Malay (113)	Kinesthetic Tactile	Visual Auditory Group Individual	NONE
Chinese (90)	Visual Auditory Kinesthetic Tactile	Individual	Group
Korean (118)	Visual Auditory Kinesthetic Tactile	Individual	Group
Thai (47)	Kinesthetic Tactile	Visual Auditory Individual	Group
Indonesian (59)	Auditory Kinesthetic	Visual Tactile Individual	Group
English (153)	Auditory Kinesthetic	Visual Tactile Individual	Group

Number = number of students responding to survey
Source: Reid 1987

The PLSP in EFL Classrooms

Since Reid's investigation, many teacher-researchers have used the PLSP informally to help their students identify their individual learning styles. Teachers have also begun to administer the PLSP surveys in EFL programs in non-English speaking countries. The investigations described in the studies below are not comparable in statistical terms: the number of students and the kinds of students (for example, secondary students, teachers-in-training) differ. Yet the data gathered can be discussed in terms of general trends and be compared in general with Reid's original study. More important, the trends described by the teachers below can be studied by other ESL/EFL teachers as they practice their own classroom research.

Egypt

With assistance from Fulbright lecturers Carol Clark (Cairo University, El-Fayoum Branch), Nancy Frampton (Suez University, Al Arish Branch), and Michael Heaner (Assuit University, Sohag Branch), Reid surveyed more than 100 EFL teachers-in-training in 1992. Figure 2-1 charts the major, minor, and negative learning styles of the surveyed students.

Figure 2–1. Major, Minor, and Negative Learning Styles of Egyptian EFL Teachers-in-Training, 1992

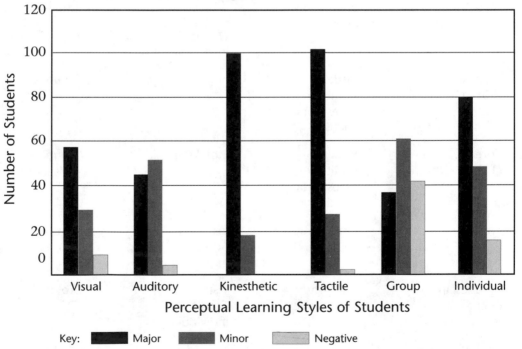

Although Reid did not separate Egyptian students from all Arabic speakers in her original research, it is interesting to compare the 1992 Egyptian results with those in her 1987 study (See Table 2–1, above). Some of the results of the Egyptian students parallel Reid's general results for Arabic students studying ESL in the United States: a great majority of the Egyptian students also strongly preferred kinesthetic and tactile learning styles. In contrast, auditory learning was primarily a minor learning style for the EFL Egyptian students, although many ESL Arabic students in the earlier study strongly preferred auditory learning. One reason might be that the Egyptian students have very limited access to spoken English outside the classroom; another might be that this smaller, more homogeneous population differs from the larger Arabic group.

In general, the Egyptian students responded more positively to the survey than did the Arabic group; very few Egyptian students identified negative learning styles. Moreover, many of these teachers-in-training indicated preferences for multiple learning styles; this may be either a cause or a result of their being successful university students.

Spain

Manuel Vicente Mata Vicioso teaches at a secondary school, the Instituto de BUP "Francisco Tarrega," Villarreal de los Infantes, in Castellón, Spain. He administered the PLSP (in English) to 193 secondary school students in first- and second-year classes, and in third- and fourth-year humanities and science specializations. The results of his research are in Figure 2-2 (note that the data apply only to major learning styles).

Reid's original research did analyze Spanish-speaker learning style preferences, but the students came from a variety of Central and South American countries as well as from Spain. The added differences, ESL vs. EFL and secondary vs. post-secondary students, indicate that Mata's results may be compared only generally.

While students in both research groups strongly preferred kinesthetic learning, Mata's students ranked tactile learning at about the same level as all the other major learning styles, dramatically lower than they ranked kinesthetic learning. Mata explains that students may have lower tactile preferences because they lack experience with tactile techniques in their educational environment; thus, only the fourth-year science students (who spent much time in laboratory classes) were strong proponents of tactile learning. Another difference found by Mata was the nearly equal preference for group and individual major learning styles. Mata clearly believes that group learning is preferable: "The individual preference is used by some [first-year] students because they do not know each other yet, so they [would] rather do things alone. Those who like group preferences [do so] because they are open and outgoing people by nature" (Mata Vicioso 1993, p. 31).

Figure 2–2. Major Learning Styles of Spanish Secondary School Students

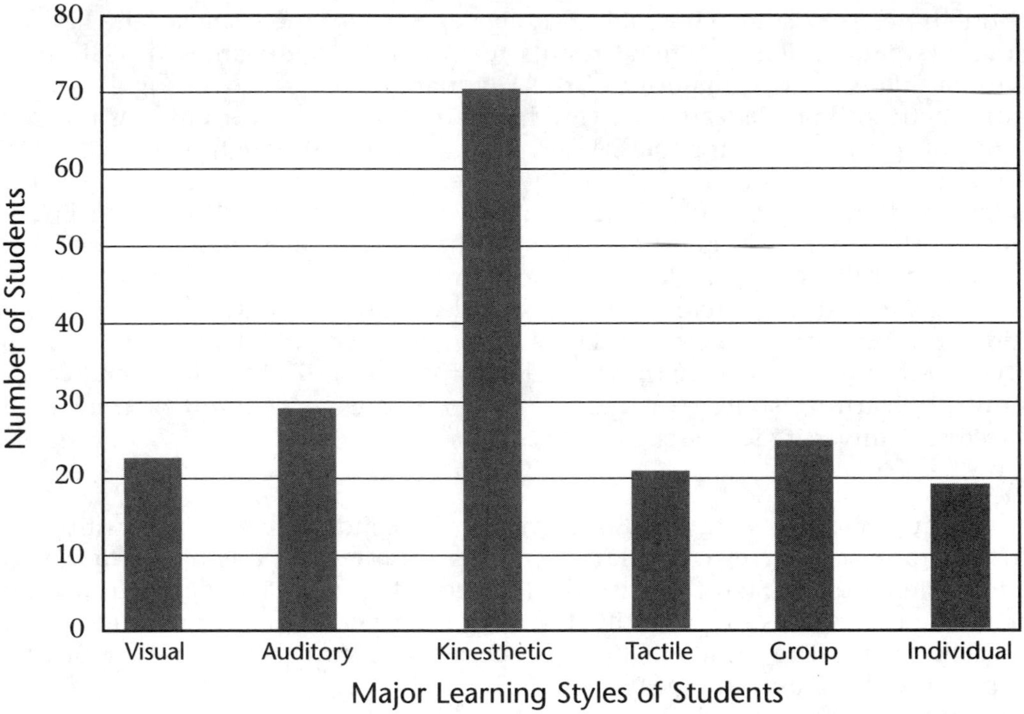

Hungary

In 1992 Éva Gedeon (ELTE English Department) and Katalin Takacs (ELTE Center for English Teacher Training) in Budapest administered the PLSP to 138 university students, whose major fields were as follows:

English	42
Science (Physics, Mathematics, Biology, and Chemistry)	51
Engineering	16
Computer Science	10
Business	15

As Figure 2–3 illustrates, these Hungarian students, like the Egyptian teachers-in-training, responded very positively to the survey; they also chose kinesthetic and tactile as their major learning style preferences, and they chose multiple learning styles. In addition, these Hungarian EFL teachers-in-training identified auditory learning as their first choice as a minor learning style preference, and, in a departure from Reid's study, a substantial number chose group learning as a learning style.

Gedeon and Takacs also found that the longer students studied English, the more auditory their preference became, a result that parallels Reid's 1987 study. As Éva Gedeon writes: "Our tentative assumption is that auditory learning style

Figure 2–3. **Major, Minor, and Negative Learning Styles of Hungarian EFL University Students**

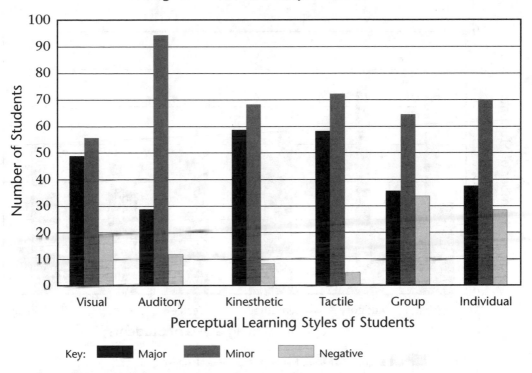

preferences have to be developed by students, especially when learning [English as] a second or foreign language. In learning, listening and understanding play an extremely important part, and modern communicative methods lay a special emphasis on developing those skills. This may induce students who want to be successful to accommodate their learning style preferences accordingly" (personal communication).

Russia

Zhanna Korotkikh, who trains EFL undergraduate majors and minors in the Foreign Languages Department at Barnual Pedagogical State Institute in Siberia, administered the PLSP survey to 193 students. Most were 20 to 23 years old, and most had had ten to fifteen years of EFL study; nearly two-thirds of the teachers-in-preparation were women. Figure 2–4 shows the general results of the investigation (note that the numbers of students surveyed differs from the other studies reported in Figures 2–2 and 2–3 above).

Reid's original work did not analyze the learning preferences of students from Eastern Europe or the former Soviet Union. Nevertheless, results of the PLSP questionnaire administered to Siberian students show several similarities to the ESL students in Reid's work. Again, the strongest learning style choices were tactile and kinesthetic; group learning was the most common negative learning style.

Figure 2–4 Major, Minor, and Negative Learning Styles of Siberian EFL Undergraduates

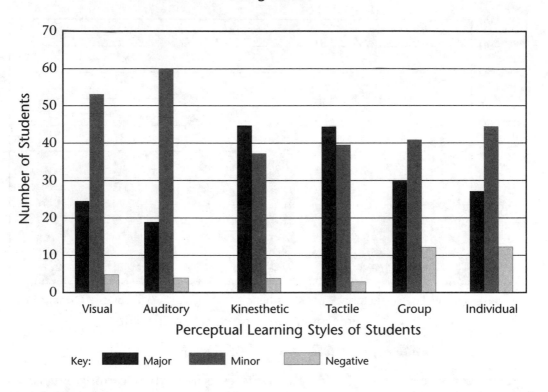

Korotkikh writes:

Intuitively I've always felt that students learn differently. Some are better in group work, others are individual learners, and so on. The information on the students' learning style preferences at the beginning of the academic year can help teachers as well as students themselves organize their work more productively. The teacher's task will be either to adapt his methods to individual learners or to help students develop other learning style abilities. The major learning style preferences for 50 percent to 60 percent of our students are tactile and kinesthetic. But we don't have any multimedia courses or a series of textbooks based on tactile and kinesthetic learning styles. If there is such a course for advanced learners, please let me know. [personal communication]

When comparing the Siberian teachers-in-training with the Egyptian and Hungarian university students, we note that

- all three groups chose kinesthetic and tactile as major learning styles.
- none of the student groups selected auditory learning as a strong major learning style.
- all groups demonstrated preferences for multiple learning styles.

In addition, the Siberian and the Hungarian results are unusual in at least one way: large numbers of the Siberian undergraduates chose minor, not major, learning style modes. This may be a factor of real and unexplained differences, or it may be that these students, like the Japanese students in Reid's research, respond more moderately to surveys. That is, they may be less willing to check "strongly agree" and "strongly disagree" than, for example, the Egyptian and Spanish students (or the other students in Reid's original study).

Conclusion

The purpose of this chapter has been two-fold. First, for ESL/EFL teachers who have questions about student learning styles (and/or teaching styles), this article, and this anthology, have been designed to stimulate "action research" (that is, reading, analyzing, reflecting, synthesizing, and making decisions within the classroom setting) that will develop greater sensitivity to learning style issues. And as teachers develop professionally in this area, their students will also benefit through knowledge about styles and strategies involved in optimizing their individual learning styles.

Second, for ESL/EFL teachers who have begun to reframe their instructional philosophy to accommodate students' learning styles (Black 1993), this article suggests that the next step is to actually administer one or more learning styles instruments, to replicate previous research. Teachers can then have the students chart, analyze, and discuss their major, minor, and negative learning styles. Next, both teachers and students might reflect upon the individual and class data in order to provide ideas for responsive instruction (Reid 1996). In these ways, teachers acknowledge the prior knowledge and inherent worth that the learner brings to the classroom (Swisher and Deyle 1987) and can offer students empowerment through equal educational opportunities to perform at their maximum potential.

For Further Reading

Learning Styles Network Newsletter. (1980–1989). New York: National Association of Secondary School Principals and St. John's University, Jamaica, NY 11439.

> Published by the School of Education and Human Services at St. John's University (Grand Central and Utopia Parkways, Jamaica, NY 11439) three times a year for nine years, this newsletter reported on the most recent research and school programs concerning learning styles. It provided practical suggestions for implementing learning styles in public school classrooms and still provides interesting material for teachers. Back issues are available.

National Association of Secondary School Principals. (1979). *Student Learning Styles: Diagnosing and Prescribing Programs*. Reston, VA: NASSP.

This book describes the pioneering work in learning styles in secondary schools; much of the information is still relevant today. In addition, it provides much practical information concerning implementation of learning styles research in the classroom.

TESOL Journal 6 (1), (1996) Special Issue: Learning Styles and Strategies in ESOL, Autumn.

This issue of the journal contains eight articles (several by authors in this anthology) that offer a classroom-based overview of learning styles use. Included are articles on Multiple Intelligences, the link between styles and strategies, sociocultural influences on classroom interactional styles, and the use of group work with learning styles. The focus of the articles is utterly practical; they are written directly to and for teachers.

Richards, J. and Lockhart, C. (1994). *Reflective Teaching in Second Language Classrooms*. Cambridge: Cambridge University Press.

The focus of this book is on teaching, particularly on changing teachers' perspectives on teaching ESL/EFL. Especially helpful are Section 3, "Focus on the Learner," and Section 7, "Interaction in the Second Language Classroom," in which the authors discuss individual student learning styles.

Chapter 3

The Triune Brain and Learning: Practical Insights for the Classroom

Emma Violand–Sánchez
Arlington (Virginia) Public Schools

> There are perhaps about one hundred billion neurons, or nerve cells, in the brain, and in a single human brain the number of possible interconnections between these cells is greater than the number of atoms in the universe.
>
> Robert Ornstein and Richard Thompson (1984, p. 21)

New knowledge about the brain is reinforcing the expectation of all good teachers: that all students can learn. Although I am not a neuroscientist, I believe recent research findings in brain research and their application to education are providing powerful insights and tools to improve learning. Yet brain research has been slow to infiltrate our teacher education programs and classrooms; ESL teachers in particular, who often concentrate on language development, can greatly benefit from these insights to enhance classroom instruction.

As supervisor of the Arlington Public Schools English for Speakers of Other Languages (ESOL) and High Intensity Language Training, I am constantly looking for practical findings that can guide teachers in improving delivery of instruction. In the past, staff development on how to incorporate learning styles has made teachers more sensitive to individual differences (Reid 1995), and has thereby helped our students better use their individual talents and abilities (Violand–Sánchez 1995).[*] The purpose of this chapter is to share additional instructional strategies that enhance learning a second language, in particular by increasing learning readiness, by improving motivation and engagement, and by eliminating barriers to learning.

---

[*] Publications such as *Integrating Learning Styles and Skills in the ESL Classroom: An Approach to Lesson Planning* (Hainer et al. 1992, Washington DC: National Clearinghouse for Bilingual Education) present samples of lesson plans developed by teachers in grades K–12 in the Arlington Public Schools.

The Triune Brain

ESL students have a variety of academic and sociocultural pressures, as well as affective needs, that can interfere with their learning processes. They struggle with the stress of their acculturation process and how to demonstrate their knowledge in an unfamiliar language. In addition, large numbers of immigrant students are reuniting with their families from whom they have been separated for a number of years; these students are struggling to establish stable family relations while meeting basic survival needs. Racial and ethnic conflicts increase stress and fear; polarization of ethnic groups and anti-immigrant sentiment affect students' views of themselves and can ignite anger. Counseling that eases these tensions is valuable, but more classroom strategies are also needed to reduce teachers' and students' tension and stress.

One major contribution from brain research is the discovery that all students (in fact, all humans) need a safe and supportive environment in which to learn. The Triune Brain theory, developed by National Institute of Mental Health researcher Paul MacLean, helps us to understand the important role of emotions in the learning process (in Kline 1988; MacLean 1978; Silvester 1995). To explain why student stress and anxiety are so detrimental to learning, MacLean demonstrates that we have three brains in one (see Figure 3-1). The oldest and most primitive part of the brain is the **reptilian** system; it is located in the brain stem, and it regulates relaxation and the stress response. The next layer of the brain, developmentally and structurally, is the **mammalian** (**limbic**) system; it is the site of emotions and long-term memory. The **neocortex** is the third part of the brain; it includes the frontal lobes (both left- and right-brain) and is responsible for many of our higher capacities such as language, the development of skills, an unlimited storage capacity, and our higher thought processes (Russell 1979).

The reptilian system is automatic; it controls vital functions such as self-preservation. It activates the body to respond in ways that ensure survival: basic needs are met before other higher functions can proceed (Caine and Caine 1991; Hannaford 1995). Because the reptilian brain controls our "flight or fight" response, chemicals in that part of the brain respond whenever students feel physically or emotionally threatened. For example, fear of deportation can become a major barrier for learning and send students into a "flight" response: they drop out of school. Under other stresses, students experience a "minimizing of cortical functioning. When this happens students resort to more automatic and limited responses. Thus, there is less capacity for rational and creative thought" (Wolfe 1996). In other words, Stephen Krashen's "affective filter" explanation holds: when students are anxious, the filter goes into effect and becomes a barrier to learning (Krashen 1981). Instead, students need to relax in order to focus their attention; a nonthreatening environment is essential for the neocortex to operate efficiently.

The mammalian (or limbic) system, located beneath the neocortex, is the seat of our emotions. This layer of the brain must be activated in order to access long-term memory (that is, all prior experiences). Emotions, and activating prior experiences, are essential to motivation; the intricate wiring of this system shows

Figure 3–1. The Triune Brain

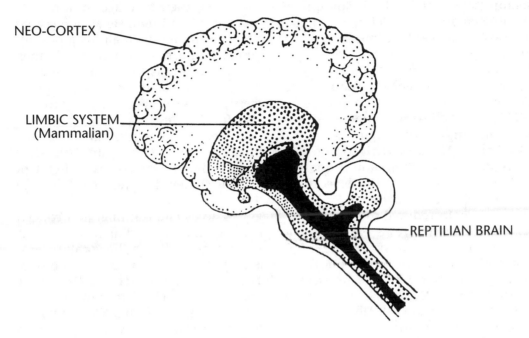

NEO-CORTEX

LIMBIC SYSTEM
(Mammalian)

REPTILIAN BRAIN

Source: Laura Ellison, *Seeing with Magic Glasses* (Arlington, VA: Great Ocean
Publishers, 1993), p. 15. Used with permission.

that in order to learn and remember something, there must be sensory input and a
personal emotional connection (Hannaford 1995). Students who lack emotional
connection to the curriculum, and who cannot appreciate its application to their
lives, are therefore less successful in school.

All incoming sensory stimuli (except smell, which is a more primitive sense)
are processed through the mammalian system. The mammalian system links the
sensory stimuli with the neocortex, allowing for emotional and cognitive
processing. That is, a person remembers some event in detail when that event is
accompanied by feelings. In the case of intense feelings (such as a loved one's
death or another student's ridicule), we cannot forget.

The neocortex is intimately tied to the mammalian (limbic) system; it uses
input from the emotional processing in the limbic system in memory and thinking
functions, for creativity and decision-making. This close relation between the
rational neocortex and the emotional mammalian system explains why learning is
more likely to occur when information is presented in a meaningful, relevant,
engaging way. That is, information will be taken in and remembered if it has
meaning to the student and if it contains an emotional "hook" (Wolfe 1995).
Therefore, bringing fun and emotional involvement to learning activates the
mammalian mid-brain centers where long-term memory is processed.

Relaxation and Learning

Bulgarian psychotherapist Georgi Lozanov was a pioneer in the 1950s in demonstrating, through his Suggestopedia approach, the advantages of a relaxed learning environment in foreign language teaching (Kline 1988). He explored ways to teach languages by eliminating fear from the classroom, maintaining a positive suggestive atmosphere, and dealing with mistakes in a nonthreatening manner. According to Lozanov, the secret to accelerating learning is to recreate a natural learning environment. He proposes that classes be conducted in an atmosphere similar to a living room. The teacher, he suggests, needs to take a nurturing role by reinforcing the learner's attempt to learn with affectionate and positive responses, while playing down or ignoring mistakes. Teachers also need to harmonize the content with nonverbal components: music, dance, drama, and physical movement. A teacher should not even suggest that the subject is difficult or boring; on the contrary, the expectation is that the student has the ability to reach the highest level of performance.

Lozanov introduced the "concert strategy" to accelerate learning. In a concert session, the teacher reads the information in a dramatic way and matches it to the musical structure of baroque, classical, or romantic music. When the vocal patterns match the music, the long-term memory is tapped because there is harmony of both hemispheres of the brain: the left hemisphere processes linguistic information while the right hemisphere processes music. This harmony generates feelings of relaxation sufficient to further lower barriers to learning (Kline 1988).

Proponents of Lozanov have written about their own successes. Laura Ellison (1993), for example, recommends that each day some precious minutes be used to build students' ability to deliberately relax; she uses baroque music to help students relax as she teaches them how the biological processes of breathing and relaxation relate to focusing attention. Peter Kline (1988) has demonstrated that when students learn to overcome fear, they perform better and improve their achievement.

Specifically, Kline recommends that teachers bring out positive feelings with an exercise called "The Good and the New." During this activity, all the students are invited to share a bit of good news or to communicate a good feeling. A koosh ball is thrown by one participant to another, indicating that person's turn to participate. ESL students in our school district have responded very well to this activity; they improve their language skills and have a positive feeling of belonging as they share their experiences and feelings. Kline also suggests another interpersonal strategy: "The Birthday Circle." The birthday person—or, if desirable, any student who might particularly benefit from the experience—sits in the center of a circle as classmates take turns saying "I am glad you were born because . . ." The birthday person simply listens and takes in compliments.

These strategies foster a safe, warm, and supportive classroom atmosphere. As our students become more familiar with these exercises, they become more sensitive to each other. Cooperative learning is a natural extension of these activities, another powerful way to foster a positive learning community in the ESL classroom. For example, "Think and Listen" is a simple cooperative strategy involving two students (Kline 1988). The underlying premise is that people aren't "listened to" enough and thus become "starved for attention." Working in pairs, students take turns talking for a specific number of minutes (three, five, or seven, depending on the needs of the class). The listener looks at the speaker and can smile and react appropriately, but never speaks. (Note: The speaker might not always be looking at the listener because when a person thinks, the eyes often travel about.) Teachers in our program have found that students who can practice "think and listen" exercises with ease generally have an easier time speaking in front of groups. Classroom practices like these, that encourage individuals to know one another, support one another, and enjoy one another, are desirable and beneficial. They activate positive emotions and thus prepare students to learn.

Movement and Learning

Insights from brain research on the essential role of physical movement can also enhance learning in the ESL classroom. In *Smart Moves* (1995), Carla Hannaford explains how movement impacts learning by "waking up" our brains and preparing them for incoming information. A neuroscientist, Hannaford emphasizes that physical movements not only strengthen the body but are crucial to brain and nervous system development and are vital for maintaining alertness and learning readiness. For example, in *Brain Gym* (Dennison and Dennison 1994), there are twenty-six exercises designed to help students relax and release tension and thus become open to learning. In my experience, the best exercise in *Brain Gym* to wake up students is "Cross-Crawl." Students stand and hold both hands up by their shoulders with their feet comfortably apart. They then alternately move one hand down to touch the opposite lifted knee, return to the original position, and touch the other knee with the other hand. A variation is to extend the leg while touching the knee; an even more difficult variation is to reach behind the body to touch the opposite foot. Teachers report that elementary school children who have the most difficulty with the exercises seem to be the ones having more difficulty in general. According to those teachers, as students' abilities to do "Cross-Crawl" improve, so does their improvement in listening, writing, and reading.

One major reason that cross-lateral movements (that is, both sides of the body moving in concert) help students is that they stimulate nerve growth between the frontal lobes of the brain, which is used for formal reasoning functions in the neocortex: language development is located in the frontal lobes. As authors Paul and Gail Dennison explain, any movement that makes a right limb touch a left limb activates whole-brain processing because both hemispheres of the brain must be used simultaneously. Crossing the "midline" (between the left and right lobes) is necessary for whole-body coordination and ease in learning. Midline (that is, cross-lateral) movements help to integrate the left and right sides of the brain and the body and so have an effect on cognitive processing as well (Dennison and Dennison 1994).

Another activity that enables the student to cross the midline is tracing a "Lazy 8" or infinity symbol in the air. The teacher begins by drawing the symbol on the chalkboard, making it easier for students to see that one continuous line has separate right and left sections and a midpoint. One variation is for students to stand while drawing the symbol in the air or to trace the figure on their desks. Students hold their left thumb up and, beginning at the midpoint about waist height, move an extended arm counterclockwise over the rounded left end of the horizontal eight and around to the midpoint again. Then the student continues to move his left thumb clockwise up over the rounded right end of the infinity symbol and back to the midpoint. The student must be looking at his thumbnail as he makes the large, continuous movement tracing the symbol in the air.

ESL teachers in our district who have been trained and who use exercises from *Brain Gym* report that their students concentrate better and seem more ready to learn. Further, our students love to move and do these simple exercises, usually for about five minutes at the beginning of a class.

Another important suggestion made by Hannaford and others is that students should drink water to enable proper functioning of the nervous system; quite simply, adequate hydration improves academic skills. The brain, which constitutes only one-fiftieth of the body's weight, consumes one-fifth of its oxygen. As the oxygen breaks down food to release the energy needed for mind/body functioning, water assists oxygen distribution to the brain. After teachers in our district learned about the benefits of water in enhancing communication and social skills, they shared this knowledge with the students. I now observe many students bringing water bottles to class!

Conclusion

The whole brain works together in amazing ways, and brain-compatible classroom strategies can promote feelings of belonging and caring among all students by relieving stress and enhancing natural brain processes that improve learning. Consequently, educators need to acknowledge that emotions play a vital role in the learning process, and they need to learn how to adopt such strategies in their curricula.

Because ESL students have diminished abilities to function linguistically while they are acquiring English language skills, and because brain research has demonstrated that external factors can inhibit language learning, teachers need to implement strategies for eliminating fear and stress from the classroom. They should know how to engage their students' positive emotions in the learning process. Once teachers in our program learned about the strategies and activities that raised the comfort level of their students, they began to include techniques that created a stress-free, positive classroom environment in which students felt safe. They introduced stimulating sensory activities, asking students to tap their physical abilities as well as their intellectual strengths in order to extend their individual skills in school and in the community.

The results have been extremely rewarding and exhilarating: more active involvement by all students in the classroom, improved ability to absorb new information, increased motivation, and the ability to work cooperatively with others. After the initial training sessions, one teacher said that these strategies were a means of humanizing the classroom and improving attention and memory.

Another teacher stated that, "This training was most beneficial because these techniques can be applied to every area of a person's life, not just the classroom."

For Further Reading

Caine, G. and Caine, R. (1991). *Making Connections: Teaching and the Human Brain.* Alexandria, VA: Association of Supervision and Curriculum Development.

> This book explores the implications of recent brain research for learning and teaching. It has a chapter, for example, that describes Paul MacLean's theory on the Triune Brain. The book is accessible to the general reader and provides a foundation for teachers who choose to use the material in their classrooms.

Hannaford, C. (1995). *Smart Moves: Why Learning Is Not All in Your Head.* Arlington, VA: Great Ocean Publishers.

> This book presents the neurophysiology of the learning process and stresses the need for movement and for respect for the emotions in learning. The book has three sections: "Ways of Knowing," which has a chapter on the roles of emotions in learning; "Smart Moves," which incorporates movement and the Brain Gym; and "Nurturing and Protecting Our Learning System," which summarizes important concepts regarding the brain and learning.

Chapter 4

Learning Style Diversity and the Reading Class: Curriculum Design and Assessment

Marian Tyacke
University of Toronto

Few language programs provide an adequate learning context for ESL/EFL learners with different cognitive styles, and fewer still develop assessment tools with cognitive styles in mind. In this chapter, I describe a project that (a) identified style groups among language program ESL students, and (b) examined the effects of various reading tasks commonly used in language teaching and testing on each style group. The results of the project demonstrated that individual responses to the reading tasks affected outcomes in both. My purpose is to show that because adult students are usually able to report quite reliably on their own learning preferences, and because those learning preferences can be categorized quite simply, consideration of such individual differences should underlie the curriculum design of language programs and the development of language tests.

Background

Cognitive style is defined by J. Kagan, H. Moss, and I. Siegel (1963, p. 76) as "stable individual preferences in modes of perceptual organization and conceptual categorization of the external environment." Samuel Messick (1976, p. 5) states that "They [cognitive styles] are conceptualized as stable attitudes, preferences or habitual strategies, determining a person's typical modes of perceiving, thinking and problem solving." These definitions stress not only the individuality but also the stability of learning behaviors. If, as both research and teacher-experience indicate, style differences cause learners to react to the language-learning context in significantly different ways, then we, as language teachers, must make allowances for such differences.

Recognizing learning style differences is only the first stage, however. Teachers must also provide appropriate learning paths in terms of syllabus design, choice of materials, and alternative assessments of proficiency. Yet diagnosing and prescribing (to use a medical metaphor) can be difficult. That is, even though effective instructors are sensitive to their students' responses to classroom activities, it is not always clear why some students respond more positively than others, or make more progress than others.

The problems of identification probably have several (often overlapping) causes. First, learning styles are complex, and the overall learning "profile" of a student may be difficult to analyze. Second, if the value of a particular learning style or strategy is relative to a particular goal (Reed 1992, p. 140), students may well use different learning styles in different learning contexts. Third, sometimes a methodological bias is imposed, either by the individual teacher or by the larger educational system, that favors one kind of learner over another: the individual, analytic learner (valued in many U.S. schools), for instance, or the rote group learner. In addition, teachers tend to respond more favorably to similar cognitive types so that, for example, a conscientious, well-organized, analytical teacher is likely to perceive students who exhibit those tendencies as "better" students.

As Ken Willing suggests, "At any period in the history of methodological fashions, there is usually the covert assumption of one particular learning style as basic. [However,] what makes the current interest in learning style new is that **several ways of learning** are now held to be equally valid" (1988, p. 6). If students learn in several "equally valid" ways, it is possible that we need to re-examine the definitions on which we based earlier research. Consequently, as I began my investigation into the cognitive learning styles of my intermediate English language proficiency reading students, I recognized the need to investigate a variety of approaches used by students in order to become "good" readers. First, though, I needed to answer two basic questions: What constitutes a "good" reader? What constitutes a "good" reading-test taker?

The "Good" Reader

Much research has suggested that "good" readers are risk-takers rather than cautious, and global rather than sequential learners (Goodman 1967; Hosenfeld 1977; van Dijk and Kintsch 1983). General classroom observation, however, reveals that there are different kinds of successful (and unsuccessful) readers. At one end of the learning style continuum, some students read slowly and carefully. These students are more inclined to use their reasoning and analytical skills, make conscious choices, compare and select, then retain or discard information. At the other end of the continuum, students take risks, read more quickly and extensively, but may be inaccurate answering questions about detail. These students have substantial synthesizing ability and verbal memories, inductively retaining unrelated "chunks" of information and making connections when it is relevant to do so. And, of course, many students "reside" on the continuum between these two extremes. In terms of assessment, the former group may appear to be more successful in traditional assessment situations, while the latter group would find traditional testing less accessible.

Even this categorization may be too simple. Carolyn Cherry suggests that reading involves complex processes: "The 'unfolding' of meaning is then not a simple, sequential process; it involves short-range and long-range cognitive processes, using different forms of memory" (1978, p. 319). Moreover, some learner types find it difficult to concentrate when anyone else is talking, while others successfully filter out distraction; still others depend upon distraction as a strategy in order to "mark time" while more subconscious processing takes place.

Although seemingly trivial, such differences can enhance or undermine the learning process for some students.

The "Good" Reading-Test Taker

Analyzing the issues of assessment and learning styles is even more murky. For example, much argument exists as to whether it is possible even to agree upon what particular reading sub-skill is represented in a testing context. Charles Alderson and Y. Lukmani (1989) found that experts could not agree on what a particular item tested; A. Allen (1992) found that there was at best a 50 percent agreement among judges of what the items tested.

Alderson also claims that

> students approach test items in highly individual ways [and] get the correct answer for a variety of different reasons [and that] even more worrisomely, in some ways, is the fact that individual students have been seen to get the answer right, yet have displayed abilities that were not supposedly being tested, nor have they displayed evidence of the ability that the test constructor believed was being tested [1991, p. 17].

This phenomenon is also reported by Samuel Messick, who states that different individuals perform the same task in different ways, and that the same individual might perform in a different manner across items or on different occasions.

It is ironic that the assessment measures we often apply both in class and on tests depend on student comprehension of short texts at an artificially detailed level (Scott 1990, p. 20), which means that more text must be processed, thus affecting reading speed. This might influence test results, as there would be an advantage for slower, sequential readers. More global risk-taking readers may be unable to use what are probably superior skimming/scanning skills that are successful in "real" reading. The recognition of such differences when assessing the product of reading comprehension (that is, answers on a test) should alert teachers to the need to account for those differences in the development of reading skills.

The Project

I carried out a three-phase investigation designed to relate cognitive type to reading behavior (Tyacke 1996). Phase 1 comprised case studies of six expert readers (three L1 and three L2) and was based on interviews and private introspection, where their different patterns of reading behavior were related to their learning style profiles. Phase 2, the subject of this chapter, identified different cognitive types of students in an intensive ESL program and related their reading behavior to their learning profiles. Phase 3 examined the interaction of cognitive type and task success on a university-entrance reading test.

The students who participated in Phase 2, the classroom section of this project, were attending the Intensive ESL Program at the University of Toronto, which attracts a large number of highly educated students and professionals from around the world. The majority of the students in the program are in their twenties, and many already possess an undergraduate degree. Although many tend to use the program to prepare for entry into post-secondary North American institutions, others see it as a way of advancing their careers in the international marketplace.

The questions to be answered in this phase of the project included:

- Is it possible to identify distinct groups of learners who represent different cognitive types?
- Does each group prefer different reading activities?
- Is there any relationship between cognitive type and performance on different reading tasks?

By providing a relatively flexible classroom environment (by allowing learner selection from a variety of materials and exercises, as well as learner control of type of feedback), it was assumed that individuals would create situations in which they could use their preferred styles and strategies, and that this would have positive and measurable effects on the learning process.

The specific setting was a series of four 8-week high-intermediate-level reading classes. The first hour of each two-hour class was teacher-directed; it included traditional reading comprehension tasks, using a variety of texts, and reading strategy training (such as separating gist and detail, contextualizing, and inferencing). The second hour of each class was learner-directed and was devoted to student-chosen activities. Students could choose from a wide variety of texts, most of which had been pre-selected by the teacher; the selection was based on the needs analysis carried out at the beginning of the course. Or students could supply their own reading material and write a "book report" consisting of a content summary and a personal response.

The classroom had movable tables and chairs so that students could create their own space. Some students gathered in groups, others worked quietly in a corner, and others stayed near my desk so that they could consult me easily. The students could work at their own speed, and they could use any of the exercise and feedback types described below. They could also use a dictionary or a thesaurus if they wished, although we avoided this practice in the teacher-directed hour. The variety allowed the students who really felt they needed my input to see me on a one-to-one basis, and it also allowed me the opportunity to join a discussion group if I were invited to do so.

Students in these classes were asked to keep a detailed record of what they read. The record included:

content area

exercise type: those normally used at this level. They fell into four main categories:

1. vocabulary in context
2. grammar points
3. true/false or multiple choice factual retrieval and inferencing
4. open-ended comprehension of main and support ideas

feedback type: three kinds were available to each student:

1. teacher-scored responses
2. group consensus after a discussion
3. an answer key that could be consulted without instructor involvement

attitude rating: whether the activity was perceived to be

interesting
useful
easy

Learning Styles of the Participants

At first, students completed the Tyacke Profile in which they used a checklist that resulted in one of the four styles defined in Table 4-1. (See Appendix 4 for a copy of the Tyacke Profile, Version 3.)

Table 4–1. Tyacke Profile Styles

Style A:	The **studier** likes structure, rules, and an expert teacher.
Style B:	The **diverger** seeks advice when needed and works out his/her own rules.
Style C:	The **explorer** actively practices with peers rather than learning rules.
Style D:	The **absorber** (also called the "free spirit") does not consciously practice or learn rules, but seems to absorb language patterns.

While there are overlaps in the self-identified characteristics, the **Studiers** (Style A) can usually be associated with the analytic, left-brained learner, while the **Absorbers** (Style D) can be associated with the global (holistic), right-brained learner. The unique combination of characteristics for each style is described below; each description was derived from the ways each group of students selected reading materials and reacted to reading exercises. (I have left Style B for the last paragraph of this discussion because it proved the most problematic of the groups.) (See Ehrman, this volume, for another perspective.)

Studiers treated language learning as a task that had to be completed by working diligently and sequentially. They were very focused and reacted negatively to distractions (which included the needs of others). They liked clear instructions rather than choice, and structure rather than open-ended situations. They usually completed what they undertook, even though in some cases they did not find the experience enjoyable. They handled paper and pencil exercises more successfully than group activities, but they did not mind participating in either. They kept lists and made notes, learned rules and tried actively to apply them, often seeking confirmation from the teacher that their performance was successful (which usually meant accurate). They preferred black-and-white answers to long explanations, and they were not as likely to seek feedback from their peers as the other groups. In general, they resented making choices of materials, preferring the teacher to give them clear directions, but did so conscientiously when required to do so.

Explorers differed from Studiers in that language learning was more of a game that they enjoyed playing with their peers. They avoided learning rules, preferring to practice in discussion groups, and enjoyed variety and choice. Moreover, they did not rely on the teacher. They referred more to outside knowledge, and they were more concerned with making themselves understood than with teacher approbation. In general, they focused on meaning rather than form, and fluency rather than accuracy. They tended to pay more attention to the functional goals of the reading task rather than to their own proficiency improvement—in contrast to the Studiers, whose main goal seemed to be self-improvement. The Explorers were more applied than theoretical, and more grounded in the real world. Finally, they were more willing to accept the responsibility of making choices from the materials than Studiers, but they tended to make them quickly, without a great deal of care and attention.

Table 4–2 illustrates the characteristics of each of the four style types and the numbers of students in the project who identified themselves as possessing those characteristics.

Table 4–2. Cognitive Type Choices and Student Self-Profiles

Type A **Studiers** (23 students)	Type B **Divergers** (18 students)	Type C **Explorers** (14 students)	Type D **Absorbers** (13 students)
realistic*	realistic	realistic/imaginative	imaginative
practical*	artistic	artistic	artistic
intellectual*	intellectual	intellectual	emotional
logical*	logical	logical/intuitive	intuitive
analytical*	analytical	holistic	holistic
serious*	serious	playful	playful
plans**	plans/spontaneous	spontaneous	spontaneous
cautious**	cautious	cautious	impulsive
convergent**	divergent	convergent/divergent	divergent

A factor analysis carried out on 427 responses to the profile suggests two underlying factors. The first (*) reflects the interplay between the world of reason and the world of the imagination: the rational, analytical self as compared to the intuitive, creative self. The second (**) reflects a willingness or unwillingness to take risks, to follow a different path.

Absorbers ("free spirits") are more difficult to describe because they demonstrated fewer overt strategies. In the reading class, they seemed to be more interested in processing the text than in completing any follow-up activities; they paid little attention to choice of materials, and they rarely completed assignments. They responded more positively to the open-ended task of an oral book report than to comprehension questions; however, some did not show up in class on the performance date. They were not really interested in discussing their opinions about texts, preferring instead to listen to the opinions of others; they responded occasionally if pressed by the teacher or a classmate. They rarely initiated, leaving such behavior to the Studiers and Explorers, but they seemed relatively relaxed. They responded specifically to underlying meaning and paid attention to context when allowed a free-range response to a text, and they were more interested in critical reading than in grammatical rules.

It is possible that **Divergers**—the most difficult of the four groups to characterize—combine some risk-taking characteristics with more cautious, analytical ones. This combination seemed to create a dissonance rather than a productive working together. In general, Divergers behaved on the surface like the Absorbers in the classroom in that they tended to be reflective observers rather than active participants. Yet they were more anxious than the Absorbers; they sometimes made quick decisions but then tended to check individually with the teacher to ensure that they were moving in the right direction. They also lost focus when distracted, and they did not seem to have the concentration of the Studiers or the confidence of the Explorers. They preferred to work alone, rather than with the group, but they did not complete assignments as consistently as the Studiers and tended to give up if they encountered difficulty. Moreover, they did not like changes in direction, needed time to make adjustments, and required more reassurance from the teacher than any of the other groups. It is possible that they needed more time to discriminate what was relevant from what was irrelevant to the task; their reliance on assurance from the teacher supports this notion.

The Results: Learning Styles and Attitudes Toward Reading Tasks

As students completed the reading tasks, they kept a record of their work; as I studied the resulting records, I commented on each student's learning styles and strategies.

Table 4-3 is a completed record of (and about) one student. This student used exercises (for example, on the "main idea" of the text) that had a key; she preferred not to work with a group or with the teacher. Therefore, her scores on the chart below are the result of correcting her exercises with the exercise keys. The ratings she gave each of the exercises were originally divided into separate scores for L (like), U (Useful), and E (Easy); rather than give all of those scores, I have given an average of the three in this table.

With regard to the general tendencies of the other students, the careful Studiers were the most positive to exercises overall, and the active Explorers were the least positive. It should be noted that both groups were successful test performers, so that a less positive attitude did not necessarily lead to failure. Studiers responded most positively to the more structured True/False and multiple-choice questions, cautious Divergers and Absorbers to the more open-ended tasks. Again, attitude and success did not seem to be linked, as these were the two groups who performed worst on the tests.

It is not surprising that overall differences in attitudes were relatively small, and there were no significant differences. This may be partially explained by the fact that the exercises themselves were too similar—all were typical classroom exercises—but creating tasks that provided greater contrasts would have interfered with syllabus design of the program, which I had decided at the beginning of the study would be intrusive.

Table 4–3. Personal Reading Record

Reading Title	Content	Exercise Type	Score (Key)	Rating (Average)	Personal Comment
What Is Apartheid?		Complete blanks	17/21	3	Do it alone.
Main idea	Fiction & Newspaper	Identifying	4/5	3	Did it alone.
Dictionary	Dictionary definitions	Scanning for specific info	8/8	4	Do it in 5–10 minutes, alone
School by Tyranny	Personal story	Comprehension questions— inferencing	2/6	2 3	Do it alone, 15 min., understand questions
Short novel	Mystery	Inferencing, double meaning	9/10	3	Worked with Francisco

My (teacher)comments about this student:
- slightly more left-brained; a little more analytical/careful than spontaneous/creative but able to move both ways.
- Assimilator: abstract thinking + observant—likes things to be clear and precise.
- Performance: did well in exercises requiring precise answers/ vocabulary/grammar; has some trouble with inferencing.
- a bit panicky and hard on herself; tended to stay outside group.

The Results: Learning Styles and Assessment Tasks

There was evidence in the project that linked success on tests of reading comprehension to the detailed student profiles, and that successful test-takers demonstrated different profiles, depending on the test-type: multiple choice, summary, and cloze. Table 4–4 summarizes these results.

Notice that no characteristics discriminate between success and failure on all three tests. This is an important finding. That is, different test types do seem to advantage and disadvantage different cognitive types. Moreover, successful performance on traditional tests could not be attributed solely to the deductive skills of the analytic learner, but might also be the result of other more risk-taking strategies, such as answering from memory without double-checking.

Table 4–4. Learning Characteristics and Test-Takers: Success and Failure on Different Test Types

Multiple Choice	Summary	Cloze
success = analytical failure = holistic	(BOTH ARE HOLISTIC)	success = holistic (creative) failure = analytical
success = careful (plans) failure = spontaneous	success = spontaneous failure = careful (plans)	success = spontaneous failure = careful (plans)
success = intellectual failure = emotional	success = emotional failure = intellectual	success = intellectual failure = emotional
(BOTH ARE DIVERGENT)	success = divergent failure = convergent	success = divergent failure = convergent
success = logical failure = intuitive	success = logical failure = intuitive	(BOTH ARE LOGICAL)
(BOTH ARE CAUTIOUS AND PLAYFUL)	success = cautious failure = impulsive	success = serious failure = playful

Some generalizations, however, can be made about successful and unsuccessful test-takers.

- A successful Multiple-Choice test-taker is (predictably) left-brained (that is, analytical, logical and intellectual), but combines these characteristics with artistic and playful tendencies.
- Spontaneous, emotional and holistic (creative) tendencies are characteristics of successful Summary test-takers and unsuccessful Multiple-Choice test-takers.
- A successful Summary test-taker demonstrates an interesting and seemingly balanced mix of left- and right-brained tendencies, tempering spontaneity and emotion with caution and logic.
- A successful Cloze test-taker also demonstrates left- and right-brain tendencies, tempering holistic, spontaneous, and divergent tendencies with intellectual and serious ones.
- Unsuccessful Summary and Cloze test-takers demonstrate a seemingly dissonant left-brain/right-brain mix in which risk-taking is hampered by a too careful, convergent approach, which suggests a measure of high anxiety in a test-taking situation.

  An intuitive, impulsive nature is combined with care, intellect, and convergence in the unsuccessful Summary test-taker.

  Unsuccessful Cloze test-takers combine a playful, emotional nature with an analytical, careful, and convergent one.

Other generalizations can be made regarding cognitive-style group performance based on gain averages:

- **Studiers** and **Explorers** clearly have an advantage in a traditional testing situation over **Absorbers** and **Divergers**, but they perhaps approach the task differently. **Studiers** may approach the task analytically; **Explorers** may approach the task more globally.

- **Absorbers** do better than **Studiers** on the Summary tests and better than **Explorers** on the Cloze tests.

- **Divergers** perform worst on all three test-types. They may be handicapped by traditional tests, perhaps because they need more time to plan and are overwhelmed by choices, which result in a lack of time to complete the test and a tendency to guess impulsively.

Discussion

One major insight that needs additional research concerns style flexing: the recommendations of so many teachers and researchers that students be encouraged to experiment with styles they do not prefer in order to be more flexible learners. But the results of this project indicate that, although adaptability and flexibility may be key factors in successful language learning, this is only part of the picture. Certain combinations of style characteristics may promote flexibility, and others may create dissonance, thereby affecting the focus and the productivity of the learner. Further, the willingness—and even the ability—to switch to a different style to suit a particular situation may in itself be an aspect of risk-taking, which in turn is typical of some styles but not others.

Based on observation, in-depth interviews, and analysis of student reports, my findings suggest that it is very difficult for adult learners to change their overall approach to a task, but that some are more capable than others of adapting strategies that are less congenial, but more successful, in a particular situation. Indeed, anecdotal evidence showed that students were quite determined to defend their own styles and strategies, and they showed little inclination to be influenced by those of their classmates. Thus, it may well be that such adaptability is built in and may not be easy to learn. The learner, therefore, may do better to hone an individual approach than try to emulate others, even though alternative styles and strategies may appear to be more "successful" in a particular context.

My recommendation, then, is to maximize the effect of the styles and strategies that the individual can already consciously and comfortably use, while at the same time increasing the awareness of the effects (positive and negative) of those styles and strategies. The global learner, for example, might simply be encouraged to do more of the same: to read quickly several times, using his/her preferred strategies and styles until more details are apprehended; the sequential learner might be well advised to sit and ponder overall meaning after s/he has completed a careful extraction of meaning from each reading selection. Ultimately, I suggest that understanding the individual and encouraging individual reflection on and implementation of preferred learning styles is more important than trying to impose "good" habits or styles.

Conclusion

Teachers in relatively short-term intensive English language courses must learn how to recognize individual learning preferences quickly and reliably, then provide a flexible program to accommodate them. Systematically providing a learning context that allows individual students to invoke their preferred learning style(s) increases the complexity of program design, but it is necessary if teachers are to deal successfully with the even greater complexities of language learning. In addition, reading assessment, both formal and informal, must consider the natural tendencies of the individual and meet those tendencies with opportunities for alternative assessment. As teachers, we are already sensitive to the needs of and differences among our students. Accommodating those needs and differences may be our greatest challenge.

Results of my investigation lead me to suggest the following general principles of course design and skills assessment.

A. The learning context should be flexible by, for example,

- allowing different physical layouts
- allowing variance in teacher/learner relationships, including
  - ° expert—pupil   ° consultant—client
  - ° therapist—patient   ° facilitator—buddy
- promoting learner autonomy by presenting students with options (that is, prepared choices) and opportunities (to choose their own learning paths)
- providing activities that allow different expressions of cognitive style
- providing students with a clear idea of their own stylistic tendencies so that they can exploit strengths and minimize weaknesses in future proficiency development.

B. The testing context should be flexible by, for example,

- including a variety of assessment procedures that allow students to choose different ways of demonstrating that they have reached the objectives
- providing checkpoints and feedback at appropriate intervals so that modifications can take place during the process
- providing test-types and test-items that allow different style accessibility
- providing students with the style awareness to make informed choices as they approach an assessment situation.

Finally, it is not true that the extremes of either analytic or holistic/global styles are innately bad, and that flexibility of learning styles is innately good. Although "productive flexibility" assumes that the learner can discriminate between strategies and styles that can be adopted successfully in a particular situation, it can be dangerous for teachers to focus on creating the ideal "all-round" learner rather than assessing the style(s) of the individual students and making that the start of the learning path.

The issue of "style flexing" is only one of many that need continued and long-term research. Because teachers have the greatest opportunity for observation and experimentation, and because we have the experience and expertise with students, we are probably the best researchers to study the effect of a particular syllabus design on the individual learner. Such research need not be intrusive, and it should allow learners to participate actively in the investigation so that they develop their own awareness in the project, which could ultimately benefit the profession as a whole.

For Further Reading

Alderson, J. C. and Urguhart, A. H. (Eds.). (1984). *Reading in a Foreign Language.* New York: Longman.

> Although not directly concerned with learning style, this anthology contains several papers that focus on the reactions of individual readers in a variety of contexts. It provides information about learner behavior and asks significant questions about the nature of the reading process, and it encourages teachers to play a more flexible and experimental role in the classroom.

Allwright, D. and Bailey, K. (1991). *Focus on the Language Classroom.* Cambridge: Cambridge University Press.

> The book offers a survey of the findings of classroom research as well as an introduction to classroom research methods and a series of practical research suggestions. It concludes with a plea for a closer relationship between research and teaching through the notion of "exploratory practice."

Skehan, P. (1989). *Individual Differences in Second-Language Learning.* London: Edward Arnold.

> Skehan critically analyzes important research into differences of language, aptitude, motivation, learning style, and learner strategies. He also draws connections between learner characteristics and types of instruction. A very readable book for both teachers and researchers.

Willing, K. (1988). *Learning Styles in Adult Migrant Education.* Research Series (Ed. David Nunan). National Curriculum Resource Centre: Adult Migrant Education Program. (Address: 5th Floor, Renaissance Centre, 127 Rundle Mall, Adelaide, South Austraila 5000)

> Willing relates learning styles research to second language teaching and discusses the implication of research to classroom practice. He provides a comprehensive survey of the literature on cognitive and learning styles as well as a report on a major study into learning style preferences among students in the Australian Adult Migrant Education Program.

Chapter 5

Computers and Collaboration: Adapting CALL Materials to Different Learning Styles

Ken Keobke
City University of Hong Kong

Ray Bradbury's collection of science fiction short stories *The Martian Chronicles* (1958) includes a tale of a man who finds a deserted alien home that miraculously adapts to his needs for water and shelter. But the ideal home soon grows tired of adapting and instead transforms the man into one of its original occupants: an overgrown lizard. The story is an appropriate metaphor for the computer's tendency to impose its style and affordances on users. In an ideal world, Computer Assisted Language Learning (CALL) software programs would intuitively adapt themselves to each learner and offer a number of possible interfaces and challenges to match individual learning styles. But neither we nor our computers live in an ideal world, and teachers and learners need to involve themselves actively in adapting software to different learning styles. In this chapter, I clarify what is meant by CALL, discuss types of CALL activities, explore learning styles as they relate to CALL, and then suggest ways in which CALL materials can be adapted to learning styles.

Defining CALL

Because of the changing nature of computers, CALL is an ill-defined discipline, constantly evolving both in terms of pedagogy and technological advancements in hardware and software. CALL materials, once basic textual gap-filling and simple programming exercises (see Papert 1980), have evolved to interactive multimedia presentations with sound, animation, and video. Speech recognition sub-programs have extended the traditional reading and writing aspects of CALL to listening and speaking. Software and hardware are today faster, more interesting, and more flexible than ever before.

In CALL pedagogy, the above changes and growth necessitate creating as broad a definition as possible: *any activity in which a learner uses a computer and improves his/her language.* Although this definition might seem unworkably large, it at least encompasses a spectrum of activities in the teaching and learning of language. More important, an awareness of this spectrum allows both teacher and learners to recognize and adapt materials to various learning styles.

Activities Used in CALL

The range of tasks and exercises available in CALL can be organized into various taxonomies based on (a) the stated focus of the software (such as grammar, vocabulary, fluency), (b) the targeted language skills (reading, writing, speaking/listening), (c) the levels of questions (from simple identification and comprehension to analytical, synthetic, and evaluative tasks), and (d) the learner characteristics based on age, gender, and level.

Another way of organizing the CALL program is by locus of control—that is, the continuum between the program's and the learner's responsibilities for decisions about the outcomes, the sequence of learning, the amount of interaction, and even the content of the program. This locus of control is summarized in Table 5-1.

Table 5–1. Locus of Control Continuum for Organizing a CALL Program

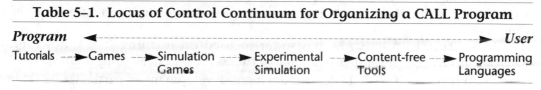

At the Program end of the continuum, as Jonnassen, Wilson, Wang, and Grabinger (1993, p. 88) demonstrate, the learner has little control or choice; the program attempts to

- eliminate extraneous information
- simplify for comprehensibility
- support individual learning and competition
- offer prescriptive sequences of instruction
- abstract instruction experiences
- focus on acquiring skills
- reconstruct/replicate knowledge.

In contrast, in CALL designs in which the User/learner is in control, the program tends to

- support natural complexity and content
- avoid oversimplification
- offer open-ended learning environments
- engage in reflective practice
- engage the learner in knowledge construction
- support collaboration
- present multiple representations/perspectives
- present instruction in real-world contexts (as authentic tasks).

Examples of learner-controlled CALL design include open activities structured around word-processing software and the use of electronic mail and the Internet. The Internet is particularly popular for various forms of learning and discourse (as summarized by Seaton 1993 and Turkle 1995). On its simplest level, the Internet allows telegraphic-style written communication that, for second language learners, can encourage writing—to pen pals, for example—as a real-world communicative task.

Defining Learning Styles

The interaction between learning styles and CALL materials is unlikely ever to be researched definitively because of the already-mentioned continuous advances in technology and related revisions to pedagogy. Nevertheless, many definitions of learners and learning styles have been offered by those studying traditional learning materials and classrooms. Carol Chapelle has studied ESL students as Field Dependent (FD) or Field Independent (FI) (1995); Madeline Ehrman (1996) has suggested synthesizing many learning styles into a profile for students; Lynn O'Brien (1989) has developed an instrument to measure sensory learning styles such as *visual, auditory,* and *haptic.* Another division categorizes learners into those who learn best by doing, imagining, reasoning or theorizing (for a summary, see Coe 1996).

Little research in L2 CALL has so far focused on learning styles, however. Patricia Dunkel (1991) summarizes some of the issues that need to be addressed.

- Which kinds of CALL lessons augment development of particular L2 skills such as reading and listening comprehension, oral proficiency, knowledge of grammar?
- Which kinds of computer environments (computer-assisted instruction, computer-managed instruction, or computer-enriched instruction) augment L2 use and learning?
- Do students perceive CALL to be beneficial to the improvement of English language skills?
- Does small-group work at a computer terminal generate conversational interactions among group participants, and, if so, what is the quality and what are the constituents of the discourse generated?
- Do certain features in the design of CALL courseware (such as locus of control) affect the quantity and quality of student learning?
- Do students' attitudes toward writing and the written product improve as a result of learning and using word processing in English?

Other areas for research in L2 and CALL include these.

- How do affective states (high anxiety, for example) and preferred modes of communication (auditory or visual, or even kinesthetic in the case of the deaf-blind) and cognitive traits influence L2 language acquisition? (On this topic, see Boyd and Mitchell 1992.)
- Do self-reported learning style instrument results reflect ideal learning styles? For example, although a student may prefer to learn through passively watching a video, might s/he learn some skills better through active participation?
- In what ways does facility in the technical aspects of the computer (keyboarding skills, a mouse, or the systems of windows and cursors) affect student learning?

CALL and Learning Styles

As CALL develops and programs proliferate, teachers are increasingly concerned with matching appropriate programs to their students' learning styles (Wild 1996). For example, students studying grammar who tend to favor rule-based learning will benefit most from programs such as Taskmaster and Gapmaster, which allow teachers, or even students, to create true/false and multiple-choice problems. More sophisticated language-learning programs, such as those by EZ Language, Berlitz, and Triple Play Plus, tend toward the approach that allows students more control and a wide range of activities from which to choose.

Among the best ways learners improve their language skills with computers is through collaborative learning activities (not often provided by CALL software) that implicitly or explicitly encourage discussion. Students with a variety of learning styles can participate successfully in such activities (Wegerif 1996). Moreover, "some of the highest pedagogical objectives can only be achieved by employing group learning activities such as group problem solving, games, case studies, and exchanges with real experts" (Derycke, Smith, and Hemery 1995).

H. F. O'Neil (1994) identifies some of these collaborative CALL activities with a taxonomy of teamwork skills that involve the complex production of language:

- *adaptability:* recognizing problems and responding appropriately
- *coordination:* organizing team activities to complete a task on time
- *decision-making:* using available information to make decisions
- *interpersonal:* interacting cooperatively with other team members
- *communication:* the overall exchange of clear and accurate information.

CALL programs used to encourage language learning often address several of these teamwork skills. For instance, most are found in programs that present learning as a quest. Some quest programs, particularly appropriate for younger students, involve making a series of correct answers that move the player along a map or save a creature in danger; students work in pairs or small groups. In general, L2 quest programs require coordination, decision-making, and interpersonal or communication skills. They often work best with group members of different language and cultural backgrounds for whom English, however limited, is the only common language. In such situations, cooperative interpersonal skills such as consensus, leadership, and queuing must be negotiated.

Designing CALL for Multiple-Style Users

The continuing changes in computer hardware and software, the different definitions of learning styles, and the broad definitions of what constitutes CALL make developing guidelines for identifying or designing effective programs and lessons difficult. Nevertheless, some general guidelines are possible.

First, the classroom environment in which effective CALL takes place must be carefully considered and designed. Currently, schools continue to be built on an Industrial Revolution model, with students sitting in rows being force-fed knowledge (Logan 1995). Computer "laboratories" are often constructed with individual carrels that isolate one computer and user from another in a forest of BE

QUIET signs; often, computer access is restricted, either in terms of time or space. The result: CALL is discouraged. Instead, the environment should match the nature of CALL activities, particularly collaborative learning.

An effective CALL environment is flexible in physical arrangement and provides computers and programs for individual students (with headphones to provide privacy) as well as shared computers for small groups. A large-screen projector system, such as a computer screen that fits over an overhead projector, can provide a common screen for group discussion, or even for a networked program that allows several more sophisticated students to work on the same document.

In addition, teachers should discuss with students which kinds of CALL lessons augment development of particular L2 skills such as reading and listening comprehension, oral proficiency, and knowledge of grammar. Teachers might also discuss different approaches to such learning, depending on the individual learning styles of their students. One way to begin is to brainstorm with students about what they think they need to learn, and how they prefer to learn it. Such discussions increase learner-centeredness (or locus of control toward the user) in which "learners are closely involved in the decision-making regarding the content of the curriculum and how it is taught" (Nunan 1994, p. 2).

Next, to match CALL software packages with student learning styles, the software should be reviewed and classified by both teachers and students. The environment must provide time, training, and materials that allow students to experiment with and evaluate software programs. Initially, teachers can collect reviews from professional publications such as the *CAELL Journal.*[*] Eventually, more personalized reviews by student-users can

- outline key aspects of the program.
- locate the program on the Locus of Control continuum (see Table 5-1).
- suggest how learners might use it.
- indicate which learning styles are accommodated by the program.

Teachers can incorporate these reviews into lesson plans that also teach critical thinking; the reviews should be posted or otherwise made easily available to other student-users.

Finally, when a CALL program is not suitable, students and teachers might examine ways it could be adapted. For example, students can work together to develop layers of tasks for existing materials to make them more challenging or more appropriate. In some cases, this might involve a student drawing up a set of questions that will guide another user. The creation of such student-made "custom-user manuals" is beneficial to future learners because the manuals are likely to focus on the essentials necessary to using the program, and it is beneficial to the student-manual author because explaining the program to others

---

[*] *CAELL Journal* is available by subscription from *CAELL Journal*, ISTE, University of Oregon, 1787 Agate Street, Eugene, OR 97403. Phone (503) 346-4414, fax (503) 346-5890, e-mail ISTE@oregon.uoregon.edu or Compuserve 70014,2117.

encourages precise language use. The same is true of another p
students might create a treasure hunt for key words and con
encyclopedia software program or use a translation program.
dictionaries that address local needs.

Conclusion

CALL is a discipline still in its infancy. Adapting CALL to individual student
learning styles therefore involves numerous challenges: some are technical; some
require examining, modifying, and even creating custom materials. Materials
development may seem complex and daunting for many teachers, but it is a task
too important to be left solely to commercial software publishers. To meet these
challenges, teachers should rely upon the resources of professional publications,
special interest groups, and the help of peers and students.

For Further Reading

Wegerif, R. (1996). Collaborative learning and directive software. *Journal of
Computer Assisted Learning 12,* 22–32.

> This article provides a good overview of recent research in the area of
> collaborative learning when using computers, and it offers examples of
> different models. The article explores how students learn when using
> computers and emphasizes the unintentional benefits of students creating
> language to deal with the computer, its software, and each other. The
> significance of undirected talk is also underlined. Teacher intervention
> may actually interrupt the dynamics and benefits of collaborative learning
> by shifting the focus from true learning to simple recitation of facts.

Wild, M. (1996). Mental models and computer modeling. *Journal of Computer
Assisted Learning 12*, 10–21.

> Wild provides an excellent bibliography on mental models of learning, and
> he suggests that learners' mental models are neither fixed when they enter
> our classes nor simply developed and transferred by teachers. Rather,
> learners' mental models are by definition incomplete and likely to evolve
> over time. There are implications in terms of accessibility for reflection of a
> learner's personal model and a model supplied/implied by a computer;
> juxtaposing a computer's mental model on a user may lead to confusion
> rather than to better understanding.

Chapter 6

Learning Styles and Strategies of a Partially Bilingual Student Diagnosed as Learning Disabled: A Case Study

Rebecca Oxford
University of Alabama

Christine Nam
Teachers College, Columbia University

> Traditional teaching methods were not serving my needs . . . I slipped through the cracks of the educational system, discovering years later that I had a learning disability.

These are the words of a university student who suffered in silence for many years before summoning up the courage, at age twenty, to go to an education specialist for a learning disability evaluation. Neither her teachers nor her parents had ever suggested that she seek diagnostic help, although she had experienced repeated learning problems.

This chapter reports on the young woman, who grew up partially bilingual (English outside the home and Thai and English at home) and who received a formal diagnosis of a learning disability only a year ago. We have altered "Louise's" name and personal-demographic features to maintain her confidentiality, but report accurately the specific data on her learning styles, strategies, and disabilities.

Definitions

Most investigators agree that a "learning disability" refers to a somewhat independent deficit in learning. That is, a person's learning difficulties are associated with one or more aspect(s) of learning, but not necessarily with all aspects of learning. It is entirely possible for a person to be learning disabled in reading and not in mathematics, or vice versa.

The term "learning style" refers to a person's general approach to learning and problem-solving (Reid 1995). Many successful learners are aware of their preferences for learning styles, which are the ones they find the most comfortable and easy to use (Oxford, Ehrman, and Lavine 1991).

A learning style . . . can run the range from a mild preference ("I'd rather learn by discovering patterns by myself") through a strong need ("It interferes with my learning when I haven't mastered the grammar patterns first—I have trouble following the material that uses them") to an out-and-out rigidity ("I have to see it before I can remember it; if I don't see it nothing sticks at all") [Ehrman 1996, p. 54].

"Learning strategy" is a technical phrase that means any specific conscious action or behavior a student takes to improve his or her own learning. Learning strategy choices are often related to preferred learning styles. For instance, a student who has a strongly visual learning style tends to use the strategies of taking notes and outlining, whereas an auditory learner tends to use the strategies of recording lectures and listening to them after class ends. Learners who have an analytic learning style often like to use strategies that involve breaking material down into smaller pieces, whereas global learners prefer strategies that help them grasp the main idea quickly without attending to details.

The Case Study

Louise was an especially interesting subject because she grew up partially bilingual and because her disabilities drew three important concepts—learning disabilities, learning styles, and learning strategies—into a focus we could examine fruitfully. We gathered information from several open-ended, learning-related interviews with Louise; from personal notes Louise wrote to us; and from a four-page essay about her own learning history that Louise wrote for a psychology class. We also drew on a narrative report written by the education specialist who first diagnosed Louise's learning disability.

In addition, we perused results from the Style Analysis Survey (SAS) (Oxford 1993). (See Appendix 8 for this survey.) This questionnaire of 110 items measures five different dimensions of learning style:

- how you use your physical senses for study and work (sensory preferences)
- how you deal with other people (extroversion, introversion)
- how you handle possibilities (intuitive-random, concrete-sequential)
- how you approach tasks (closure-oriented, open)
- how you deal with ideas (global, analytic).

The education specialist also administered a battery of tests, each of which yielded results that we used in our study.[*]

Louise's Background and History

Louise is a 21-year-old university student who grew up in a prosperous suburb in New England. Both her parents are native Thais who came to the United States

---

[*] These tests included the Woodcock-Johnson Psycho-Educational Battery–Revised (WJ-R), including the Extended Cognitive Abilities Tests and the Tests of Academic Achievement; Rey-Osterreith Complex Figure Drawing; Nelson-Denny Reading Test; Informal Writing Sample; and Wechsler Memory Scales–Revised.

earlier in their lives. At home the family speaks mostly English and some Thai. Louise has one sister. The other family members have no discernible learning disabilities. From our interviews with Louise, we gathered some information about her "culture" in the home: her parents are upwardly mobile; they want Louise and her sister to succeed academically; and they did not realize that Louise has a learning disability.

When Louise first went to the education specialist for evaluation and diagnosis, she was a university senior majoring in English. She explained that she had difficulty gaining meaning from lectures, writing coherently, understanding what she read, and dealing with word problems. Her university grade point average was 2.85 on a 4.0 scale, indicating B- or C+ work. On her Scholastic Aptitude Test, taken for university admission, Louise had scored 520 on the verbal section and 520 on the math section. Her high school grade point average had been 3.3, or B+.

There had been early hints of learning problems. Louise wrote in her learning history essay:

> I do not know the exact day when I began having trouble at school. Maybe it started in first grade, when my teacher had to consistently move my seat because she noticed I was glancing over at my neighbor's paper. . . . Perhaps, it was in third grade, when my teacher put me in an ESL class, even though I spoke English perfectly. During this time, I was also placed in the highest level math, since I was good at numbers, but after a while I was moved to the mainstream class. Or maybe it became noticeable in fifth grade, when I was placed in a remedial history group, because of the trouble I was having imbibing information. Or perhaps it was in sixth grade, when everyone took a mandatory reading lab class, and I was never able to read at the same speed as the rest of the students. I just took my time and did the most I could do, and at the end of the class, I flipped to the back of the book and filled in the answers to the ones I didn't get (of course leaving a few wrong answers).

Later, Louise had to have a tutor for Spanish. This indicates that whatever problems existed in her English language learning spilled over into the learning of Spanish, a foreign language.

Louise's Favored Learning Styles and Strategies

The results of the SAS demonstrate that Louise has very strong learning preferences, and she confirmed orally that the results accurately reflect her own perceptions of her learning styles and strategies. Louise's results show (a) very definite visual and hands-on preferences (she prefers to learn through books, videos, graphics, and she enjoys conducting experiments, building models, and working with objects) and (b) very weak auditory inclination.

Louise's essay about her learning history substantiated these results and indicated that her distaste for listening is related to a real dysfunction in listening ability.

I sat dumbfounded in lecture halls from all the information that was being thrown at me . . . I was unable to take notes, since it was difficult for me to remember facts long enough to write them down. This also affected any oral questions that may have been directed towards me. My auditory problems, along with my high anxiety level made the processing of information take a lot longer. . . . I was not able to tune out any extraneous noises.

[In] *disciplines that depended solely on tests or lecture style instruction, I was barely able to keep my head over water. In high school, I somehow got by, cramming* [using the visual sense] *the night before an exam and regurgitating the information the next day.*

The results of the SAS on extroversion and introversion indicate that Louise is an extroverted learner who enjoys a wide range of social contacts and interactions; she prefers not to work alone. Although Louise's low preference for auditory learning might make some group work difficult for her, she described certain learning strategies that involved other people: "I made sure however, to attend all TA sessions, student study groups, or had friends that were patient enough to explain concepts that did not seem to connect."

Nevertheless, Louise's natural extroversion was sometimes hidden, especially in small classes where she did not feel she could answer questions or participate effectively due to listening problems. She wrote:

In classes that were more discussion-oriented, they were smaller in class size, [and] based more on papers, which was beneficial to me, but higher in stress level, since individual attention would increase and there would be more time to call upon students. If such were the case, I usually picked a seat in the last row, directly behind another classmate and hardly uttered a sound.

The SAS results also demonstrate that Louise has a concrete-sequential preference rather than an intuitive-random preference. That is, she prefers one-step-at-a-time learning activities, wants to know where she is going at every moment in the learning process, dislikes ambiguity (Chapelle 1983; Ely 1989), and avoids abstract theories. She prefers to have clear rules and directions established by an expert or authority figure. Louise wrote:

I need information presented in a clear, step-by-step linguistic framework. I feel more comfortable when a person tells me exactly what to do, this feeling stems from my lack of confidence. Thus, the more structure I have, the more secure I feel.

Similarly, Louise is definite in her preference for a closure-oriented rather than open-ended orientation to learning. That is, she focuses carefully on all tasks, meets deadlines, plans ahead, works systematically, prefers neatness and structure, and wants rapid decisions. As Louise stated in her learning history essay, she uses many closure-oriented strategies to learn better, especially since her learning disability diagnosis.

After my diagnosis [of specific learning disabilities], . . . *I started studying for exams weeks ahead of time, using structured reviewing, mechanical devices, such as flashcards, groups, studying with a partner or large study groups . . . I became extremely "anal retentive" in the way I dealt with certain matters, everything had to have order or closure, which compensated for the lack of organization in my mind.*

Finally, Louise's results demonstrate that she is definitely an analytic learner rather than a global learner. The analytic preference suggests that she likes to break down ideas into details, seeks perfection and accuracy, and is uncomfortable and impatient with "main ideas" that appear too general or fuzzy to her. Her analytic bent sometimes prevents her from seeing the big picture, causing her to get lost in a welter of details. She wrote:

If the teacher, however, were to ask me to apply what I had just learned [through the cramming of details the night before the test], *he/she would have seen that I did not comprehend how things fit into the larger picture.*

Louise's Test Results

In the ability and achievement tests administered by the psychologist, Louise's results demonstrated scores across the continuum, as shown in Table 6–1. These standardized test results indicate unquestionably sharp deficits in three aspects of auditory memory, as well as in auditory inferencing, listening comprehension, overall oral language, labeling pictures, and two aspects of writing (usage and fluency). Louise's very mixed pattern of learning disabilities underscores the fact that the problem is highly complex and that learning deficits appear alongside cognitive strengths. The pattern also suggests that while some learning problems occur somewhat independently, other disabilities may be interrelated.

The education specialist's narrative report states that Louise has serious difficulties with "phonological awareness": "This would affect Louise's note-taking ability as well as her ability to follow instructions [and revealed] difficulty with short-term [auditory] memory [and] her ability to inference meaning verbally in order to provide missing words to short paragraphs."

Deficits in auditory processing no doubt cause Louise some additional problems in long-term and short-term memory. If an individual cannot process effectively through the aural mode—that is, if the person cannot listen successfully—the auditory memory will be affected negatively. These serious auditory problems were confirmed by Louise's learning history essay:

In the beginning of each class, I would start by telling myself that I would pay close attention to what the professor had to say. But, as soon as there was an opportunity for me to divert my attention, I was lost in either reverie or frustration, from not being able to tune out any extraneous noises.

The more severe deficits that Louise demonstrated on the standardized tests might also be related to speed problems in processing and using language. The very low scores on writing fluency, memory for (oral) sentences, picture vocabulary, and listening comprehension are likely to be partially linked with

Table 6–1. Louise's Ability and Achievement Test Scores

Ability	Achievement
Above Average	*Above Average*
long-term retrieval of visual-auditory learning	basic reading skills
visual memory and delayed recall	broad reading skills
verbal memory	
Average	*Average*
verbal analogies	basic writing skills
visual matching processing speed	all subtests of mathematics skills
overall processing speed	
Below Average	*Below Average*
overall long-term retrieval	reading passage comprehension
short-term memory for reversed numbers	overall broad written language
Deficient	*Deficient*
overall auditory processing	overall short-term memory
picture recognition	word usage
overall (oral) comprehension–knowledge	writing fluency
cross-out task showing processing speed	overall oral language
overall auditory processing	memory for sentences
overall broad written language	listening comprehension

issues of speed and timing. Indeed, the education specialist noted difficulties "in the speed with which she reads and writes," and, in her diagnosis, she stated that Louise "needs to be identified as a young woman with mild language-based and short-term memory learning disabilities. As a result of her disabilities, [she] works more slowly with language-based tasks." Therefore, the psychologist recommended many psychoeducational interventions, the most relevant of which for this chapter are as follows. Louise should

- be given time-and-a-half to complete exams requiring reading or writing, including math tests with word problems.
- take all standardized tests in an untimed manner.
- use her strong visual skills and learn semantic mapping techniques, which would assist in comprehension and in organizing tasks.
- use a note-taker (a personal assistant to take notes for her).
- talk to her professors to ensure she has gained all pertinent information from lectures.
- review notes with other students and preview lectures with her teachers.
- sit up front during lectures.
- join discussion or study groups to review materials so that she does not have to reread entire texts two or three times.

- take notes as she reads, asking questions of the text and cross-referencing when possible.
- work with a strategies tutor to help identify main ideas and organize large amounts of information.
- consider audiotaping lectures.
- avoid pop quizzes based on verbal information because she needs to preview and organize material before any exam.
- review instructions with her professors to be sure she is on task.
- discuss with a doctor the possibility of medication to aid her attention and auditory memory skills.

Reflections

When we examine all of the data on Louise, it is impossible to escape the obvious auditory processing problems. These problems are exacerbated by and help create the auditory memory difficulties Louise experiences. It is likely that the auditory processing and memory deficits take their toll on Louise's reading and writing as well. This does not mean, however, that all her academic problems can be attributed solely to these gaps in auditory processing ability or auditory memory function. Certain other factors, such as anxiety and initial lack of knowledge about appropriate learning strategies, play roles as well.

Throughout her life, Louise had been frozen with anxiety and fear when faced with learning tasks that failed to meet her stylistic requirements. She needed structured tasks that were filled with visual stimuli and accompanied by explicit teacher-given instructions. Moreover, she did not always have access to appropriate learning strategies. When under stress, she sometimes chose strategies that reduced her anxiety level in the immediate situation (especially in listening-related circumstances) but did not create learning.

After the diagnosis of learning disability, Louise has learned to use her knowledge of learning styles to help her choose specific learning strategies. When a learning task was inadequately structured by the teacher, for example, Louise began to take charge by structuring the task, and she organized herself at the same time. She has also learned to use strategies that focus on her natural inclination toward the visual and hands-on learning styles, and she looks for teachers who use visual aids and hands-on activities offering authentic applications of knowledge.

Discussion

Many researchers have asserted that successful language development for any student depends partially on appropriate use of learning strategies that fit the individual's learning style. Joy Reid (1995) and Madeline Ehrman (1996) focus on the roles of styles and strategies. Roberta Vann and Roberta Abraham (1990) have found that unsuccessful language learners did not necessarily use fewer language-learning strategies than their more successful peers; rather, they simply employed strategies in a haphazard fashion, inadequately relating the task at hand and their own learning style preferences. Oxford, Ehrman, and Lavine (1991) stress the importance of recognizing one's own learning style and finding the most style-comfortable strategies, but also note the need to stretch beyond one's favored style occasionally. That is, the most comfortable strategies for a given person's learning style might or might not be the best for the particular language tasks, so some degree of style-stretching or style-flexing might be needed. This is best accomplished through the conscious use of learning strategies that do not fit one's own learning style(s) but that might well be relevant to the task at hand.

In contrast, some researchers do not see the value of understanding language learning styles and strategies. For instance, R. L. Sparks and L. Ganschow (1995) disparage research on learning strategies and learning styles and treat learning style conflicts and poor choice of learning strategies as virtually irrelevant to language problems. These investigators suggest that an understanding of learning strategies and learning styles is relatively useless in terms of improving language development among learning-disabled students, that only a very small sub-set of phonologically-based linguistic factors—and no non-linguistic factors—can explain the etiology of learning disabilities related to language.

We hold a much more moderate view. We believe that learning strategies are among a large group of factors that influence language development in learning-disabled students and "normals" alike (Oxford and Green 1996). Learning styles and strategies are not the only explanatory or diagnostic factors, of course, and knowledgeable researchers have never claimed them to be. While learning styles and strategies do not represent a total explanation or a panacea, some researchers (Cohen 1990; O'Malley and Chamot 1990; Oxford 1997) have suggested that they are well worth considering and optimizing in the language classroom. Many linguistic, affective, and social factors are implicated in learning disabilities as well.

Conclusions

After the learning disability diagnosis, Louise wrote that she felt stronger, better informed, and more hopeful. Shortly thereafter, she took a psychology class that stressed learning styles and learning strategies, along with affective factors like motivation and anxiety. In her learning history essay, she felt secure enough to give suggestions to teachers dealing with learning disabled students like herself.

> *The feeling was as if I were starting from square one. The result of this discovery* [the learning disability diagnosis] *has been my greatest struggle and my greatest accomplishment. I have learned more about myself this past year, in assessing my own learning styles and strategies and have excelled in my classes. In the past, the way I dealt with my dormant learning disability was acquiring many compensatory methods that shaped my personality, as well as aiding me along through the years of academia. Now, I have honed the ones I had acquired and adapted* [adopted] *new ones.*

> *I have become more analytic than global, since I must break broad concepts into smaller manageable units, in order for me to process information. As a teacher, one way to target both groups could be to write class notes in an outline form, so students can see both the details and how* [they] *fit into an overall theme.*

All students have sensory preferences. Therefore, educators should assess their students' strengths and incorporate learning strategies [more precisely, teaching strategies] into their lesson plan. Due to a weakness in my auditory short-term memory, I depend on visual aids and hands on projects. Strategies that helped me, were teachers who used resources such as overhead projectors, chalkboards, dittos, as well as hands on activities that applied classroom instruction to authentic material. In this way, teachers can accommodate to all types of learners.

For those students who may be either extroverted or introverted, instructors should give students the option to either work in groups or individually. I personally benefit from hearing my classmates' input and am able to brainstorm ideas better when listening to their suggestions. This also appeases my short attention span . . .

Educators should always give options, options, options to his/her students. Traditional, well-organized teaching should not be disregarded (especially for closure-oriented and concrete-sequential students like me), but to [sic] those students who are open or intuitive-random can be easily pacified with creative projects that deal directly with the text at hand.

As we can see, tapping into one's learning styles and strategies help[s] all students, not only second language learners, but gifted students, mainstream students, and those with special needs. The problems I have encountered could have been alleviated if I were given options, rather than trained to conform to a single mode of learning . . . With this new knowledge I have gained about myself, I am beginning to refill the cavities that had been left to decay. Fortunately, education is slowly revolutionizing and teachers are being equipped with the right tools to serve the needs of their students. Educators realize that there is no one correct way to teach a child and that there are innumerable manners in which for them to learn. If both student and teacher [are] able to identify their strengths, they can work as partners toward scholastic achievement.

Louise was right: *there is no one correct way to teach a child*, people learn in *innumerable manners*. She showed tremendous optimism in believing that today's educators realize this profound concept.

This optimism might not be fully justified because many educators have not yet come to the conclusion that there is more than one way to teach or to learn. Such educators tend to follow the instructional behaviors displayed decades ago by their favorite mentors. Reflexively, these educators teach the way they were taught, oblivious to the needs of their own current, flesh-and-blood, diverse students. As a result, many learning-disabled students are caught in a secret web of undiagnosed cognitive deficits and affective difficulties.

The educational revolution Louise described is slow and sometimes tortuous. As the revolution continues, increasing numbers of educators might discover the multiplicity of ways in which people actually learn and the corresponding multiplicity of forms that good instruction could and should take. We hope this case study about Louise—an exceptionally courageous, insightful, and ambitious student—helps propel the revolution along its trajectory toward the possibility of optimal learning for all students. Louise is now advancing toward the start of her graduate studies, with the goal of becoming a special education teacher to help others like herself. As a teacher, no doubt she will nudge the educational revolution with her unflagging, newly energized spirit.

For Further Reading

Journal of Learning Disabilities

This is the best place to find information on learning disabilities. The journal is up-to-date, incisive, and interesting. It contains all the latest research of note on learning disabilities, and it publishes articles by authors from around the world. Many of the investigations on learning disabilities published in journals in the foreign and second language field are elaborations of earlier investigations that appeared in "mainstream" learning disability journals like this one.

Oxford, R. L. (1996). *Language Learning Strategies Around the World: Crosscultural Perspectives*. Manoa: University of Hawaii Press.

This is the only existing volume about language-learning strategies that intentionally includes dozens of cross-cultural contrasts regarding strategy use. The preface explains the great importance of cultural influence on learning, particularly on strategies. The first section contains a variety of chapters on strategy assessment. The second section explores innovative techniques and methods for strategy instruction. Teachers and researchers interested in the learning of any second and foreign language can benefit from this book.

Chapter 7

Field Independence, Field Dependence, and Field Sensitivity in Another Light

Madeline E. Ehrman
Foreign Service Institute, Arlington, Virginia

Dominic, Henry, Lester, Nell, and Victoria are students in the same language class, one that is taught with the aim of producing both communicative fluency and linguistic precision. Each of these students reacts in a different way to those two goals. Dominic and Nell are particularly responsive to activities that require them to use the language they are learning in complex contexts. On the other hand, they don't learn much from grammar lectures or discrete-point exercises. Lester, on the other hand, prefers an orderly program in which he can deal with each linguistic item separately; he loves grammatical explanations, but he is overwhelmed by too much authentic input. Victoria has never found a language class in which she did not do well; Henry, on the other hand, has a difficult time with both communicative fluency and precision.

Much of the variation among these five students can be explained by the construct of field independence and a related one of field sensitivity. We shall meet the students again later in this chapter.

Background

Every natural experience consists of a great range of perceptions: auditory, visual, kinesthetic, olfactory, and so on. All of us have the ability to discriminate and to focus, to some degree, on a stimulus that is important to us, such as a physical object, a certain sound or sequence of sounds, an idea, or a grammar rule. The term "field independence" refers to discrimination and focus that is "at least a preference and at most an ability" (Ehrman 1996, p. 78).

The construct of field independence–field dependence (FI–FD) has been intuitively attractive to researchers and teachers in second language acquisition for years. At the same time, the field independence model has been theoretically controversial and elusive as a practical tool for teachers. The greatest weaknesses of the construct are its definition (how broad or narrow) and its measurement, which has been accomplished through a test of ability—Herman Witkin's (1969) visual task of disembedding figures—that may not apply well to language learning.

The FI–FD construct is a work in progress. No matter what the definition, practitioners—teachers, student counselors, and learning style researchers—persistently see differences among students that relate to how readily they can work with material **out of context** and impose some amount of cognitive reconstruction on it. At the same time, there is confusion about whether FI–FD is a style or an ability, whether it should include personality factors or refer strictly to cognitive functioning alone, whether field dependence is the absence of field independence or a processing style in its own right.

In the absence of agreement in the field and a satisfactory measure, practitioners resort to very inclusive descriptions of every possible behavior associated with the construct, as is the case for most of the discussions of FI–FD in Reid (1995). When researchers attempt to narrow FI–FD definitions, they make use of descriptions of global vs. analytic processing (see Oxford, Ehrman, and Lavine 1991; Oxford 1995) or analytic vs. relational processing (such as Kinsella 1995). In the former case, the focus is on the difference between the general and the particular; in the latter, it is on the degree to which an individual isolates information or links it to other data.

In this chapter, I treat FI as a learning style representing a preference for dealing with materials out of context. In contrast, many learners prefer to learn material **in context**; this preference can be described as "field dependence" or "field sensitivity," a distinction pursued in the questions and answers that follow.

Questions and Answers

The following is an attempt to progress further in making this intuitively appealing construct practical for the classroom. The discussion is organized by some of the areas of difficulty that a variety of researchers have identified.

1. *What is field independence?* At its most general, FI is related to an ability to distinguish and isolate sensory experiences from the surrounding sensory input. In Herman Witkin's original research, the construct began as differential ability to perceive the vertical, either for one's own body position or for external objects. That ability was found to correlate with extraction of simple geometric figures from a more complex field, a task that involves cognitive restructuring as well as perceptual differentiation. Since Witkin's research, each step away from the original definition (perception of one's own vertical position) broadened the definition of FI, making it applicable to a wider but increasingly less precise range of situations.

Researchers have also suggested a personality dimension in the vertical and disembedding of geometric figures. FI individuals are described as task-oriented rather than person-oriented, inclined to set their own paths in life rather than to be compliant, and to interact with others in a cool rather than a warm way. A variety of cognitive processing behaviors have also been linked with the construct. In this chapter, I limit FI to **lack of need for context.**[*]

---

[*] Witkin also observed that subjects who excelled on perception of vertical and disembedding of geometric figures had personality characteristics of the sort described in this chapter: task-orientation, interpersonal independence, and cool interactions.

As it is used now in second language acquisition studies, the term FI includes perceptual factors, aspects of fluid intelligence, personality, and classroom behaviors. It is both an ability, measured by a test of visual disembedding, and a stylistic preference, addressed

2. *What is field dependence?* The term "field dependence" can mean a relative absence of field independence, either as a behavioral tendency or as a lack of an ability. When FI–FD is measured, it is invariably through tests of FI. If we treat FD as an outcome of the usual measures, we can accurately define it only as an absence of field independence (Brown 1994). Practitioners have observed that many of the behaviors characteristic of FI learners can be contrasted with a set of behaviors shown by many non-FI individuals. Beginning with Witkin, therefore, they describe the FD learner as interpersonally oriented, compliant, dependent on external structure, and in need of context.

The term "field dependence" is also used to indicate responsiveness at some level to the surrounding background. I use the term "field sensitivity" (FS) for that characteristic, reserving the term "field dependence" (FD) for absence of FI. An FD learner cannot extract material from context.

3. *What is field sensitivity?* "Field sensitive" is a term originated to sidestep the negative connotations of "field dependence" in U. S. culture (Ramîrez and Castañeda 1974) and to suggest that such learners have a positive array of skills, not just deficiencies (that is, they are not just non-FI). Under the "global" rubric, researchers (such as Oxford 1995) have suggested such positive learning qualities as the ability to guess from context and to work with incomplete data.

As mentioned at the beginning of the chapter, the ability to discriminate among perceptions is universal, although it is not realized equally well in all contexts for every individual. Similarly, at least to some degree, all of us need to be able to tell what is going on in the background as well as pulling perceptions into the foreground. Complex social situations, including real language use, demand some capacity to attend to context, as do such effective learning approaches as peripheral learning.

In parallel with the use of the term **FD** for the absence of **FI**, I suggest that we describe learners who are not field sensitive (**FS**) as "field insensitive" (**FN**).

4. *What are the relationships between FI–FD and FS–FN?* **FI is a learning style representing a preference for dealing with material out of context. FS is a preference for addressing material as a part of a context.** In Ehrman (1996), I describe FI as a spotlight focusing sharply on one thing, and to FD as a floodlight illuminating everything. Some learners are comfortable with both approaches to learning, some to one or the other, and some work well in neither mode. These possibilities can be mapped as shown in Figure 7-1.

Each of these types represents a continuum: learners are more or less FI, FS, FD, and FN. Further, much variation is possible within each of the types. Many of the learners with whom I work fall in a borderline area (such as someone who is mostly Type 4, with indications of some Type 3 functioning if all other learning

descriptively. In Ehrman (1996), I attempt to cope with this confusion at least in part by referring to FI–FD as abilities, while using the terms "global" and "analytic" for the learning style preference poles. While I still believe the distinction between ability and style to be valid, I have come to feel a need to further define the "global" and "analytic" concepts, as they are used to represent a wide range of stylistic variables (Ehrman & Leaver 1997), and therefore I use the term FI to indicate a style in this chapter.

style needs are met). Similar variations are possible for the other types. Moreover, an individual does not operate at the same point on *any* preference continuum all the time and under all circumstances. The field-independence and field-sensitivity scales are no exception. For instance, students who display Type 1 characteristics can lose their "mobility" and access to their skills under stress.

Figure 7–1. Relationships Between FI–FD and FS–FN

	Field Sensitivity	
Field Independence	High	Low
High	Type 1	Type 2
Low	Type 3	Type 4

Source: Ehrman 1996, p. 80. Used with permission.

5. *Can a learner be both FI and FS?* If, as suggested above, FS is not the same as FD, then the answer is clearly <u>yes</u>. Many of the best language learners probably fall into the Type 1 (FI, FS) category. These are the learners that Herman Witkin and D. R. Goodenough (1981) have called "mobile," indicating that they can use either style as needed. They can both discriminate what is important from the background and also be aware of the cues in the context that modulate language use.

Victoria is a Type 1 learner. She takes a field-sensitive (FS) approach in that she stays open to everything in her learning setting. She expresses a strong preference for learning new things in context, especially a personal one. When she undertakes a new experience, she likes to be exposed to the whole picture. In the classroom, she expresses considerable comfort with open-ended, highly contextual activities whose outcomes are not predictable.

As a Type 1 learner, Victoria also operates in a field-independent (FI) way. She likes puzzles and inductive grammar analysis; when her curiosity is aroused, she focuses her spotlight intently on word families, cultural points, and grammar patterns. She is highly adept at planning her study, easily selecting what she thinks is the most important thing to focus on—that is, she has no trouble discriminating among tasks and setting priorities. Also characteristic of FI is Victoria's detached approach to her classmates and the target culture.

6. *What are the characteristics of the Type 2 learner?* Type 2 learners (FI, FN) may excel at analyzing language, but tend to have trouble using a new language in a real sociocultural setting. Type 2 learners are often good classroom learners when the tasks and tests involve material out of context, as has frequently been the case in classrooms. Type 2 fortes are accuracy and precision; their approach can be quite detached.

Lester is a Type 2 learner. He likes grammar and drilling, and he wants the teacher to correct all his mistakes. He expresses considerable discomfort with reading or listening to materials over his head, guessing from context, and reading between the lines ("not my cup of tea"). He does well with the formal portions of the language class, but resists field trips unless there has been thorough advance preparation to minimize surprises. Lester is not an outstanding learner, but he is competent when classroom activities meet his preference for avoiding too much confusing background input.

Type 2 learners can run into trouble with others with their single-minded focus on the task they have selected to concentrate on. If they alienate teachers, classmates, and native speakers of the language, they may be cut off from interactions that would otherwise enhance their learning. At some level they may sense this rejection and thus become inhibited in reaching out and making opportunities to continue learning. Lester's classmates, for example, perceive him as somewhat cold; some of that is the effect of his needing to think about what he says before responding, which in itself represents a kind of detachment. Of course, many Type 1 and Type 2 learners are very personable and at ease with people.

7. *What are the characteristics of Type 3 learners?* In contrast to Type 2, the Type 3 learner (FD, FS) picks up a great deal from context, both social and linguistic, but is often handicapped by not being able to discriminate among all the many components of his or her intake. Type 3 learners can be excellent communicators in real interactions, but they may stumble in situations requiring a great deal of accuracy. Such learners often enjoy great success in work with speakers of the language they are learning, and they enjoy themselves enormously overseas. When faced with the need for precise language, however, they take evasive action or resort to communication strategies that hide their inaccuracies.

Nell had some previous language learning experience when she was abroad for a student exchange program. While living overseas she enjoyed meeting people and trying out what she knew from the brief preparatory language training she had had prior to her trip. When she returned home, she enrolled for an advanced language class in the same language. The placement test showed that she had a very large vocabulary and seemed to engage others readily in conversation. The trouble was that she was "abominably fluent": her speech was full of errors of every sort.

The activities in Nell's class are aimed at increasing accuracy, and Nell, her classmates, and her FI teacher are increasingly frustrated. Nell brightens up when the class does role plays, simulations, and field trips; its grammar and focus on form "get her down." Nell knows that she needs to "clean up her act," but it's hard when there are so many interesting things to talk about or watch on the videotapes she borrows to use at home.

Type 3 learners come in a variety of "flavors." That is, there are multiple combinations of high field sensitivity and low field independence. Dominic, like Nell, is FD and FS. Like Nell, he learns best from context and picks up language as he is using it. He differs from her, however, in his much more practical and concrete approach to learning and his relative lack of interest in cultural topics. Dominic's preferred learning strategies include a substantial amount of rote learning and mechanical practice, and he avoids inductive, analytic learning. Open-ended discussion is not for Dominic. He likes his contexts to be practical and related to real language use, although he prefers that topics and practice be relatively concrete and applied. He is somewhat too quick to turn away from input he thinks is impractical or irrelevant; he endorses hands-on kinesthetic activities.

8. *What about the Type 4 learner?* The Type 4 (FD, FN) learner is unaware of the important points and of environmental signals; this learner has the benefits of neither FI nor FS, and has little with which to be mobile among styles. The Type 4 has the worst of all worlds, with few strengths in the FI–FS domain, although s/he may have considerable compensating strengths in such areas as self-discipline, auditory acuity, and so on.

Henry is a Type 4 learner. He lacks the discrimination skills and analytic skills of the FI learner, and he finds it difficult to learn through heavily contextualized material as the FS student can. He is thus disadvantaged on both scales. He has difficulty setting study priorities and extracting what is important from lesson material because of his FD; at the same time, he does not benefit from the language being used around him (FN).

This is the kind of student who most needs support from the training setting to provide scaffolding while he develops a language base and learning skills. Henry wants a closely structured program to provide the controlled input that he does not have the strategies to work out for himself.

9. *What are the weaknesses of the other learner-types?* The Type 1 learner (FI, FS) has all the advantages of mobility but may be tripped up by excessively rigid classrooms. The Type 2 learner often rejects contextualized language use and so limits himself or herself to activities that are discrete, closed-ended, and finite. The Type 3 learner, who is weak in accuracy and precision, is probably the most likely to "fossilize" (to cease to learn any more language other than vocabulary).

10. *If tests of embedded figures are not a good measure for language learning, how can we assess FI and FS?* So far, no test of abilities has emerged to provide an unambiguous measurement for FI or FS in learning second languages. In my own work with adult language learners, I now use a combination of instruments. The first line of inquiry is the Modern Language Aptitude Test (MLAT; see Carroll and Sapon 1959). An MLAT profile that scores high in Parts 3 (Spelling Clues) and 4 (Words in Sentences) suggests FI. If Part 2 (Phonetic Transcription) is high relative to Parts 3 and 4, I anticipate an FS learner. Field sensitivity is further confirmed through the Hartmann Boundary Questionnaire (HBQ; see Hartmann 1991) through which I assess flexible ego boundaries and tolerance of ambiguity (Ehrman 1993, 1996). I hypothesize that a tendency not to compartmentalize experience ("'thin' boundaries") is conducive to such FS manifestations as peripheral learning, simultaneous processing, and non-linear input, whereas compartmentalization of experience ("'thick' boundaries") relates more to a need for system, order, and tuning out the surrounding environment, except where it is clearly related to task.

The Myers-Briggs Type Indicator (MBTI) (Myers and McCaulley 1985) adds further information from which to infer FI and FS styles, as do specific learning activities endorsed in the Motivation and Strategies Questionnaire (MSQ) (Ehrman

1996). For example, I have found that MBTI "feeling" types tend to endorse FS learning approaches, whereas "thinking" types more often pursue FI strategies. On the MSQ, endorsement of learning activities like group discussions suggest FS, whereas orientation to grammar learning suggests an FI approach. (For the MSQ, see Appendix 5.)*

11. *Why is FI–FS research so inconclusive?* Despite the intuitive appeal and the applicability of the FI construct to learner differences, research on its relationship to language-learning success has been inconclusive. It is my belief that this phenomenon is the result of several factors. First, FI is invariably assessed through embedded figures (see Witkin 1969), which may not provide a good measure of the characteristic for verbal learning, so the initial sorting of subjects may be somewhat flawed (see Chapelle 1992; Chapelle and Green 1992; Griffiths and Sheen 1992; Sheen 1993). Second, many of the earlier studies (such as Stansfield and Hansen 1983) found superiority of FI on discrete-point tests and closed-ended tasks of the sort formerly common in the second language classroom; in many programs, these tasks are no longer the primary criteria for success.

Third, even a very recent study such as A. R. Elliott (1995) used FI as one potential predictor for pronunciation learning, but Elliott may not have accounted for the fact that there are at least two strategies for achieving good pronunciation. One is the focused attention that FI students are comfortable with (distinctive features, pronunciation drill, contrast exercises, articulation modeling). The other is a kind of osmotic process that FS learners employ: through simple exposure and an openness to sounding like speakers of the target language, many learners never have to use pronunciation drills and conscious attention. As a consequence, FI and FS learners may well have canceled each other out in Elliott's study.

In order to get useful results with the FI–FS construct, we need to find reliable and valid ways to assess it, to define our terms clearly, and to ask the right questions. If we understand that FI–FS represent styles and are thus available for "flexing" under the press of circumstances, we will need to define the circumstances carefully and to evaluate for the characteristics that belong to FI–FS, and not to some other variable like introversion, impulsivity, intuition, or feeling.**

12. *How can I use the FI–FS typology to work with my students?* No model, however interesting, is of value to teachers who cannot apply it. I have found the FI–FS model described in this chapter to be increasingly helpful as I try to understand how students learn and to help them make the most of their learning opportunity. Based on experience, I offer the following brief suggestions for teachers and students.

---

* Extended discussion of this approach to assessing FI and FS is found in Ehrman (1996). Chapter 5 of that volume also explores the four-type model in depth.

** FI is often treated as an ability related to cognitive restructuring, a key component of "fluid intelligence." (Fluid abilities allow one to deal with relatively unfamiliar tasks that demand problem-solving, in contrast with "crystallized" abilities, which are built on developed skills, including vocabulary, world knowledge, and so on.) This may be a result of the usual measurement of FI through embedded figures tests. If we want to measure FI as an ability, we need to extract the ability from the others with which it is mixed in the present assessment approach, particularly fluid intelligence.

- Type 1 learners (FI, FS) have access to both worlds, and they can usually adapt to multiple teaching styles and curricula. But Type 1 learners often need plenty of learning space. Too much external structure may cramp their ability to use both the spotlight and the floodlight.

- Type 2 (FI, FN) learners can sometimes become entangled in specifics. They will benefit by lifting their eyes from the botanical categories and looking at the ecology of the entire forest. They appreciate a well-organized program, but they may need to work on development of tolerance for ambiguity and a relaxation of their tendency toward perfectionism. I have found many Type 2 learners to be responsive to reframing their goals in the light of the possible, not the impossible. Type 2s may need to understand that if they are learning language for use in real situations, they are unlikely to reach the point where they can be perfectly precise; "global" strategies are not only permissible, they are essential.

- Strong field independence in the Type 1 and Type 2 learners may entail social independence that can be interpreted as non-compliance by some teachers. When a Type 1 learner is a "good citizen" of the classroom, the best thing a teacher can do may be to stay out of the way and let the learner take the lead in managing his or her own program. But if an FI learner (Type 1 or Type 2) is too unaware of the social environment, the solution is appropriate classroom management.

- Type 3 learners, in contrast to Types 1 and 2, may need help to (metaphorically) sort out all the trees into genera and species, to decide which species to select for building a cabin, and to set priorities on which task to begin. They can use help with developing their accuracy, but teachers should respect the very real, although unconventional, talents such learners bring to the classroom. These Type 3 learners tend to appreciate external structure, such as a lesson plan, syllabus, or textbook, because that kind of planning and prioritizing does not always come naturally to them. To the degree possible, provide meaningful context for everything Type 3 learners are exposed to.

- Henry shows us how to assist Type 4 learners: provide plentiful external structure and what he calls "reinforcement of material." Offer consistent, frequent, regular feedback on progress and what is needed/expected. Let the Type 4 learner check what he has learned and build a sense of mastery before moving to new material. Review, review, review. Many Type 4 students need help with such basic learning techniques as flashcards and sound-symbol matches. Henry wants/needs a lot of intensive practice and drilling. Help Type 4 learners build up to as much learning autonomy as they can manage.

Conclusion

In this chapter, I have attempted to review some of the difficulties researchers and practitioners have had with the FI–FD–FS construct and suggest some ways to make it more practical. Because our understanding of FI–FD is in process, I view my contribution here as a kind of way station as the concepts and assessments become refined. My aim has been to shed a little more light on the FI–FS construct; the reader can decide if it is a spotlight, a floodlight, both, or neither.

For Further Reading

Brown, H. D. (1994). *Principles of Language Learning and Teaching,* 3rd ed. Englewood Cliffs, NJ: Prentice Hall Regents.

> This volume describes a great number of factors, both internal and external to the learner, that affect second language acquisition. Brown is particularly interested in learning styles, including FI–FD. The volume is especially helpful for its overview of some of the main individual difference variables and some of the most important literature about each. Brown has stayed in touch with developments in the field, so this third edition includes relatively recent findings as well as the "classics."

Chapelle, C. and Green, P. (1992). Field independence/dependence in second language acquisition research. *Language Learning 42*, 47–83.

> This article is probably the most complete exposition of the FI-FD construct in second language learning research. Included are a history of the construct, beginning with the work of Herman Witkin and his colleagues on perception of the vertical (Witkin and Goodenough 1981), and describing several decades of efforts to make FI–FD useful in second language learning. Chapelle and Green also address the question of overlap between FI and fluid intelligence and treat some of the controversial issues associated with the construct. This is a thorough, scholarly treatment of a difficult subject. Many of the difficulties with the construct are also explored in the controversy published in *Applied Linguistics* (Chapelle 1992; Griffiths and Sheen 1992; Sheen 1993).

Ehrman, M. E. (1996). *Understanding Second Language Learning Difficulties.* Thousand Oaks, CA: Sage Publications.

> This volume addresses the broad range of individual differences that affect second language learning success. It is full of case material, which illustrates the many models and concepts in the book. Cases are accompanied by suggestions about how to work with students of the sort illustrated by the case. Two short chapters treating data-gathering through observation and interviews are followed by discussion of learning styles (including a chapter devoted to field independence), affective factors, biographic background, learning strategies, language aptitude, and learning disabilities. A questionnaire is included that teachers can use to evaluate student learning styles through the kinds of learning activities their students prefer. This book can help teachers, teacher-trainers, and students understand their learning processes.

Chapter 8

"Keep the Fire in Me": Teaching Advanced ESL Learners Through Their Learning Styles

Prem Ramburuth
University of New South Wales

Meeting the language and learning needs of students in an ESL class is usually a challenge, but sometimes I am faced with a group of students who also challenge my perceptions of the learning and teaching context. This chapter examines a range of strategies that I developed to address the language needs and learning styles of advanced ESL learners who came from a mixture of Asian and European backgrounds, and who had high levels of language proficiency, extremely high expectations of their course, their teachers, and themselves, and varying orientations to learning.

Background

The ESL learners described in this chapter were enrolled in an intensive English program at a university-based language college in Australia. They were studying at the advanced level (the highest level at the language college) in a course designed to enhance general English language proficiency in the macro-skills of reading, writing, listening, and speaking. The students had come from Asian and Southeast Asian countries, such as Japan, Korea, the People's Republic of China, Hong Kong, Thailand, and Indonesia, and European countries, such as France, Germany, Italy, Switzerland, and Sweden.

Such students bring with them not only a diversity of cultures but also a learning and language diversity that needs to be addressed, particularly since students at the advanced level tend to experience the highest levels of frustration in their language learning when learning needs, learning styles, and expectations are not met (Gray 1990; Vincent 1990). Further, many students at this level are field independent in their learning styles and need to go beyond the traditional classroom curriculum. In working with these students, I attempted to cater to their various language needs and learning styles by making curriculum changes in three areas:

- internal adjustments from within the core curriculum
- extensions beyond the core curriculum (the Independent Learning Program)
- expansion of the learning environment beyond the classroom context.

While these changes have been divided into three convenient sections for the purpose of discussion, the development and implementation occurred concurrently and were interrelated.

Adjustments to the Core Curriculum

Experience and studies in Organizational Theory (Morgan 1989) had convinced me that if I were to implement change, I had to begin from a point of stability and familiarity to lessen the threat to those involved in the process of change. I therefore retained the set 10-week course of topics, themes, content, and teaching methodologies[*] as the framework for classroom learning and teaching. At the same time, I made several "internal" changes to match the different language levels and learning styles of my students. These included (a) adopting a more "learner-centered" approach to curriculum development and (b) using graded materials and varying approaches in my teaching.

At the outset of the course, in addition to the traditional Needs Analysis, I invited the students to provide direct input into the curriculum through suggestions about topics, content, activities, and learning and teaching strategies that they regarded as appropriate for their course. These student contributions followed intensive class discussions and self-evaluation of language levels, learning backgrounds, learning styles, learning needs, and cross-cultural differences. I also asked the students to complete a writing task outlining their expectations of the course, and I encouraged them to be creative, thought-provoking, and analytical in their responses. Most student replies were similar to this excerpt from Andy, a Swiss student.

> Actually, I think quite positively about learning English. I hope these feelings aren't only the enthusiasm of the starting days. . . . It might be a problem that I want too much in too short a time, and could be frustrated if I don't feel I'm making progress. This is why one of the most important things will be to keep this "fire" in me. You can help me in this area if you arrange variable and creative units, and if you are able to produce new and original ideas . . .

Such responses not only provided cues but also presented a challenge to respond appropriately or risk a high level of student frustration!

Another strategy I used was the introduction of graded materials to address the issue of variation in levels of ability in the four macro-skills of reading, writing, listening, and speaking, and in the different orientations to learning. Examples:

Reading

To each reading class I took two sets of reading materials, one set at the accepted advanced level for all students, the other at a much higher level for those students who wanted to extend their reading and comprehension skills further. This enabled students to work on task-based activities at their own pace and their own level; slower readers often requested copies of the more advanced reading texts to complete as homework and thus challenged themselves without feeling pressured.

---

[*] The set 10-week course and the Needs-Analysis survey, which was administered to identify the learning and language needs of the students, are available from the author upon request.

As an extension of this strategy, I introduced a set of readers, simple novels, and novels for native speaker proficiency levels for reading in class or for home borrowing. This reading strategy was linked to the Independent Reading Program, which encouraged students to take responsibility for selecting their own reading materials. Finally, I linked these classroom strategies to external resources through membership in the local library and visits to the state and inter-campus libraries.

The effectiveness of these strategies for the autonomous learners in the class is evidenced by the response of Wakki, a Japanese student who had never read a "complete" book or novel in English prior to joining the class.

> I think I'm beginning to find out how interesting reading is and how helpful it is in improving my language skills. Although I've read just 5 books, I've really enjoyed reading. Once I started to read a detective story, I couldn't stop because I wanted to know what would happen next and next! I chose a very thin book with a few stories this time, and if I get used to reading this size of novel, I'm going to try to read a thicker one, step by step.

It is difficult to imagine how a traditional approach to the teaching of reading skills could have taken Wakki to this level.

At the same time, some of the students who needed more direction and structure did not feel comfortable with the level of learner autonomy. For example, Erina, a Japanese student who had the highest class score on the English language entry test, found the independent reading strategy difficult to cope with.

> I went to the library to borrow some books. It is difficult to choose one or two from so many books. Maybe I should read everything that comes my way. But it will be easier if you give me some lists. Who are the popular authors in Australia? Which novel is popular among young students? Are there any classical novels which everybody has read once?

At first I found Erina's response surprising, as I had already taken her to the library, discussed strategies for choosing books, and even provided a suggested reading list drawn up by the librarian. It seemed that, despite Erina's high level of English language proficiency, her field-sensitive learning style and lack of confidence made it difficult for her to choose something to read. I then went a step further and brought in a sample of popular classical novels, and she made her choice: an abridged version of *Jane Eyre*, which she thoroughly enjoyed. From the safety of the reading list we devised together, Erina's extended reading program began.

Writing

As the students read the novels and short stories of good writers and experienced the joys of reading widely, most felt confident to engage in such extended activities as

- writing their own short stories
- writing poetry
- setting up their own ESL class magazine (called *What's Up?*)
- writing letters and postcards in English more frequently and confidently to family and friends in their own countries
- writing freely and confidently in their reflective learning journals.

Speaking

I developed a wider than usual range of activities for different levels of learners in the speaking class and personalized the discussion activities. For example:

a. Classroom discussions led to the formation and enactment of committees and forums (meetings with the class) in which students took on roles to present different points of view on topics of interest. The nationality mix of students provided an ideal context for international forums on challenging topics such as world health, environmental issues, and the Olympic games. These sessions were sometimes videotaped and formed the basis of follow-up speaking and discussion skills lessons.

b. Classroom practice in the language of argument led to the formation of debating teams and participation in in-class, inter-class, and eventually inter-campus debates. In these activities I paired the reflective, visual students with students more willing and able to argue verbally, in order to provide help researching topics and formulating questions.

c. Classroom role-play and drama activities prepared students who preferred this kinesthetic learning style to participate in end-of-term concerts and inter-campus theatrical performances.

These extended activities enabled students to maximize their learning not only on the basis of their level of language proficiency but also in accordance with their level of "readiness" to engage with the language and their learning style preferences.

Listening

It was a little more difficult to address the range of levels of and needs for this macro-skill in class, although I attempted to grade the tasks (such as listening and note-taking activities, and listening comprehension questions) based on audiotapes played in class. As an extension to classroom-based activities, I loaned taped materials to some of the field-independent visual students who had difficulty learning through the auditory mode so that they could practice the skill at home. Further, I developed a collection of children's stories, rhymes, songs, lectures, and news items for both in-class use and home borrowing.

The Introduction of Electives

To further extend the learning experiences of the students and to cater more effectively to their diverse needs, I introduced a selection of short "elective" courses to the Advanced Course. The electives were devised in conjunction with colleagues who had expertise in subject areas such as Australian Studies in English, Business English, English for Translation/Interpreting Skills, Language and Literature, and Drama. Each elective ran for approximately six hours per week, and students could choose any one elective from a selection of two or three that were offered each term.

Extensions to the Core Curriculum

Changes from within the Advanced Course certainly helped to address some of the differences in levels of English language proficiency and learning style preferences,

but the changes were still limited to the core curriculum and th
classroom context. In seeking further strategies to extend student lear
these limitations, I was influenced by several projects carried out wit
level learners in which learning environments and resources outside tł
were linked to class work (Gray 1990; Kumaravadivelu 1991; Nunan 1989; Tudor
1993; and Vincent 1990). Using this approach, I developed the Independent
Learning Program (ILP), a program that proved to be most effective in providing
for and accommodating the differences in the language levels and learning styles
of my students.

Initially, I set my students simple tasks to perform outside the classroom in
their free time (such as speaking to a native English speaker, reading a
book/novel/newspaper article written in English, or watching the news on
television), and they reported back in informal class discussions. As I began to see
the value of the resources outside the classroom and the opportunities for my
students to extend their study and use of English in a wider context, I formalized
the tasks in the format outlined below and included it as a component of the 10-
week Advanced Course. The set tasks were to be completed by all students on their
own time outside the classroom context, with a two-hour feedback session
scheduled each week (with the flexibility for increased time if needed). The
program was as follows:

Independent Learning Program (ILP)

Carry out the following tasks each week. Keep a record of your work by making
brief notes in your learning journal, and report back during class discussions
each week. You may adjust the topics to suit your interests and language level.

Week 1:   Discussion and negotiation of the ILP
Week 2:   Theme-related research topic: **Introduction to Australia**
            Find out as much as possible about Australia's

location	climate	places to visit
population	capital cities	other information

            For your information:
              ° go to the library
              ° read newspapers, magazines, brochures
              ° go to a travel agent or tourist office
              ° ask your friends, homestay family, etc.

Week 3:   Talk to a native speaker of English (e.g., homestay parent,
            neighbor). You may choose to have an informal conversation or a
            formal interview. Reporting could include comments on:
              ° who you spoke to
              ° what you talked about
              ° what language difficulties you experienced/how you
                coped
              ° whether you found the conversation interesting,
                challenging, etc.

Week 4:   Read an article (from a newspaper, journal, magazine) on any issue of interest or concern. Reporting could include comments on:
- ° what the article was about/why you selected it
- ° the style/genre
- ° any language difficulties and how you coped with them

Week 5:   Watch a TV program/movie/play/video. Reporting could include comments on:
- ° the type of program and reasons for your choice
- ° aspects you enjoyed most/least
- ° the level and type of language used
- ° some of the difficulties you experienced
- ° whether you would recommend it to other students and why

Week 6:   Evaluate your progress in developing your English language skills in reading, writing, listening, and speaking. You will be able to share this information in class discussions and in an interview with your teacher.
- ° consider the progress you have made in these skills
- ° comment on areas of most/least improvement
- ° identify strategies used in improving your language skills
- ° identify areas for further improvement
- ° make suggestions to help other students

Week 7:   Personal experience: Describe an interesting/humorous/sad/worrying or other experience you have had while living in Sydney. Exchange information with other students in your group and try to identify experiences that are similar and those that are different.

Week 8:   Student suggestion/free choice. This could be a joint task in which you can work with a partner or a group on any topic or project of your choice. Please discuss your ideas with your teacher.

Week 9:   Discuss a novel or short story you have read during this term. Comment on:
- ° your choice of story (the plot, characters, style of writing, etc.)
- ° aspects you enjoyed most/least
- ° whether you would recommend it to others and why
- ° similarities/differences with a novel or short story you may have read in your home country

Week 10:   Evaluation of the Independent Learning Program:
- ° group discussion
- ° completion of questionnaire
- ° suggestions for further development[*]

---

[*] See Nunan, this volume, for additional ILP information.

Implementation of the program required students to

- carry out the task set for each week.
- record responses in the learning journals.
- discuss the learning activity and responses in a two-hour report-back session in class each week (topics were discussed in a variety of modes: individually, in pairs, groups, and by the whole class).
- submit the learning journals each week after the class discussion.

The learning journals provided an excellent mechanism for monitoring student progress and providing a sense of structure to the program (despite the workload in having to have them marked and ready in time for the next task!).

The ILP was particularly effective in that it gave students the opportunity to take charge of their own learning—to determine (via a set of guided tasks) their own content, learning styles and strategies, level, pace, and depth of learning. It also drew the attention of learners to the existence of a much wider learning environment and a richer pool of resources for language learning and development.

For the most part, student responses to the ILP were amazing. Many of the students experimented with a variety of learning styles and strategies. For example, for the speaking skills task (Week 3), students used an impressive range of activities: some developed detailed questionnaires and used them to interview people in shopping centers, in the workplace, and over the phone; others interviewed several families and made cross-cultural comparisons; some called service-oriented companies (such as telephone companies and travel agents) to inquire about "deals" they were offering to would-be customers, and then made comparisons; still others interviewed Australians in pubs, on picnics, and on the beach. The students who found the task of approaching native Australian speakers too daunting instead interviewed a close friend, a homestay parent, or a friendly and supportive teacher.

In the challenging task of evaluating their progress in language learning (Week 6), students benefited from the process of meta-learning, that is, understanding how they engage in the learning process (Biggs 1987). The following extract is from a Japanese student's evaluation of his progress, for which Hiroaki devised a question/answer format:

Q5: Could you tell me how you study in each skill such as speaking, listening, and reading?

A: As regards speaking, I talk to my host mother a lot, and I pay attention to what other people are saying, then I pick up an interesting sentence and I use it. . . . Referring to listening, the most important thing is concentration and curiosity. I've found I could listen to what people were saying if I was interested in them. Besides I try to keep on practicing by watching videos, the TV and listening to the radio. I've found one more thing. At first I could catch just a few words, then I could get to catch the sentence and then imagine the written words. I think this is an interesting process.

Students who participated in the ILP displayed learning styles and strategies that Joan Rubin and Ian Thompson (1982) have identified as those of "good or efficient learners." The students were autonomous, made their own learning opportunities, organized their own information, were creative and innovative, took risks and experimented with language, and found opportunities outside the classroom to practice their language. Even those students who were more field sensitive and reflective found that the structure and the precision of the assignments appealed to their learning styles.

The general satisfaction with this aspect of the course, particularly its nature of being both free and structured, is indicated by this response from Taiwanese student Anna:

> Our class level is very high, much higher than I expected. But I like it because we have to push ourselves higher. . . . The independent learning actives [sic] are very useful because every week I can focus on one part. . . . Usually teachers say "study at home," but this is not concrete, not tangible. This learning program is good, now it is concrete, tangible.

There were a few students, however, who found aspects of the ILP difficult and so may have been better suited to a more traditional classroom program. Yuki, a Japanese student, wrote:

> Sometimes it was difficult to keep up to the level. . . . Also, it was hard for me to speak to people or give my opinion because Asian people like me don't talk. . . . But I'm getting used to it.

Extensions to the Learning Environment Beyond the Context of the Classroom

The third area of change involved accessing new opportunities for student learning by linking with other courses and resources in the wider learning environment. Students who needed to be challenged even further, or those who had been unable to fully address their learning needs and preferences, were encouraged to join a range of external courses offered in different departments of the college at which they were studying. For example, students who were interested in examination preparation (as were most European students) joined the Cambridge English Examination class. Those who were practicing teachers or planning to teach in their home countries could join either the TESOL Training course or the Introduction to Language Teaching course. And those students who wanted to further improve their English for work purposes in the business field could join either Business Writing Skills or Business Speaking Skills. Most students evaluated their participation in such courses as did René, a Swiss student.

> For me the evening Cambridge class is a very good class. It challenges me more than the day time class. . . . I need it for my exam preparation. Also, I can interact with native speakers.

Conclusion

The extent to which it is possible to address the language needs and learning styles of every student in an ESL group or class is difficult to measure. Yet by implementing changes to the Advanced Course and its core curriculum, and by extending the boundaries of the classroom learning environment, the foundations have been laid for students to engage in their language learning at their preferred level and through their preferred learning styles. In doing so, the students are more likely to fulfill their expectations of their course, themselves, and their teachers. The results of the Independent Learning Program, and of the additional opportunities offered to these advanced students, have encouraged other teachers in the program to look beyond the resources of the traditional curriculum and classroom structure to develop similarly challenging approaches. I take as continuing encouragement this comment from Barbara, a Swiss student, who was asked to write suggestions for improvement of the course: "My suggestion would be to keep on going. You're on the right track."

For Further Reading

Dunn, R. and Griggs, S. A. (1995). *Multiculturalism and Learning Style: Teaching and Counseling Adolescents*. Westport, CT: Praeger Publishing.

> This recent publication provides a comprehensive description of current research relating to the learning styles of students from diverse cultural backgrounds. It discusses the implications of research findings, and describes teaching and counseling strategies appropriate for accommodating the varied learning styles of diverse students. It also reports on schools and programs that have effectively addressed issues of achievement, confidence building, and successful learning in relation to students from minority groups.

Sims, R. and Sims, S. (Eds.). (1995). *The Importance of Learning Styles: Understanding the Implications for Learning, Course Design, and Education*. Westport, CT: Greenwood Press.

> This anthology contains several chapters relevant for curriculum designers and classroom teachers. Its focus on the integration of learning styles to enhance college/university instruction ranges from frameworks for matching teaching and learning styles to the "changing face of the community" and the diversity of current student populations.

Chapter 9

Bridging the Gap Between Teaching Style and Learning Styles

Maria Hsueh-Yu Cheng
Chinese Military Academy, R.O.C.

Kingsley Banya
Florida International University

Teacher behavior in the classroom can significantly affect learner achievement. Specifically, teachers have styles that they use as they plan and present material to their students. Often, they mirror their learning styles in their teaching styles (Oxford 1990). That is, most teachers teach the way they were taught or the way they learned. Yet research has demonstrated that higher student achievement relates to a match between student learning styles and teacher teaching styles (Cornett 1983; Dunn and Dunn 1979; Dunn and Griggs 1995; Ellis 1989; Griggs and Dunn 1984; Oxford, Ehrman, and Lavine 1991; Smith and Renzulli 1984). The purpose of this chapter is to explore the relationships between the perceptual learning styles of English as a foreign language (EFL) students in Taiwan and the learning/teaching styles of their teachers.

Background

Learning and teaching styles are the result of both nature and nurture (Ellis 1989). Some are biological and stable, such as the individual's response to sound, light, and temperature. Others are developmental and flexible, such as perceptual preferences, motivation, and reflectivity; that is, they can be trained and extended. Research suggests that most people have only six to fourteen strongly preferred learning styles, though at least twenty-one have been categorized (Dunn, Gemake, Jalali, and Zenhausern 1990). Moreover, learning styles are influenced by such factors as subject matter, context, age, prior knowledge, gender, motivation, and ethnicity (Dunn and Dunn 1979; Oxford and Ehrman 1995; Reid 1987). For example, in a formal learning setting where the target language is learned as a foreign language and linguistic accuracy is the major concern, students tend to be more visual, while in an informal learning situation in which communicative fluency is emphasized, students may tend to be more auditory or kinesthetic.

Research also indicates that cultural background plays an important role in learning style preferences (Rossi-Le 1995). Asian students are highly visual (Reid

1995b), especially Koreans (Erhman and Oxford 1995), while Hispanics are frequently auditory, and many non-Westerners are tactile and kinesthetic learners (Oxford 1992). Finally, a teacher's style can have great impact on students' learning style preferences (Cornett 1983; Marshall 1991).

My Study

A total of 140 male freshman cadets at the Chinese Military Academy completed seven questionnaires.[*] Among them was the Perceptual Learning Styles Preference Survey (PLSP) (Reid 1984) (see Appendix 3 for this survey). In addition, the PLSP questionnaire was sent to Taiwanese English teachers in Taiwan universities; 35 of those English teachers responded anonymously, and their surveys were used in the study. Based on their self-reported surveys, both teachers and students preferred auditory, tactile, and individual learning styles. Table 9-1 demonstrates the results, with the bold type indicating the preference between two contrasting styles.

	Number	Visual	Auditory	Balanced	Kinesthetic	Tactile	Balanced	Group	Individual	Balanced
Table 9–1. Comparison of Teachers' and Students' Perceptual Learning Style Preferences										
TEACHERS	35	7%	**70%**	13%	39%	44%	17%	39%	**52%**	9%
STUDENTS	140	**41%**	**43%**	16%	38%	43%	19%	36%	**48%**	16%

NOTE: When two scores were equal, students were labeled "balanced."

Three interesting results from this study deserve mention. First, notice that the Taiwanese military cadets indicated that they don't have markedly strong preferences for any single learning style. One reason is that they provided more answers of *agree* or *disagree* than *strongly agree* or *strongly disagree*. Perhaps these students did not feel "strongly," or perhaps the word "strongly" was too strong for them to use: in general, based on Confucian philosophy, Chinese students are expected to behave moderately rather than sharply.

Their teachers, in contrast, reported somewhat more definite preferences in many of the styles; indeed, the teachers reported being substantially less Visual and more Auditory than their students. These results may be an indication that the teachers were more practiced at taking surveys or were more experienced in identifying their learning styles. Or, as Cornett (1983, p. 18) states, "It is likely that the teacher's learning style will have a greater variation than that of the students because the teacher has had many more experiences."

---

[*] The other questionnaires are the Motivation Attitude Questionnaire (MAC) (Cheng 1995); Beliefs About Foreign Language Learning (BALLI) (Horwitz 1988); Strategy Inventory for Language Learning (SILL) (Oxford 1989); Foreign Language Classroom Anxiety Scale (FLCAS) (Horwitz, Horwitz, and Cope 1986); Second Language Tolerance of Ambiguity Scale (SLTAS) (Ely 1995).

Finally, in a society in which group cohesiveness is thought to be essential, in which Chinese students are supposed to de-emphasize self and to be concerned for the group, these Taiwanese teachers and students preferred Individual learning. This is not a surprising result, however. While Chinese students are taught to have socially acceptable behavior without "acting out" or "speaking out," individual success rather than group performance is rewarded more in Chinese society. Hence, when Chinese students want to learn by modeling, it is acceptable to work with others during the process, but at the outcome stage, individual achievement is valued. The complicated characteristics of Chinese (group in theory but individual in practice) suggests that Nelson (1995, p. 16) is correct: "When teaching Japanese or Chinese students, ESL/EFL teachers might consider decreasing the amount of small-group work they do in class. . . . If the purpose can be achieved in another way, it may be better not to use groups."

Statistical analysis of the PLSP and other surveys provided much information about interrelated preferences. Results of interest to teachers included the following:

Perceptual Learning Styles Results
- Students who preferred kinesthetic learning have more confidence as well as more positive attitudes and beliefs about foreign language learning than students with other perceptual learning style preferences.
- Students with the Individual preference style use more language-learning strategies, and they are less tolerant of ambiguity.
- Students who identified themselves as Tactile learners seemed to be more anxious about learning English.
- Students with an Auditory preference like to make friends with and speak with foreign language speakers (in this case, English speakers).

Results from Other Surveys
- Many of the students in the study were field independent.
- Extroverts more often preferred Group learning than Introverts.
- Attitude, motivational intensity, learning strategies, anxiety, and beliefs are related to students' English achievement.
- Students with positive attitudes and beliefs toward English learning use more effort, utilize more language-learning strategies, are less anxious, and tend to have better language achievement.

Differences Between Teachers' and Students' Styles
Based on the self-reports of their perceptual learning styles, both teachers and students preferred the perceptual learning styles of Auditory, Tactile, and Individual learning. In addition, one significant difference between teachers' and students' learning styles was demonstrated in this study. The teachers were substantially more Auditory than the students (70% to 43%). We can therefore expect that these teachers feel comfortable instructing by lecture, which supports Lynn O'Brien's article (1989) in which she claims that 80 percent of instruction is

delivered in an auditory fashion. In contrast, their students, with their significantly greater Visual orientation, reported that they learned more by reading textbooks than by listening to lectures. Those students might learn more effectively from approaches and activities better suited to the Visual and Tactile styles.

Implications for Teachers and Students

Of course, in any classroom, mismatches do exist between teachers' and students' styles. Teachers need to make conscious efforts to improve this teaching/learning conflict.

- Teachers have to be aware of students' learning styles as well as their own learning/teaching styles. If student styles do not match the teacher's, both the students and the teacher should be aware of the differences and the possible consequences of those differences.

- Teachers have a responsibility to provide multiple opportunities for their students to investigate and identify their learning styles.

- Teachers need to take risks to integrate more teaching styles into their class preparation even though they may not feel entirely comfortable using them. For example, teachers of the students in this study, knowing that many of their students (43%) like to work with their hands, might plan language lessons in which students can participate in "hands-on" ways.

- Teachers should also encourage their students to "stretch" their learning styles in order to become more empowered in a variety of learning situations (Reid 1995b). For example, teachers could prepare some lectures that are interesting and related to subject matter being taught. This would give an opportunity to Auditory students and provide an opportunity for other students to vary their styles.

- Students need to be aware of their own learning styles. They also need to know what learning styles are appropriate in special learning situations and for special learning purposes.

- Students need to cooperate with teachers in matching teaching and learning styles. For example, students should learn appropriate ways of informing their teachers when classroom approaches and activities are not meeting their needs.

- Students should also learn to become more tolerant of ambiguity in the complex situation of foreign language learning. Such tolerance will serve them well in adjusting to different learning styles, and will allow them to work to strengthen their weaker learning style preferences.

- Students need to go beyond their "comfort zones" (Nelson 1995) and to open themselves to more chances to move from one preferred learning style to another, to expand their learning style repertoires in order to become more autonomous in their learning.[*]

---

[*] See Tyacke, this volume, for a different perspective.

Conclusion

Both teachers and students will be comfortable in class if the teaching style(s) match the learning style(s). If a learning style conflict does occur, the affected students may become bored, inattentive, discouraged, and do poorly on tests (Felder and Henriques 1995). And teachers, confronted by students' unresponsiveness, poor attendance, or low test grades, may become frustrated and depressed and even question their own ability to be good teachers.

Therefore, to help teaching and learning become more effective, both teachers and students should share the responsibility for solving the learning style conflict. Both must be aware of that fact that no one style can work all the time. That is, a teacher's preferred learning/teaching styles cannot benefit all of her/his students in every teaching environment. Nor can a student's learning style preferences always help her/him solve problems in all learning situations.

Effective teaching requires teachers' awareness of students' individual differences and teachers' willingness to vary their teaching styles to match with most students'. An eclectic approach to classroom teaching is the rational solution. The more able and willing the teachers are to observe their students and to integrate appropriate material presentation and class assignments that match their students' learning styles, the more easily and efficiently their students will learn (Smalley and Hank 1992). That is, students learn more from teachers who are interested in their subjects and their students, and who are more flexible and tolerant in their teaching.

For Further Reading

Cornett, C. (1983). *What You Should Know About Teaching and Learning Styles.* Bloomington, IN: Phi Delta Kappa Education Foundation.

> This book provides a clear exploration of learning styles, teaching styles, the relationship between learning and teaching styles, and an extended discussion about the advantages of matching learning and teaching styles in the classroom.

Reid, J. (Ed.) (1995). *Learning Styles in the ESL/EFL Classroom.* Boston: Heinle & Heinle.

> This anthology contains 15 excellent chapters that deal with cognitive, sensory, and personality learning styles. Rich curricular materials and instructional implementations are presented, and surveys about learning styles, language learning strategies, tolerance of ambiguity, etc., are included as well.

Chapter 10

Designing ESL Classroom Collaboration to Accommodate Diverse Work Styles

Kate Kinsella and Kathy Sherak
San Francisco State University

Small group learning is widely recognized as one of the most advantageous practices in contemporary education. Although classroom collaboration is beneficial in improving outcomes for all students, it is particularly helpful for second language learners, especially those ESL students with a dire need to become more proficient in the target language who have scant opportunities for sustained and varied practice. This chapter addresses some of the educational, social, cognitive, and perceptual factors that greatly influence a student's needs in a collaborative classroom learning environment.

Background

Carefully structured student-student interactions provide a classroom forum for extended, meaningful exploration of ideas, which exposes ESL students to more varied and complex language from their peers than does traditional teacher-fronted classroom interaction (Pica and Doughty 1985). The increased frequency and complexity of linguistic input and output resulting from group work contribute to substantive gains in communicative second language competence (Christison 1990; Long and Porter 1985; Pica 1987; Pica, Young, and Doughty 1987). In addition to promoting use of a wider range of communicative functions, group work helps students develop their subject area knowledge. A major premise in the use of peer working groups is that students learn new material more efficiently and effectively by doing something with it. Collaborating with classmates to solve a problem, explore an issue, or create a product requires that students assert and justify their own viewpoints, and it exposes them to alternative perspectives and approaches. This process of active listening, interpreting, clarifying, organizing, and applying course material facilitates comprehension and retention of focal lesson concepts and terminology (Bejarano 1987; McGroarty 1992) and also nurtures in students the fairly elusive yet widely stated educational goal of "learning to learn."

Further, sustained teamwork in heterogeneous groups can provide a stable and supportive environment for learning for students from various ethnic and linguistic backgrounds. This potentially unthreatening and humane instructional format may offer underprepared language minority students the academic and social support that will help them experience more school success (Holt 1993). Finally, in addition to affecting cognitive learning and interactional skills, small group collaboration influences student attitudes and relationships. When students from diverse backgrounds meet regularly to tackle structured meaningful tasks together, the interdependence that develops promotes positive prosocial behaviors (Kagan 1986).

ESL Student Reticence to Enter the Collaborative Classroom

Because of the compelling pedagogical and social benefits of classroom pairing and grouping strategies, it stands to reason that peer collaboration has become an essential tenet of contemporary learner-centered ESL instruction. Methodology and curricula in ESL classrooms have departed dramatically from traditional approaches that relied primarily on whole-class discussions, lectures, and individual seatwork. Nevertheless, most experienced ESL instructors have discovered that the students themselves seldom enter this new instructional arena with unbridled enthusiasm. In fact, many adolescent and adult ESL students are apt to respond initially with visible dismay. In our work with high school and college ESL students, we have come to realize that furrowed brows and plaintive sighs are not merely signs of obstinate or reactionary learners. Instead, linguistically and culturally diverse students often bring to the cooperative classroom a background of disappointing collaborative classroom experiences that is frequently compounded by the stellar academic track records they attain by working independently in a traditional instructional milieu. For too many ESL students, impressions of seemingly chaotic, unproductive, and at times unpleasant task-based learning with peers stand in striking juxtaposition to vivid memories of more secure, structured, and successful transmission and mastery of material in a teacher-fronted classroom.

Conscientious ESL classroom practitioners are thus faced with a formidable instructional dilemma: How can peer learning groups be successful if the students do not have the philosophical underpinnings, the skills, or in many cases even a remote desire to participate in a collaborative learning venture? Classroom collaboration is undeniably a constructive response to linguistic and social diversity, yet the use of learning groups can be justified only by their efficacy in improving student outcomes and attitudes. In second language schooling there is admittedly more than one relevant definition of success in the learning situation, but critical components certainly include linguistic and academic gains along with learner satisfaction. It is unfortunate that small group activities are not always structured for active and equitable participation and/or with assessment of observable gains in language development and academic achievement.

Moreover, well-intended ESL teachers frequently ask classmates to put their heads together to identify and solve problems or to integrate new material with prior knowledge, without first taking into consideration the cognitive, affective, and subjective dimensions of peer collaboration. A teacher cannot simply throw diverse ESL students together with limited preparation and guidance and expect a successful joint learning venture to result. Classroom experience and research suggest that peer collaboration is far more than a creative seating arrangement, and that many things can and do go wrong when teachers incorporate group work into their lessons (Fiechtner and Davis 1992). Similarly, advocating task-based peer collaboration and carrying it out effectively in a heterogeneous ESL classroom are two distinct matters. Unless group work is thoughtfully designed to affirm and build upon students' individual learning histories, biases, and abilities, its pedagogical and personal potential will be realized by all too few.

Previous Schooling and ESL Student Receptivity to Classroom Collaboration

Some ESL student reluctance and disorientation in this interactive learning format stem from their prior educational experiences. Many international and immigrant students enter U. S. secondary and higher education lacking the linguistic and pragmatic machinery in English to embark confidently upon collaborative endeavors with native English speakers and more fluent bilinguals. The ESL students may have a limited repertoire of English language functions, such as offering opinions, disagreeing, interrupting, or requesting clarification, and are consequently poorly equipped to accomplish their communicative purposes and contribute dynamically to the group process.

Adolescent and adult ESL students' insecurity about their communicative competence in English is frequently exacerbated by limited classroom experiences learning with and from peers. Although ESL newcomers to high school and college classes do regularly form study groups with fellow classmates outside the classroom, few tend to have engaged in pair or small group learning on a consistent formal basis as part of an organized course curriculum. The majority of these mature learners have excelled, or at least survived adequately, in classes where instruction was largely delivered in what Jim Cummins (1989) refers to as the "transmission" mode. In this educational paradigm, the teacher assumes the bulk of the responsibility for generating and transferring knowledge, which students are expected to passively record, memorize, and later recall. Thrust together with peers to engage in collaborative inquiry and problem-solving, some students will no doubt feel cheated and actually blame their teachers for withholding course knowledge or simply not performing their professional duties.

For many ESL students, teaching effectiveness has to a great extent been based upon efficient delivery of information rather than on active minds at work. Students who have completed the bulk of their formative schooling in a traditional learning forum will understandably require a compelling rationale and meticulous preparation for a successful transition to a model of teaching and learning that invites students to become "active generators of their own knowledge" (Cummins 1989) and to work together to maximize each other's achievement (Johnson, Johnson, and Holubec 1994).

Individual Classroom Work Styles

Individual learning and working styles are not entirely innate or unalterable, but they are ingrained and affirmed by years of conventional classroom roles and norms. When given the opportunity to specify learning and working preferences, an adolescent or adult who has experienced consistent academic success within a relatively authority-centered and competitive classroom is not likely to indicate group work as a methodological preference. Culturally absorbed ways of acquiring and displaying knowledge are not readily "unlearned." Moreover, positive group work experiences cannot be limited to the students who already value and thrive in this active, collaborative educational context. Rather, they must be based on instructional design principles that take account of individual learner differences and increase possibilities for all students to learn how to learn more successfully.

An extensive body of research on learning styles offers some critical direction for thoughtful and responsive integration of partner and group work in heterogeneous classrooms. Multiple elements that include perceptual, cognitive, and social needs within a learning context compose an individual's unique learning style. This part-biological and part-developmental set of characteristics influences a student's general pattern of preferences for academic task completion and can be said to constitute an individual *classroom work style*. Because students vary considerably in the ways that they process, understand, and retain information, it stands to reason that they would also vary in the ways that they feel comfortable and productive building and applying skills in inquiry, analysis, and problem-solving to achieve a learning goal.

A learner's strengths in receiving and internalizing information will undoubtedly shape the conditions that support her/his active engagement and achievement in various forms of task-based learning. Moreover, personality characteristics and information-processing strengths have been found to be the most stable components of an individual learning style, and the least subject to change in response to intervention by the teacher (Claxton and Murrell 1987). Thus, one critical reason for deliberately focusing on work style preferences and pitfalls is to bring these factors into the open. By critically examining the work style characteristics that are apt to most directly affect student attitudes and abilities with regard to group work, an informed and proactive teacher-facilitator can enhance the potential for all learners to reap the purported benefits of peer collaboration.

Analytic Versus Relational Learning Strengths

Although various theories and models exist to conceptualize learning strengths, the **analytic/relational** learning style construct provides a particularly useful framework for applying educational research to collaborative task design and grouping strategies. The genesis of this widely researched construct is Herman Witkin and his colleagues' (1975, 1977) pioneering cognitive-style research in the area of visual perception, which employs the bipolar global categories of field independence and field dependence to refer to the ways in which individuals process and structure information in the environment. These researchers investigated how people learn and memorize when faced with complex situations or material by using the Embedded Figures Test. Subjects were shown a simple geometric shape within a complex design, then asked to isolate the simple figure from the potentially distracting design or field.[*]

---

[*] For a fuller discussion of field independence/dependence, see Ehrman, this volume.

Although studies in field dependence/sensitivity and field independence initially focused on visual perception and information-processing orientations, this learning style framework is now also associated with social and personality factors in an educational context, and is commonly referred to as analytic and relational learning. A number of researchers studying linguistically and culturally diverse populations in the United States have delineated distinguishing characteristics of learners who cluster near each end of the analytic/relational continuum (see Anderson 1988; Cohen 1968, 1969; Hale-Benson 1986; Ramírez and Castañeda 1974; Shade 1989). This overarching construct is a characterization of a student's subjective requirements for classroom learning. The comprehensive profiles of analytical and relational learners summarized in Table 10–1 (p. 90) highlight intellectual, curricular, and social-relational characteristics with a clear potential for inhibiting or enhancing a student's ability to work willingly and productively with classmates.

One can note from Table 10–1 that analytic learners favor left-brain approaches to processing information and are therefore more comfortable with linear, focused, rational, and objective presentations of material. Generally quite cautious and systematic in their approach to thinking tasks, analytic learners appreciate predictable classroom routines and activities. These reflective and structured problem-solvers excel at tasks demanding analysis, induction, and attention to detail. In addition, analytic learners typically favor independent task completion and are prone to competitiveness. Highly task-oriented, these students are able to focus their attention on the relevant aspects of an assignment and persist autonomously to achieve a learning goal, rarely soliciting assistance or qualitative feedback from classmates and instructors. Analytic learners also predictably gravitate toward subject matter and activities more abstract, factual, or practical in nature, and consequently see less intrinsic value in understanding how curricula relate to the lives and interests of others in the classroom.

Unlike analytic learners, who tend to match the prevailing instructional mode and expectations of traditional secondary and higher education, relational learners place a greater emphasis on affective and experiential learning. These holistic thinkers favor right-brain information processing and consequently search for immediate connections, relevance, and personal meaning in what is taught. They demonstrate their right-brain strengths on tasks requiring intuition, risk-taking, and application to individual experience rather than trial-and-error or discovery learning. More easily distracted and less able to concentrate on a single task for an extended period of time, these students appreciate variety in instructional pacing and activities. Further, because they prefer a social learning environment and are particularly sensitive to the perspectives and feelings of others, relational learners enjoy working closely with classmates to achieve a common goal. They are additionally motivated by displays of confidence, praise, and support from their peers and instructors. These students also characteristically approach both independent and collaborative assignments with a global perspective rather than with a detailed and systematic process. Relational learners thus serve to benefit from a fairly explicit organi-

Table 10–1. Comparison of Analytic and Relational Learning Styles

Analytic Learning Style	*Relational Learning Style*

Perception and Information Processing

Left-brain strengths:	**Right-brain strengths:**
analytical, linear, sequential, rational, objective, abstract, verbal, mathematical	relational, holistic, pattern seeking, spatial, intuitive, subjective, concrete, emotional, visual
Focuses on detail; finds it easy to detach a perceived item from its given background	Experiences a distinct item as fused item with its context, as part of an overall impression
Reflective and cautious in thinking tasks	Impulsive in thinking tasks, trusts hunches
Dislikes excessive input; responds to selective, low-intensity stimulus	Responds to rich, varied input

Learning Strengths

Exhibits sequential and structured thinking	Exhibits intuitive and improvisational thinking
Better at analytical problem-solving	Better at collaborative problem-solving
Prefers predictable routines and familiar activities	Prefers variation and creativity in activities
Able to persist at unstimulating tasks	Prefers to withdraw from unstimulating tasks
More easily learns material that is abstract, factual, impersonal, and practical	More easily learns material with a human, social content characterized by experiential/cultural relevance
Has an affinity for focused and systematic instructional strategies	Has an affinity for instructional strategies in which various features are managed simultaneously and realistically in significant context
Likes to work independently or with a partner who has a compatible learning style	Likes to work with others to achieve a common goal
Likes to set own learning goals and direct own learning	Prefers more explicit structure, modeling, guidance, and feedback for task completion
Benefits from narrow examples, from trial and error, and from rules and definitions	Benefits from repeated exposure to associative patterns, not from specific rules and error correction

Interpersonal Relations

Personal identity and social role to a large extent self-defined	Greater tendency to defer to social group for identity and role definition
Self-esteem is less dependent upon the opinion of peers	Learning performance is improved if group or authority figure offers praise and support
Task-oriented; relatively inattentive to subtle emotional cues in interpersonal interactions	Socially oriented; sensitive to verbal and nonverbal cues in interpersonal interactions

Source: Adapted from Anderson (1988), Cohen (1968, 1969), Ramírez and Castañeda (1974), Witkin and Moore (1975)

zational and procedural framework for task completion, along with consistent modeling and coaching.

It is critical to emphasize three aspects of this (and other) learning styles delineation. First, our classes do not comprise only two types of learners: analytic and relational. Rather, a learner has a natural and pervasive set of characteristics that places the individual at a particular point along this descriptive scale. Second, no value judgment should be made by either teachers or learners about where a student falls on this continuum because analytic and relational learners have the same intellectual capacity. The critical differences become evident in their ways of processing and using material. Third, all students are quite capable of using both analytic and relational faculties. Some students are simply less willing or immediately able to venture into unfamiliar pedagogical terrain, while others are decidedly more comfortable and experienced with adjusting their learning and working approach to both contextual and task demands.

The analytic/relational construct, like any learning style theory or scheme, is both less and more complex than the learner reality it is intended to depict. Nevertheless, this research-based framework has tangible descriptive value with respect to classroom learning and working differences, as well as instructional expectations and needs. Exploring this learning style construct can help concerned educators become more aware of critical work style differences and guide them to better provide for those differences in task design and implementation, thereby improving classroom collaboration for all students.

Implications of the Analytic and Relational Learner Profiles for Inclusive Group Work Design and Implementation

Analytic and relational classroom learners differ strikingly in their perceptual ability and information-processing strengths, as well as in their task orientation and social-relational values and skills. Students with pronounced analytic or relational learning orientations are thus likely to bring strengths and challenges to different aspects of a small group task and process.

From the composite description of highly analytic learners in Table 10-1, it seems probable that these students will enter into collaborative endeavors with some decided reservations. These independent and competitive learners have experienced a great deal of success establishing their own learning goals and plans of attack for task completion within and outside the classroom. They will need a convincing pedagogical justification for getting together with classmates to arrive at mutual understandings and solutions, through a process that will inevitably at stages be rather chaotic and unsettling. Further, the instructional rationale for engaging in task-based learning with peers will be greatly undermined if the outcome of their collaborative effort is not clearly superior to what they could have produced more efficiently on their own. Drawn toward objective, abstract, and practical curricula, analytic learners are apt to perceive little or no academic value in schema-building or application activities that primarily draw upon classmates' relevant experiences and personal reactions.

Similarly, strongly analytic learners may feel that valuable instructional time has been squandered on group tasks that appear to be pointless "games." These linear and highly structured learners are also sure to become flustered in seemingly unstructured brainstorming or trouble-shooting sessions that lack a readily apparent direction or connection to the course curriculum. In general, more structured and achievement-oriented than their relational classmates, analytic learners need to be assured that any class time devoted to peer learning will be viably assessed, and that all group participants will be held responsible for contributing equitably to the final product.

In contrast, for relational learners, the learning context is of maximum importance. Relational learners thrive in dynamic, participatory classroom settings and therefore appreciate a lively instructional pace and variety in learning formats. These socially oriented learners enjoy sharing perspectives, hearing from their peers, and applying new concepts and skills to personal experiences and interests. They are usually less motivated by and adept at tasks that require objective analysis and attention to detail, such as proofreading a peer's written work for grammatical and mechanical errors. And they are decidedly less comfortable with competitive independent learning formats or aspects of small group tasks that require systematic analysis, abstraction, linear organization, or trial-and-error.

Although highly relational learners welcome breaks in traditional classroom routines that allow them to interact with peers, these students regularly require meticulous assignment design and set-up in order to get started in a timely and productive manner, and to continue to stay focused on the task at hand. Because they approach tasks in a holistic and relational manner, these learners may struggle with conceptualizing the various components in a particular assignment, establishing a realistic work schedule, and determining the most efficient process for completing each step. When a small group is solely composed of extremely relational learners who are grappling with a complex or relatively ambiguous assignment, the team is apt to take almost the entire class session just to figure out how to proceed. Because of their strengths in visual perception and hands-on experiential learning, these students benefit from clearly articulated and recorded assignment directions followed by step-by-step modeling, particularly for new or challenging tasks. They are also reassured and motivated by the presence of an active and available teacher-facilitator who provides constructive feedback throughout the small group process.

Guiding Principles for Inclusive Group Work Design and Implementation

Although students with extreme analytic or relational learning orientations bring distinct reservations and strengths to the small group process, both styles of learners can benefit from similar instructional design principles. Several recurring themes emerge from the preceding analysis of learner needs and preferences within this overarching construct. The following instructional design principles take into account these salient patterns and, if followed, will provide flexible and responsive opportunities for ESL classroom collaboration that will maximize the performance of diverse learners. Group work should be designed to include

- a compelling rationale for task-based classroom learning with peers.
- highly structured tasks, with explicit objectives, procedures, and outcomes.
- tasks that invite multiple responses and build collective knowledge rather than favor independent analysis and a single best answer.
- a variety of task types and/or tasks with multiple parts, involving analysis and creative problem-solving as well as personal relevance and meaningful application.
- collaborative tasks that are tied to on-going course content, preferably incorporated into a thematic unit with a variety of other independent and unified-class activities.
- a clear and adequate time frame for task completion.
- unified-class debriefing after task completion in order to clarify what was learned and accomplished in light of the course goals, on-going curricula, and future assignments.
- assessment of individual and small group participation and performance.
- an equitable distribution of classroom participation formats throughout the course curriculum (independent, partner, small group, unified class).
- consistent and manageable integration of partner and group activities within the course curriculum rather than sporadic lengthy collaborative assignments.
- an active and involved teacher-facilitator who checks progress and helps keep students on task, while offering both academic and affective support.

Conversely, the composite descriptions of analytic and relational learner needs within participatory learning formats point to a set of instructional maneuvers that, when employed individually, would seriously undermine the productivity of small groups, and in combination would virtually ensure small group **failure** in a heterogeneous ESL classroom and erode the credibility of any future classroom collaboration for even the most social/relational learners. To be avoided are

- an unwieldy and/or a loosely structured task with no tangible final product or expected outcome.
- a task that is skewed only toward analytic or relational learning strengths.
- a fairly analytical task that does not invite multiple possible responses or approaches and that could be completed more efficiently independently.
- a task that lacks a vivid connection to the course content and goals.
- vague directions for task completion with no instructional modeling.
- no clear or compelling rationale for working in collaboration rather than independently to complete the task.
- inadequate time to complete the task successfully.
- an instructor who assumes either an authoritarian and disruptive role, or a passive and unavailable stance during the small group process.
- inadequate or no class time devoted to debriefing and processing what was learned or accomplished by engaging in this collaborative process.
- no follow-up assessment of the affective or cognitive dimensions of the individual and small group efforts.

Task Design for Inclusive ESL Classroom Collaboration

To support neophyte collaborators with diverse work styles and distinct reservations about interactive classroom structures, teachers must carefully and systematically consider the task type and design. Several excellent instructional resources have addressed the necessity of preparing ESL students philosophically and linguistically for group work by formally teaching students the role expectations, organizational tactics, and language strategies for team learning (see Coehlo 1994; Cohen 1994; Kessler 1992). Little has been written, however, about the actual nature of the task, and the extent to which a task design is biased in favor of a particular learning orientation and its potential for undermining group process.

Despite the best efforts of teachers to introduce ESL students to the collaborative process with a convincing justification, structured role responsibilities, and strategic language practice, some students become frustrated with small group endeavors because the task is unstimulating and fails to capitalize on their distinct learning strengths. In our informal survey of ESL textbooks across the skill areas and grade levels, we noted that many texts contain a plethora of activities designated for partner and group work; however, upon closer examination, many of these activities do not actually provide a forum in which all students, regardless of their learning strengths and biases, will be engaged and productive.

As an illustration, both a highly relational learner and a highly analytic learner may be equally frustrated by a group assignment that actually requires a high degree of independent objective analysis. The following classic example highlights the hidden problems in this type of task.

> For one modified cloze exercise found in a grammar textbook, students are asked to work together to complete a story by filling in the blanks with the correct article. The analytic learner, who is comfortable and confident systematically tackling such structured tasks which draw upon verbal/analytic abilities, may resent having to relinquish an opportunity to excel by independently determining the series of correct answers. In fact, this so-called group activity could much more easily and efficiently be completed by students working alone or at home. Being forced to complete it in collaboration may annoy the more competitive student who values less distracting and solitary task completion. And the highly relational learner, who prefers the interactive and collaborative process, may protest the fact that this activity does not really lend itself to multiple perspectives and negotiation of meaning.

A predictable negative scenario would be the more analytic learner completing this detailed cloze task silently and independently, while the other group members passively await the correct responses or muddle through the process collectively.

Another common situation when group work can be less than fulfilling for many students occurs when no classmates are asked to share their experiences and thoughts, most notoriously before or after an assigned reading. In contrast to the above exercise with its anticipated correct answers, these types of tasks are intentionally open-ended to encourage maximum participation. Frequently, however, these pre- and post-reading tasks consist of little more than open-ended questions with no specific listening focus or tangible final product. The following is a hypothetical example of a fairly typical type of interactive task in an advanced reading class, one that is a definite red flag for an unproductive group process.

The students have just read a newspaper article about divorce and blended families. Their task is to now freewrite about their own family, describing the various relationships within the family, then to get together with a group of classmates to share individual freewrites. Not only is this writing and discussion topic too broad; it is also very personal and potentially sensitive for many individuals. While some highly relational learners might enjoy this opportunity to focus on interpersonal relationships, a more analytic student who favors abstract and impersonal curricula would recoil at the amount of self-disclosure necessary for engaging in this seemingly intrusive discussion. Further, with no concrete product assigned as an outcome of this discussion, this unstructured group venture would have immense potential for wandering into incoherence and irrelevance, which would further exasperate the analytic learner.

From an instructional point of view, such schema-building or application activities are appealing because they provide a springboard for students to express a multitude of perspectives. However, the above example helps to explain why diverse learners are less than forthcoming when assigned this sort of free-form and personal interactive task.

In striking contrast to the two preceding poorly conceptualized peer collaborations, the following activity is designed to engage and support students with both analytic and relational learning orientations.

The students in a low-level adult ESL class have been studying the language for food shopping and dining. Their small group task is to plan a dinner party for the class. The teacher will give each group a copy of a supermarket advertisement, and the students must use the ad to choose items that appear to be good "buys" that week. Then, based upon these observations, they will collectively decide what to prepare for the dinner party. The final responsibility for each small group is to describe their jointly planned dinner to the rest of the class. Subsequently, the unified class will apply nutritional criteria developed and discussed in class to choose the most healthy and appealing dinner from the options presented by the groups.

This multi-faceted task truly lends itself to a "meeting of the minds" and diverse perspectives. This activity also requires the use of varied input and has the clear potential for yielding more fruitful results when completed with classmates than alone. In addition, instead of catering to one learning and work style, this activity allows students with diverse capabilities to flourish and contribute dynamically to the collaborative process. The initial phase of this activity, when students are scrutinizing the advertisement, requires the use of detail-oriented verbal/analytical skills, while the meal planning based on these selections draws upon creative problem-solving skills. In addition, this assignment stipulates a specific and viable final product, which enables the more analytic and task-oriented students to feel comfortably focused on a serious academic pursuit, and at the same time helps to ensure that the social/relational learners harness their creative brainstorming and maintain time on task.

Fostering Learner Flexibility in the Collaborative ESL Classroom

Asking students to complete tasks in ways that are not consistent with their preferred approaches places unfamiliar social and academic demands on many students. Therefore, partner and group work should not enter into ESL classroom instruction capriciously or incidentally. Enthusiastic yet haphazard task design and implementation is more likely to backfire and fossilize negative preconceptions about particular classmates and the collaborative process in general. Instead, interactive classroom structures must be developed that will make students feel safe to experiment with new methods and help them to learn how to learn more effectively.

One constructive way to solicit greater buy-in for ESL classroom collaboration from reticent participants is to begin the school term by offering students a structured opportunity to reflect upon their natural tendencies for academic task completion. The Classroom Work Style Survey (Kinsella 1996), found in Appendix 6, was designed to give teachers who serve linguistically and culturally diverse learners a quick and manageable vehicle for eliciting some of their students' preferences for completing assignments in class. Most students appear excited by the prospect of identifying and discussing their habitual classroom learning preferences and discovering more about their peers. This straightforward and accessible survey prompts ESL students to identify aspects of their natural academic work style, and also to recognize that not all of their classmates share these same preferences.

After administering and interpreting the results of this survey in class, the teacher has gained preliminary insights into students' perceived learning strengths and attitudes about peer working groups. The survey results and subsequent discussion can help a teacher begin to determine the range of work style preferences within the class, and to better gauge the kinds of adjustments in group formations and task design that may facilitate the collaborative process for various students. Finally, this nonjudgmental exploration of diverse learning and working strengths serves as a natural segue to an introduction to the social and academic advantages of consistent, though not exclusive, task-based classroom learning with peers.

Supportive classroom experiences like these can help less confident and adaptable students expand their repertoire of learning and working modes. Even though students have preferred ways of learning and working in the classroom, they should ideally be able to adapt these styles when necessary. Some students, however, are so entrenched in particular approaches that experimenting with difference can cause major learning blocks; they lack the ability and/or willingness to become flexible learners.[*] While the long-range goal should be increased learner flexibility, Bonham (1989) notes that a realistic view of a given learning situation takes this lack of flexibility into account, and that responsive teachers strive to be

---

[*] For additional discussion of some students' inability to "stretch" their learning styles, see Tyacke, this volume.

as informed and as insightful as possible concerning students' preferred styles and developmental stages. If, for example, a highly analytic and independent learner expresses vehement objection to group tasks, that student might initially be allowed to work with a single partner of choice. To stimulate all students toward more productive and more enriching collaboration, small group activities and assignments need to be offered in purposeful, carefully conceived, systematic, and manageable doses. Optimally, a sequence of pleasant, purposeful, and productive task-based collaborations may prompt some reticent group members to reassess their work style preferences, and equip already receptive social learners with a more complete set of tools for collective inquiry and problem solving.

Guidance for Educators in Collaborative Learner-Centered Classrooms

It is far easier to advocate classroom collaboration than to orchestrate consistently productive and enriching group work experiences for students whose work styles differ, sometimes dramatically. While teachers may perceive partner and group work as a decided advantage for all learners in their classes, they may not necessarily attend to all of the crucial variables that promote or undermine fruitful team efforts. For example, teachers who rigidly adhere to primarily collaborative classroom formats with diverse student groups can alienate just as many second-language learners as the teacher who will not stray from conventional didactic formats.

The Instructor Self-Assessment Form: Group Work Design and Implementation (Kinsella and Sherak 1994) found in Appendix 7 provides teachers who are committed to providing an inclusive setting for peer collaboration with a tool for on-going proactive scrutiny of their small group instructional efforts. This assessment instrument adheres to the design principles for classroom participation structures outlined in this chapter, and is intended to encourage reflective and responsive practice.

Conclusion

Collaborative activities are typically more intellectually, socially, and emotionally demanding than routine individualized ESL classroom tasks such as following a grammar presentation, taking notes, or practicing a new structure. Axiomatic to this learner-centered model of instruction is a deliberate and informed effort on the part of the instructor to use information by and about the students when making critical decisions about course content and methods.

Yet most international and immigrant students have seldom experienced anything but a more didactic teaching approach, and they have learned to be successful in this traditional educational atmosphere. They have either primarily or exclusively been formerly (and formally) educated by teachers who do not ascribe to the notion that social interchange and dialog within the classroom play a pivotal role in fostering intellectual development. Within this comparatively traditional, hierarchical system, students are taught to accept anything from an instructor as unmitigated truth, and never to seriously entertain opinions different from those of the content expert. It is therefore understandable that these ESL students may not be excited about classroom collaboration, and may indeed be reluctant to practice it. A student's previous educational experiences and perceived learning strengths significantly shape his/her views about the most effective ways to approach and ultimately complete an assigned task. Consequently, after years of formal lectures and individualized seatwork, it is rather difficult for students to identify and experiment with potentially promising methods like group work.

Merely increasing opportunities for discussion and problem-solving will not result in positive changes in students' social-relational skills or attitudes about active and constructive learning with peers. Instead, group work needs to visibly increase both the efficiency and effectiveness of classroom learning for students with distinct work styles, and with different social and academic preparation for peer collaboration. One way to build a classroom environment that provides the necessary confidence to experiment is by asking students to identify and discuss their major work styles, and by planning collaborative activities that allow students to succeed in solving problems with their peers. Within this collaborative teaching model, the instructor has an equal responsibility to coach students into becoming more flexible learners who are better prepared to succeed within a diversity of academic and professional settings. By both acknowledging and accommodating students' individual learning strengths and potential challenges in group work design and implementation, an ESL teacher can support and sustain rather than sabotage classroom collaboration.

For Further Reading

Coehlo, E. (1994). *Learning Together in the Multicultural Classroom*. Markham, Ontario: Pippin Publishing Limited.

> The author strikes a careful balance between theory and practice, discussing the value of collaboration as a tool for promoting a positive multiracial and multicultural classroom atmosphere, then providing specific strategies for initiating students into the group work process, crucial considerations for designing group work tasks, and suggestions for implementing structured practice and strategies for accountability and assessment.

Cohen, E. G. (1994). *Designing Groupwork: Strategies for the Heterogeneous Classroom*. New York: Teacher's College Press, Columbia University.

> This text is an invaluable resource for teachers working with diverse student populations. The author clearly explains the theoretical framework for small group instruction in terms of students' gains in academic learning and social development, as well as the advantages for classroom management. She also addresses in depth the educational disadvantages of dominance and inequality in the classroom. The theory underlying classroom collaboration is translated into practice by means of specific

strategies for preparing K–12 students in the language, roles, and behaviors necessary for effective team learning. Another valuable feature of this reference tool is the extensive discussion of the teacher's role before, during, and after group work.

Keller, E. and Warner, S. T. (1988). *Conversation Gambits*. Hove, U.K.: Language Teaching Publications.

The most comprehensive of its kind, this text offers English learners a series of stimulating activities for practicing the myriad language functions necessary for successful classroom interaction.

Kessler, C. (Ed.). (1992). *Cooperative Language Learning: A Teacher's Resource Book*. Englewood Cliffs, NJ: Prentice Hall Regents.

This outstanding collection of chapters by leading cooperative learning theoreticians and practitioners represents a comprehensive examination of the critical issues affecting second-language learners and teachers in this interactive learning format. Several chapters are devoted to practical suggestions for successful group work implementation with linguistically and culturally diverse students in a variety of content areas and grade levels, from elementary classrooms to graduate teacher preparation programs.

Chapter 11

Developing a Survey for Multiple Intelligences: A Collaborative ESL Class Project

Christopher Sauer
Divine Word College

Howard Gardner's theory of Multiple Intelligences (1983, 1995) has already been widely accepted in the field of K–12 education as a theoretical framework for the development of curriculum and classroom methodology.[*] As Gardner (1995) points out, traditional intelligence tests have relied almost exclusively on assessing the linguistic and mathematical/logical intelligences of test-takers and ignored other areas of intelligence (musical, spatial, bodily/kinesthetic, intrapersonal and interpersonal) equally vital and useful to the individual. The result has been the disenfranchisement of those individuals who possess abilities in areas that are not assessed by traditional tests and are neglected by traditional methods of instruction and school curriculum. Because administrators and teachers have a responsibility to cultivate the whole student in the classroom, an increased awareness of each student's abilities is necessary.

As a teacher, it is tempting for me think that I already include enough varied materials and learning experiences to stimulate every student in my classes, but do I really know my students? Do they know themselves? To answer these questions, I developed an intelligence test following Gardner's theory, and I tailored its administration so that it became a consciousness-raising experience for my students.

The Challenge

How can a student's wide scope of intelligences be measured reliably? The major issue for the conscientious Multiple Intelligence (MI) survey developer is that individuals may express a particular intelligence in different ways. One person may enjoy singing, another playing the flute, and a third listening to the Schumann piano concerto. All are expressing a strong musical intelligence, yet a survey that asks "Do you play a musical instrument?" neglects other areas of musical intelligence. If the survey seeks to evaluate the strength of each intelligence

---

[*] See Christison in this volume for detailed descriptions of Multiple Intelligences.

relative to other intelligences, then it is important to present equal opportunities for multiple aspects of each intelligence to be evenly assessed.

Another challenge for the teacher is the validity of the survey instrument, that is, does the survey measure what it says it measures? One threat to validity can occur when the survey-respondent is asked to reply to general intelligence statements that are divorced from the concrete, real circumstances of everyday life. The student might, for instance, imagine that s/he is quite a "people person" (that is, high in interpersonal intelligence) in the classroom, but when presented with a sentence-long classroom situation in a survey, the student might choose a course of action that suggests the opposite. Moreover, a student may *desire* to be high in an intelligence; consequently, s/he may self-report on a brief survey in ways that do not correlate with reality. To avoid these problems, the survey writer needs to provide situational problems in which possible responses are provided in a real context that is familiar to the survey respondents.

The Survey Project

The fifteen students participating in this collaborative project were enrolled in a "remedial" composition class for international students at Ohio University. All were Asian, and each had self-selected the class; while they varied substantially in their academic English skills, each perceived a need to improve her/his academic English skills. All were undergraduates and had scored a minimum of 500 on the TOEFL, and all had produced an acceptable (4.5) score on the Test of Written English (TWE) writing sample.

I believed that increasing each student's awareness of her/his individual strengths would help to improve student academic performance by encouraging them to rely on those strengths, thereby improving their self-confidence. The development and administration of the instrument was done in the context of self-directed exploration and discussion, both in the classroom and via e-mail.

Developing the Survey

To develop the survey, I first constructed a World Wide Web site with a section containing a general description of each intelligence and links to other WWW sites that further explained the theory of MI.[*] After reading the material on my Web site, the students e-mailed me an evaluation of the theory and a self-assessment of their own dominant intelligences. (I used these self-assessments to determine the validity of the instrument.) A student-led discussion in class the following day focused on the concept that every student possesses individual talents and intelligences that the student can rely on to reach academic and personal goals.

I then wrote the items for the survey, taking care to be as free as possible from any culturally unfamiliar content, to present no significant lexical or grammatical challenges, and to stimulate the interest of the student respondents. Comments from colleagues who used Andrew Cohen's "Guidelines for Evaluating Assessment Instruments" (1994, pp. 105–110) and from students in the class led to an initial

---

[*] Readers can access this information at http://oak.cats.ohiou.edu/~cs882288, 1996.

revision of the instrument. For example, a question that asked respondents to decide if they had "good taste" was dropped because some of the Asian students were clearly reluctant to praise themselves, and other questions were re-evaluated to remove any situations in which students would be asked to self-praise. Further discussion with students and colleagues also led to the revision and clarification of instructions for the survey, changes in the spacing between items, and an increase in the survey's length. Table 11-1 shows sample questions from the survey.

Table 11–1. Sample Survey Questions

5. If I had some time to enjoy myself, I would

_____ take a walk by myself.

_____ play chess (or a similar game) with someone.

_____ listen to music.

_____ go running or do some other physical exercise.

Explanation: _____

10. Your academic department needs a student to represent it at an important meeting with the university president. You have been nominated for the position, but you may refuse if you wish. What will you do?

_____

_____

_____

Survey Administration

As I explained to the students, it is important when administering any survey that students be allowed time to read through the instrument and ask questions about any difficult vocabulary or instructions. Further, time should not be a factor in completing the survey; students should feel completely relaxed and unhurried. Several of my more advanced students finished the survey early and returned to other written work. Most respondents took the entire 45 minutes to complete the test, but none appeared to be under any time constraint.

In accordance with Gardner's concept of interrelated intelligences, the survey instructions allowed students to choose up to two answers for each of the multiple-choice items. In addition, a brief (one- or two-sentence) explanation of their answer was elicited for each item, providing students the opportunity to elaborate on their answers. I then collected the completed surveys and scored them myself, compiled the scores, and developed individual intelligence profiles.

Survey Results

Students received a score for each of their intelligences; I rated the answer choices on a 7-point Likert scale. For example, for question 2 on the original instrument, the answer "I read whenever I get the chance" was given 7 points for linguistic intelligence, and the answer "I read only when I must" was given only 1 point. Some choices were given scores for more than one intelligence. The answer "take a walk by myself" in question 5 received 5 points for intrapersonal intelligence and 4 points for bodily/kinesthetic intelligence.

Short-answer items that allowed greater flexibility and creativity for each respondent's answers presented the greatest challenge in the answer-rating. In several cases, student point totals were slightly modified by their explanations. For example, question 4 gives only six choices of shops to visit in a mall (it would be impossible to list all possible shops). If a student chose "music store" and then wrote "But I'd rather go to the clothing store" (not listed as a choice), I awarded the student 7 points for spatial intelligence (the first choice) and 4 points for musical intelligence (the second choice). Of course, this subjective scoring necessitated the checking of the consistency and the reliability of the scoring.[*]

Once the items were scored, I totaled the points for each of the intelligences and constructed a graph that demonstrated for each student the relationship of intelligences in her/his personal profile. The survey results provided an interesting overview into the wide variety of different intelligence profiles in the class. Table 11-2 provides an overview of the dominant intelligences found in the class, with the total points awarded following each intelligence.

Table 11–2. Overview of Dominant Intelligence

Student	Strongest (score)	Next Strongest
1st	Linguistic (37)	Interpersonal (35)
2nd	Interpersonal (40)	Linguistic (30)
3rd	Intrapersonal (36)	Math/Logical (26)
4th	Linguistic (39)	Intrapersonal (36)
5th	Spatial (29)	Intrapersonal (26)
6th	Spatial (47)	Linguistic (26)
7th	Linguistic (42)	Intrapersonal (29)
8th	Math/Logical (36)	Linguistic (35)
9th	Interpersonal (30)	Intrapersonal (28)
10th	Linguistic (43)	Intrapersonal (29)
11th	Math/Logical (39)	Interpersonal (33)
12th	Spatial (33)	Intra/Interpersonal (25 each)
13th	Linguistic (32)	Intrapersonal (28)
14th	Linguistic (49)	Interpersonal (42)
15th	Interpersonal (28)	Musical (25)

[*] See htpp://users.mcwi.net/~sauer for more information about checking the reliability of survey results.

As the two intelligence profile examples in Figures 11-1 and 11-2 illustrate, students varied a great deal in the relationship between their intelligences. In Figure 11-1, Student 1 reported a very high score in both linguistic and interpersonal intelligence, indicating these intelligences to be dominant. In Figure 11-2, Student 15 reported relatively high scores in interpersonal and in music intelligence.

Figure 11–1. Intelligences Profile for Student 1

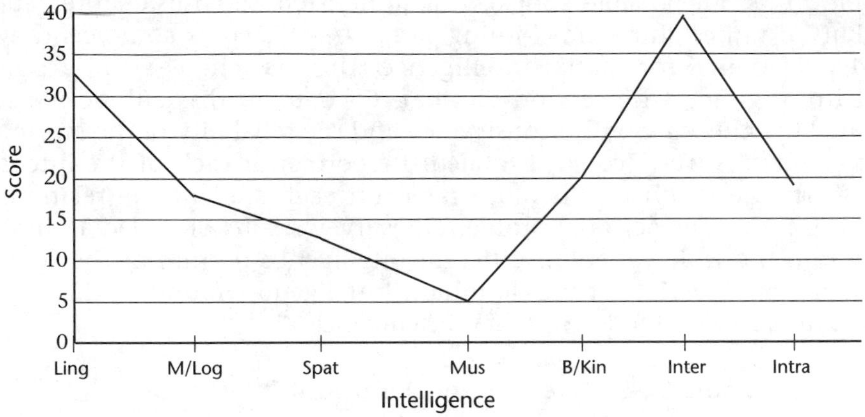

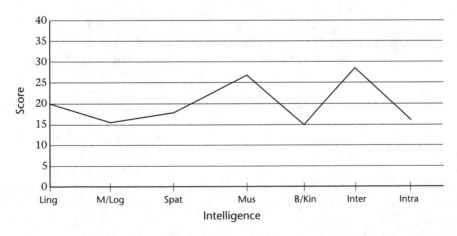

Figure 11–2. Intelligences Profile for Student 15

It is important to note in both profiles that the point totals are not as important as the relationship between intelligences, which are indicated by their relative strengths (Armstrong 1994; Campbell, Campbell, and Dickenson 1996). In the two student profiles above, notice that the score for each student's interpersonal intelligence is different: Student 1 scored 39 points, and Student 15 scored 28 points. Yet this does not mean that one student has a "stronger" or "better" interpersonal intelligence than the other. It only means that in Student

1's intelligence profile, interpersonal intelligence is the strongest. Therefore, when I shared the results with the students, I made clear that there was no maximum number of points, just as there were no correct or incorrect answers. This embraces Gardner's criticism of traditional tests of intelligence that have been used to compare and rate individuals' abilities, often to the detriment of the individual.

In short, because of the statistical limitations of the survey and the underlying premises of MI theory, student scores should not be used to compare students: a survey instrument can never hope to fully report a person's intelligence. But as an awareness-raising activity used to increase personal insights into strengths and abilities, the MI survey can be a useful tool. Students can be encouraged to identify, analyze, and use their strengths to succeed in their academic studies, to develop their personal relationships, and to learn language.

Evaluating the Survey Results

To determine the overall validity of the survey instrument, I used several methods, including students' initial personal e-mail responses, in which they chose one or two of their intelligences they felt were especially strong. I discovered that the students had been reluctant to choose a dominant intelligence in their e-mail messages—perhaps because they were unwilling to praise themselves. Instead, they often pointed out intelligences they felt they were weak in. For example, Student 8, whose MI survey responses indicated high linguistic and mathematic/logical intelligences, said:

> I know I don't have the bodily-kinesthetic intelligence because I don't like hug a lot, even though I like sports, I don't want to became an athlete. I don't like acting and dancing. So I am pretty sure I don't have bodily-kinesthetic intelligence.

Student 10 was willing to choose an intelligence only after detailing the intelligences he didn't have:

> I doubt that not only I but also my family does not have Logical-Mathematical Intelligence at all. I do not think I have a prominent intelligence of these seven intelligences. However, I assume that Linguistics and Musical Intelligences of myself are better than others.

This student's self-assessment correlated with the dominant intelligence identified by the instrument (linguistic).

Some student feedback did provide insights into the MI theory for ESL instructors interested in applying MI theory in their classrooms. Student 3's response indicates a sophisticated understanding of the importance of the interaction between and among intelligences.

> In fact, it's hard to decide which intelligence is the most effective one in human beings life, but I do think that each of seven intelligences can be affected in human's life in different situation because these seven intelligences have a particular characteristics each other and help to shape human's life.

Appropriately enough, Student 3 received her highest score in intrapersonal intelligence (32 points). Student 7 (whose strongest reported intelligences were linguistic and intrapersonal) pointed out the problems she had experienced with traditional intelligence tests.

> Intelligence can't be measured, as Gardner said, an individuals has multiple intelligence. Especially, IQ test is non-sense, because the test is focused on the ability of linguistic and math. Although the test predicts good students in school, it ignores other students with intelligence except linguistic and math. Intelligence of an individual is valuble, so we can't measure one.

Student responses in my class generally indicated that the exercise as a whole resulted in their heightened awareness of the personal strengths and intelligence characteristics. Student 10 discovered a contrast between MI theory and a traditional Japanese aphorism.

> Although we have a famous saying that means "God never gives us more than one tallent" in Japan, I was wondering that was not true. I know that many people who have more than one tallent.

Conclusion

The development of a well-written survey instrument is a difficult task; the development of an instrument to measure a person's multiple intelligences effectively is even more challenging. I found that input from students and colleagues was essential. Moreover, the entire exercise functioned as a successful awareness-raising activity; conducting the MI survey development in the context of student research and discussion became an opportunity to help students self-discover and focus on their intelligence strengths.

The teacher who takes the time to administer such an instrument also benefits from the insight that every student in the class possesses a special combination of intelligences. As a result, teachers can tailor the class curriculum to better facilitate learning by capitalizing on the resources students bring to the classroom.

For Further Reading

Armstrong, T. (1994). *Multiple Intelligences in the Classroom*. Alexandria, Virginia: Association for Supervision and Curriculum Development.

> An excellent bridge between Gardner's theory and every teacher's classroom. Each intelligence is clearly presented, with numerous activities for effectively implementing MI theory. Armstrong explores the application of MI theory to issues in classroom management, assessment, and special education, areas sometimes neglected in other MI texts.

Brown, J. D. (1996). *Testing in Language Programs*. Upper Saddle River, New Jersey: Prentice Hall Regents.

> A must-read for teachers who test. Brown concisely presents basic testing theory that is immediately applicable in the language classroom. Plenty of examples are included to demonstrate methods of ascertaining reliability, validity, and related statistical functions.

Chapter 12

Teaching Modals to Multistyle Learners

Barbara Harthill and Connie Busch

University of Denver

In this chapter, we describe an intermediate grammar unit on the use of past modals that we use in our classes at the University of Denver's English Language Center (DU ELC). Because a majority of our international students matriculate to undergraduate or graduate degrees at universities in the United States, we structure our intensive courses to prepare them for academic work. The unit described below incorporates activities to engage all learning style preferences, and it has also been sequenced to move from low-risk to high-risk activities, thus providing an optimal learning environment for the unique needs of our students. A brief summary of the learning style theories underlying the lessons is followed by a detailed description of five lessons in Barbara's class, and a detailed analysis by Connie of the learning style preferences addressed in each of the activities.

Background

In the DU ELC, we have developed and refined a learning styles approach based on David A. Kolb's *Experiential Learning Theory* (1984), which identifies four basic learning styles.

1. Divergent Learning Style

   The student

   - learns through concrete experience and reflective observation (CE/RO).[*]
   - [her/his] greatest strengths are in imaginative ability and awareness of meaning and values.
   - views concrete situations from many perspectives and is able to organize many relationships into a meaningful *gestalt*.
   - emphasizes observation rather than action.
   - performs well in situations calling for the generation of alternative ideas and implications.
   - is interested in people.
   - tends to be imaginative and feeling-oriented.

---

[*] Kolb uses these abbreviations to describe these learners:

Concrete Experience (CE)	Reflective Observation (RO)
Abstract Conceptualization (AC)	Active Experimentation (AE)

2. Assimilative Learning Style
    The student
    - learns through abstract conceptualization and reflective observation (AC/RO).
    - [her/his] greatest strengths are inductive reasoning and the ability to create theoretical models by assimilating disparate observations into an integrated explanation.
    - is more concerned with ideas and abstract concepts than with people.
    - values soundness and precision of ideas and theories rather than their practical value.

3. Convergent Learning Style
    The student
    - learns through abstract conceptualization and active experimentation (AC/AE).
    - [her/his] greatest strengths are problem-solving, decision-making, and the practical application of ideas.
    - does best in situations like conventional intelligence tests where there is a single correct answer or only one solution to a question or problem.
    - relies on deductive reasoning for problem-solving.
    - is controlled in expression of emotion.
    - prefers dealing with technical tasks and problems rather than social and interpersonal issues.

4. Accommodative Learning Style
    The student
    - learns through concrete experience and active experimentation (CE/AE).
    - [her/his] greatest strengths are doing things, carrying out plans and tasks, and getting involved in new experiences.
    - emphasizes opportunity-seeking, risk-taking, and action.
    - is good at adapting her/himself to changing immediate circumstances.
    - is willing to discard plan or theory when it does not fit the facts.
    - solves problems in a trial-and-error manner, relying heavily on other people for information rather than her/his own analytic ability.
    - is at ease with people and is sometimes seen as impatient and pushy.

Students may self-report their learning style(s) using Kolb's Learning Styles Inventory (LSI). But it is important to keep in mind that the inventory only measures a preference toward one or more learning styles; it is not intended to stereotype a student as one rigid unalterable learning type. In fact, all students use a wide variety of learning tactics, and they may change their learning orientation over the course of time as they mature and broaden their experiences. Therefore, we do not recommend that teachers actually test their students with the LSI, but rather that they utilize its key concepts in developing lesson plans in order to impact all learning styles, regardless of the particular learning style profiles of a particular group of students.

Native English Speakers, ESL Students, and Learning Styles

For the ESL classroom, studies have shown that learning type preferences are often influenced by culture (Oxford 1996; Smith 1986). In one study, Shelley Smith (1986) surveyed a sample of international students from five different ethnic groups (Asians, Southeast Asians, Middle Eastern, Hispanic, and Northern European). Survey results showed significantly higher scores for the **RO** (Reflective Observer) learning style and significantly lower scores for the **AC** (Abstract Conceptualizer) style as compared to U. S. students. The international students in Smith's study preferred a highly synthetic or holistic approach to learning as opposed to analysis of individualized detail. Many of the students also showed an aversion to highly extensional tasks such as oral presentations, group discussion, role-playing, and interviewing.

The RO style tends to predominate in high-context cultures (those cultures which are often relatively homogenous, in which there are many rules for behavior), in which relationships are highly valued and inappropriate action could easily produce embarrassment to others (Hall and Hall 1990; Oxford 1995). In countries with high-context cultures, such as Korea and Japan, the ability to internalize information through reflective observation is a socially valuable cognitive function; this skill requires a keen awareness of the situational and environmental context.

Because research has demonstrated that learning type preferences are often influenced by culture (Oxford, Hollaway, and Horton-Murillo 1992), teachers must become more aware of the reasons that their ESL students respond differently in class. Smith (1987) notes that RO ESL students are often perceived by their teachers to be exceptionally quiet, slow to ask questions, and slow to speak up in class. At the same time, their answers are generally seen as thoughtful, although sometimes tangential. Also important for ESL teachers, students with lower AC scores have less practice using analysis as a form of understanding experience.

Framework for Barbara's Lesson and Connie's Analysis

Background

Modals are often difficult for students to conceptualize and use correctly. Especially difficult is the use of past modals because they are not only different in structure but often have vastly different meaning from their present forms. Among the most difficult are the ones that are described (according to their function) as modals of speculation and conclusion about the past. They include *may have, might have, must have, could have,* and their negative forms.

The lessons described below are part of a three-week unit on past modals in our Intermediate Grammar class at DU. It occurs toward the middle of the quarter, and is preceded by (a) an in-depth unit on verb tenses and verb forms, and (b) a brief review of the forms and functions of present modals. The activities described in each 50-minute lesson can be condensed or expanded as needed.

My objective is to familiarize students with the forms and functions of modals in the past, and to give the students a clear understanding and ample oral and written practice. The textbook, *Focus on Grammar* (Fuchs and Bonner 1995), does an excellent job of presenting these modals in their functional context, and of providing high-interest materials illustrating their usage.

Teacher Preparation

- Become familiar with the meaningful, but rather unique, way *Focus on Grammar* classifies these modals.
- Review Betty Azar's modal charts (1989, chapter 2)* and note the differences in terminology. NOTE: You may want to integrate the Azar charts into your lessons. If so, cross-reference them for the students.
- Collect written material that uses the target modals in a high-interest context (for example, articles on the Bermuda Triangle or UFO sightings).
- Check *TV Guide* for programs on ancient mysteries (on the Arts and Entertainment, Discovery, or History channels).
- Keep a flip chart in the classroom on which to categorize the modals to be taught, and the context in which they are used in order to record sample sentences.
- Collect "mysterious" objects that students cannot readily identify for the "archeological dig."
- Find books/pictures on petroglyphs/Nazca lines in Peru, and so on.

Student Preparation

I introduce the students to the concept of past modals of speculation and conclusions about the past by discussing mysterious events in the past for which we have no definitive answers nor enough evidence or eyewitness accounts to come to a definitive conclusion. Elicit examples from the students' countries of origin. NOTE: Students should be fairly proficient in the forms and functions of present modals before attempting the much more difficult past modals.

Class 1 Introduction of Modals of Speculation and Conclusion

The unit in *Focus on Grammar* begins with a reading entitled "Close Encounters," which summarizes Erich von Daeniken's theories regarding the Nazca lines in Peru and the giant statues on Easter Island (Van Daeniken 1972). Realizing that this reading would be very challenging for my intermediate students, I searched for material that would be of equally high interest to the students but would introduce them to the subject matter in a less daunting format. I found a wealth of suitable material in Public Broadcasting Company (PBS) and The Learning Channel (TLC) television documentaries as well as in the Arts and Entertainment (A&E) and Discovery channels. They included the series "Ancient Mysteries of the Past" on

---

* The Azar modal charts also appear in her *Understanding and Using English Grammar Chartbook* (Englewood Cliffs: Prentice Hall Regents, 1993).

PBS and documentaries such as "The Bermuda Triangle: Secrets Revealed," "Secrets of the Pyramids and Sphinx," and "Close Encounters of the Fifth Kind" on TLC (shown between June 23 and June 29, 1996). For the lesson described here I chose a segment of one of the PBS series, the subject of which was Atlantis.* (Another time I would probably choose the documentary on the Bermuda Triangle because my students seemed both familiar with and intrigued by this topic.)

All the videotapes I used speculated frequently about past events, using the structures I wanted to teach. The segments were full of *might have, could have,* and *must not have,* and were therefore an ideal low-risk, high-interest introduction to the grammar material. As I had anticipated, the students were glued to the VCR, and as they focused on the high interest content, they were introduced to the target structures in the framework of scientists speculating on the likelihood of the existence of Atlantis and the possible reasons for its demise. In a brief introductory segment of the video, past modals of speculation were used no fewer than five times!

I showed short, five-minute segments of the video, at first asking the students to watch for the main idea only. Then I questioned students on content, using such target structures as "Do scientists believe that Atlantis could have existed? Where do scientists believe Atlantis might have been located? What might have been the causes of the disappearance of Atlantis?"

In terms of learning styles, the **Assimilative** learners, who process information reflectively, seemed especially motivated by the video, probably because the act of watching is primarily an internal process that requires active listening and observation without immediate public response or performance. They also responded well to the video because it presented a great amount of scientific information, both fact and educated opinion, from international experts in the field. Since Assimilative learners enjoy details and data collection, they seemed to relish the opportunity to take this enormous amount of information provided by the video and draw conclusions based on facts and expert opinion.

The **Divergent** learners also responded extremely well to the subject matter of the video because CEs have a great interest in people and culture, and they learn by observing others in concrete situations. The Divergent learners' favorite question is "Why?" and the mysterious quality of the lost city of Atlantis gave them a chance to raise many "Why?" questions in their own minds. Their enthusiasm was obvious in the discussion that followed. Moreover, the discussion itself further piqued their interest because Divergent learners enjoy and learn from hearing others' points of view.

The discussions following the video segments helped the other two learner groups, **Accommodative** learners and the **Convergent** learners as well because both tend to process information actively rather than reflectively. Further, they were thoroughly involved in the subject matter, which captured their imaginations.

---

* For copies of the "Atlantis" video, call 1-800-423-1212 or write to A&E Network, 235 E. 45th Street, New York, NY 10017. Phone: (212) 661-4500.

Class 2 Clozes and Charts

In the next step of the grammar lesson, the students again watched segments of the video and filled in a cloze exercise I had prepared. My strategy was to have the students listen and fill in information gaps, but the sentences contained the structures to be learned because my focus was still on recognition rather than active usage. Example:

> According to recent theories, Atlantis *might have been destroyed* by a
> _____ ("giant earthquake" is the looked-for
> information here).

The cloze exercise, as a quiet, individualized activity, appealed to the Divergent and Assimilative learners who need time to process information reflectively. The Divergent learners particularly responded to the structure of the exercise, which required them to think carefully through all the available data and respond in a concise manner by selecting exactly the right words to fill in the blanks. In a similar way, Accommodative learners liked the cloze exercise because they saw it as a problem or puzzle to be solved in an application-oriented way.

After the students had had adequate practice in recognizing the structures and understanding their functions, I gave a short lecture to develop the structural framework. The Summary Chart of Modals and Similar Expressions (Azar 1989, pp. 110–111) is ideally suited for students who rely on written reference guides to help them analyze grammar. The grammarians in the class studied it and referred to it constantly. At times, they challenged and questioned information in our textbook when it deviated in the slightest from THE CHART. Therefore, annotating the chart with the appropriate references in our textbook proved very helpful, as did the various fill-in-the-blank exercises in their text. These exercises asked students to use the structures in the context of speculating about various mysteries in the past. One exercise asked them to speculate on such mysteries as the extinction of the dinosaurs and the kidnapping of a man by Bigfoot.

Learners who perceive information abstractly, the Assimilative and Accommodative learners, benefited most from this activity. Assimilative learners in particular are comfortable with traditional classroom material like this; they appreciate being able to examine the details and find out what the experts think. They also enjoy the intellectual recognition that comes from examining the facts and challenging any logical discrepancies. Likewise, the Accommodative learners respond well to information presented systematically, as in a chart or model, since they value concise thinking and have only a limited tolerance for fuzziness.

Class 3 Class-Generated Modal Chart/Oral Group Work

Another helpful activity was the preparation of our own modal chart on which to record the various uses of the structures we encountered in both the videos and the textbook reading. We used a large flip chart and organized the material according to types of modals and their functions. We added examples from class materials as they came up. Eventually, some students volunteered to make a master chart, which was then displayed prominently in the classroom for the duration of the lesson on past modals.

The Divergent and Convergent learners, who perceive information concretely, seemed most motivated by this activity. It gave the Divergent learners an opportunity to learn by sharing their ideas and becoming personally involved in an activity that required insightful, imaginative thinking. The Convergent learners, who tended to be quiet during the Azar chart session, came alive when they could apply their own language experiences to an intellectual exercise. Convergent learners like to get things done and see results, and this activity allowed them to create an application-oriented grammar chart that made sense to them. It was interesting that even though some Convergent learners didn't grasp the details of the abstract Azar grammar chart, they nevertheless were able to draw accurate conclusions about grammar usage based on their own knowledge and experience when creating our chart.

At this point, the students were able to recognize the target structures and talk about them, but in natural speech they came up seldom, if at all. It was time for a more communicative practice of these structures, which is one of the most important facets of intermediate grammar at the ELC. (Written usage is stressed in the grammar-writing class.) *Focus on Grammar,* with its many communicative activities, is ideally suited for this purpose. The students enjoyed working in small groups with the exercises that asked them to speculate on the uses of ancient artifacts, such as an elaborately decorated Chinese wooden pillow. To add a touch of competition to this activity, I awarded a prize to the group with the largest number of reasonable speculations.

To supplement the exercises, and because several students had asked about petroglyphs, I brought to class a number of library books with wonderful pictures of petroglyphs. I asked students to speculate about the meaning(s) of various figures and objects in the petroglyphs. Several students became so interested in these petroglyphs that they planned and together went on a trip to Utah to see them during the following break!

As active processors of information, the Accommodative learners gained a great deal from this group activity. The Accommodative learners were able to satisfy their desire to integrate theory and practice. As practical problem-solvers, Accommodative learners need to know how things work, and this activity tested their problem-solving skills in an active, fun setting. The competitive nature of the activity also appealed to the Accommodative learners, who wanted to get right to the point and were not afraid of blurting out answers quickly. Similarly, the Convergent learners became engaged in the activity because they were highly motivated by the social nature of the exercise. Many of the Divergent learners also took a personal interest in the real-life mystery of topic and so were also enthusiastic about the activity.

Class 4 Archeological Dig/Group Work/Oral Reports

Because the students had enjoyed the archeological activities, I created our own "dig" as a final class activity. I searched my house for objects that might not be familiar to my students; as my husband and I are avid cooks, most of the objects came from my kitchen. A German pasta maker (*Spaetzlehobel*) was one of the many objects I hauled to class. Before the activity, I taught the students the structures necessary to question assumptions about the past by using "Could it really have been used for X?" or "This couldn't possibly have been X because . . ."

Then I distributed the "mystery" objects to small student groups and gave them the following tasks:

- Give a detailed description of the object.
- Speculate on what the object might have been used for.
- Speculate on who might have used it and how it might have been used.

After a specified time, the class came together as a whole, and students from each group presented their objects and their speculations to the rest of the class. Students delighted in questioning the assumptions of their classmates; they used the appropriate structures frequently and with ease. To my surprise, one very shy (RO) grammar student excelled at this particular activity; in fact, every student in the room was actively involved. To say this was a high-interest exercise is an understatement: my colleagues in adjacent classrooms commented (enviously) on the ruckus coming from my class.

The Divergent, Accommodative, and Convergent learners were motivated for many of the same reasons that they had excelled in the previous group activity. The Assimilative learners seemed to respond better, however; the reason may be that the "archeological dig" allowed RO students the maximum opportunity for detailed, hands-on inspections as well as challenging others' assumptions about the objects with thorough questions. They were also willing to re-examine the object when disagreement arose within the group, and they tended to rely more on the instructor to maximize their own certainty about their conclusions.

Class 5 Past Modals Test

To test the students on this grammar lesson, I combined more standard exercises with short readings and pictures of mysterious happenings, about which the students had to speculate. The strongest "grammarian" in the class complained that the non-traditional sections of the test "were not about grammar," but he got his first "A" on the test; that is, he had made the jump from theoretical knowledge of the structures to actually using them correctly in a communicative, contextualized setting. To my delight, the shyest student also got his highest grade on this test. In all, the average test score was higher than that of other tests, but not out of line— an indication, perhaps, that in this particular lesson I had successfully engaged the various learning styles preferences of my students.

The Divergent learners seemed to feel comfortable with this test because it challenged them to think creatively about a concrete situation. The Accommodative learners liked the problem-solving aspects of the test, and the practical nature of the test appealed to Convergent learners. Some Assimilative learners appeared frustrated by the test because its non-traditional format tested functional rather than abstract grammar, and some students did not clearly understand how their knowledge was being tested.

Conclusion

It is important to note the sequencing of the modals lesson. It started with low-risk activities (video-viewing, the cloze exercise, and the modals lecture). Gradually, more high-risk activities were added, such as small group and whole class oral discussion, as the students gained confidence in their knowledge-base. The gradual movement from low- to high-risk activities is crucial, especially for the Divergent and Assimilative learners who need time to process information reflectively before acting/speaking. Of course, it is also important for students of any learning style preference who are shy by nature, who lack self-confidence, or who come from educational systems in which speaking in class is not encouraged.

Perhaps the best example of the success of the sequencing was the Assimilative learners' amazing success at actively questioning the assumptions of other classmates during the oral speculation activity as well as in the high quality of all students' oral presentations. The following comment from a student evaluation of the grammar course echoes the comments of many other students in the class: "I really like Barbara's grammar class. She always teaches us completely."

For Further Reading

Celce-Murcia, M. and Hilles, M. S. (1988). *Techniques and Resources in Teaching Grammar*. New York: Oxford University Press.

> This book offers a wide variety of approaches and techniques in teaching grammar. It is, therefore, very useful in planning a sequence of lessons that engages the learners' individual learning styles preferences.

Ur, P. (1988). *Grammar Practice Activities: A Practical Guide for Teachers*. New York: Cambridge University Press.

> This is a classic! It offers a great variety of activities to practice grammatical structures. Ideal for a wide variety of learning style preferences.

Ur, P. (1992). *Five-Minute Activities: A Resource Book of Short Activities*. New York: Cambridge University Press.

> Great warm-up activities!

Chapter 13

Transforming Texts Through Graphic Responses

Roberta Vann
Iowa State University

Teachers and textbook authors have long valued visuals in teaching reading, but only recently have we begun to recognize the power and potential of having students transform their ideas about a text into combinations of pictures, diagrams, symbols, and space. In a recent study, P. E. Whitin (1996) shows how native English speaker middle school students, by constructing and sharing their own non-text visual responses to literature, open new potential for making meaning, generate new perspectives on individual experiences, and create meanings through social interactions.

Various kinds of graphic representation have also been successfully used with students learning English as a second language (Amer 1994; Bassano and Christison 1995; Tang 1992/93). Learners at all levels of second language learning can benefit from drawing in response to texts. In this chapter I offer an example of its use with young adult international students studying English for academic purposes.

Background

In their article summarizing the reading strategies that have empirical support and so can be recommended in the teaching of reading, Pressley et al. (1989) suggest that summarization (including graphic summaries), the use of mental imagery, and prior knowledge activation are key strategies to maximizing text comprehension. That is, students who are taught to summarize, to picture what they read, and to draw on what they already know can improve their comprehension of texts. That graphic responses to texts demonstrably incorporate summarization, imagery of the text, and prior knowledge activation provides theoretical support for incorporating this technique with young and older adult learners.

Finally, when used in group sessions, visual responses offer possibilities of new perspectives on a text. Shy students who may lack the confidence to share their ideas about a text find the support of a visual helpful in explaining their ideas for others. In turn, their highly verbal classmates who are trying to understand their peers' interpretation of a text find visuals a useful clarification tool. As students share their ideas and negotiate meaning, both sides expand their own views of the text.

A few years ago, several of us at Iowa State became interested in the work of visual theorists such as Arnheim (1969), who discusses the visual nature of verbal concepts and explains the integration of perception and cognition. We also examined recent popular visual techniques such as "mind mapping" (Margulies 1991), which fuses cartoon-like drawings, symbols, and sometimes words, to visualize thoughts (see Figure 13-1).

Figure 13–1. Mind Map

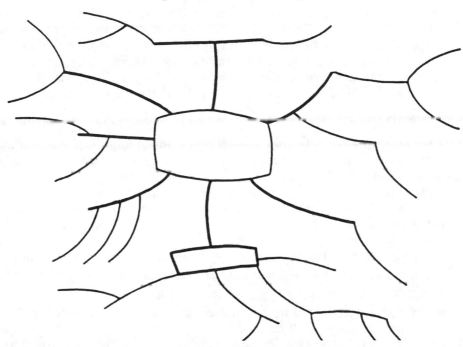

MIND MAPS can branch out in any direction. Curving the lines makes it easier to write every word right side up. Boxes around words are useful.

Source: Margulies 1991, p. 55. Used with permission.

Graduate student Maria Shahidi, colleague Helen Hoyt Schmidt, and I began to examine ways of incorporating alternative learning strategies, including drawing and kinesthetic learning, into our university-level ESL classes. While we often found our young adult students initially self-conscious about drawing and somewhat skeptical of its value in learning an academic subject, most eventually responded as enthusiastically as this student of Maria's who admitted having a life-long dislike of drawing.

> Do you believe that your class is the best delight of my school life? From p.m. 2:10 to p.m. 3:00, I have a great joy. The time is more delightful than lunch time. In fact, I don't like to draw. But in last week, I was happy when I drew the picture . . .

While using art to teach language may appeal most to younger students and to those who recognize themselves to be visual or tactile learners, graphic responses offer all learners a chance to articulate their views in ways that purely verbal means do not. One reason may be that when a student depicts visually what s/he has read, s/he is engaging in high-level cognitive skills, that is, synthesis and analysis. When s/he shares her/his own picture of the text with classmates, or helps construct one jointly with them, s/he is transforming those ideas into a readily-understandable medium. As one student commented, "Drawing can help me describe a situation, and my thinking in English improves."

Because graphic responses encourage synthesis and analysis, they can offer readers responding to a text a welcome alternative to the traditional "Answer the following questions about the passage you have just read" or simply "Summarize this passage." Therefore, while graphic responses do offer highly visual and tactile learners a way to gain self-confidence among their more orally articulate classmates, graphic representation is also an important analytical tool for students with other learning styles who are studying English as an academic language.

Getting Started

Reader-created graphics can be used as part of a reading response to or summary of any kind of text, but short texts taken from popular easy-to-read publications such as *USA Today* offer a good starting point.

We introduce the idea of representing a text graphically by first convincing students of its value. We do this by talking about the usefulness of graphics in information processing (noted above); we also share excerpts from the book *Mapping Inner Space* (Margulies 1991) like the one in Figure 13-1. The points we want to make to students are that while drawing may seem like child's play, graphics

- can help us develop new ways of perceiving and analyzing texts;
- can help us more actively engage in learning;
- have been recognized by researchers and students as useful in retaining and understanding information.

Then we model the process for our students. We tell the students that we're going to try to represent a text graphically. We provide a short text from the newspaper or a text from class materials that students have already read. Together with the students, we construct the text on an overhead, using multiple colors, pictures, symbols, and words. I begin by asking: "What happened first?" The students, maybe several talking at one time, answer. If they disagree, I ask someone to look back to the text for verification. Then I might ask: "What shall I draw first?" I draw the first suggestion and proceed in similar fashion to complete the sketch, encouraging student input, negotiation, and textual confirmation.

An important point here is that the drawings we model should not be artistic, even if the teacher is capable. Instead, the teacher needs to model simple, unsophisticated sketches (such as stick figures) that assure students that the quality of the drawing is not important. As the teacher is drawing, s/he might say something like "I have trouble drawing people, so I'm just going to use this stick figure." Similarly, symbols and words can be incorporated (as in Figure 13-1). Finally, the teacher can show the students examples of flow charts, pie charts, and picture diagrams, and can explain how any or all of these can be used in graphic summaries.

The Graphic Summary Exercise

Then we give the students a short text such as the one below, adapted from a journal article, and ask them to read it in preparation for drawing a visual summary.

POST-PEPPER PAIN

One young Israeli man with a taste for hot chilis may never be able to eat them again. It started when he and his brother decided to have a contest to see who could eat the most peppers in the shortest time. The winner ate 25 chili peppers in 12 minutes, but two hours later he was in acute pain. Two hours after that, when he arrived at the hospital, he was vomiting and reported having terrible abdominal pain. Doctors discovered a hole in the man's digestive tract. They believe that capsaicin, the active ingredient of red peppers, caused the problem [adapted from Landau *et al.* 1992].

After students spend a few minutes reading the text, we divide them into groups of three to six and give each group an overhead transparency or large sheet of paper and several colored marking pens. We ask each group to visually summarize the key events in the text on the overhead, using pictures, mathematical or other symbols, as well as space, line, and perhaps an occasional word to convey the main ideas of the text. One person in the group may volunteer to draft the design, or the overhead transparency may be passed around, but all group members should help decide what to put on the sheet. In our experience, students actively engage in designing and negotiating the contents of the graphic, although the actual "final" drawing is often handed over to one member.

After 5 to 10 minutes, we collect the visuals and ask one member from each group (but not the group artist) to present and explain their group's visual summary to the whole class. We encourage others to make comments, including expressing disagreements about events, inferences made, sequence, and so on. Figures 13-2, 13-3, and 13-4 are three student responses to the "chili pepper" text.

Figure 13–2. Student Graphic Summary

Figure 13–3. Student Graphic Summary

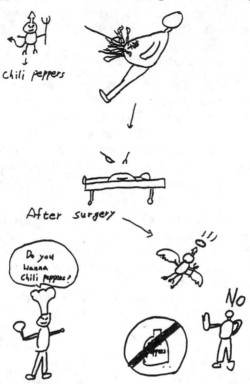

As students present the visual summaries to their classmates, we find that ordinarily shy and/or reflective students seem to find speaking with a visual less threatening than speaking without one. One particularly reticent student found the visual she created was the prop she needed to boost her self-confidence in speaking. Other students have told us that drawing "helps the memory."

Meanwhile, the audience (their classmates) tends to engage in each presentation. Even students who admitted not liking to draw report that they enjoy looking at the drawings made by their classmates, sometimes because they are humorous, but also, we think, because student-drawings are inevitably unique personal expressions of personality. Some drawings are loose and colorful, others tightly drawn; some students incorporate mathematical symbols and other elaborate diagrams, and others cartoons.

Each visual response also is engaging because it is potentially controversial. That is, because the interpretations of the text are visual, they become concrete and easy for other students to understand and perhaps dispute. By comparing the various visual interpretations of the text, students note common underlying patterns contributed by the author, see how other classmates picture the text, and delight in the varied responses. In addition, differences in the understanding of the text become clear, and if unimportant details rather than main ideas are the focus, or if material not in the original text is introduced, the problems become apparent to all the students. Class discussion then can focus on those problems:

Figure 13–4. Student Graphic Summary

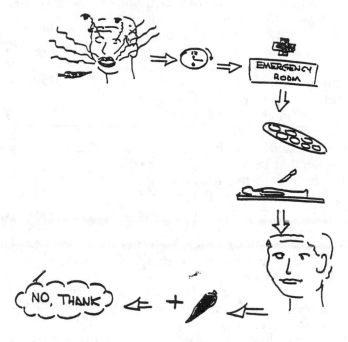

- Did all students understand the sequence in the same way?
- Did they focus on main ideas?
- Did they introduce anything that was not in the original text?

Extensions and Variations

Sharing graphic summaries of reading can be an end in itself, or the summaries can be extended into more focused academic skill-building by following up with an academic reading from a textbook or other publication. For instance, the sequence that develops from the chili pepper article is a series-of-events chain: that is, one event precedes (and sometimes causes) another event, followed by another and another (see Figure 13-5). This pattern often shows up with biological topics such as the life cycle of an animal or the steps in a procedure (how to do something), with a sequence of events (how World War II began), or with the events in the life of a historical figure or the events in a novel (Jones, Pierce, and Hunter 1988).

In our classes, we show a "scientific" version of picto-graphs such as Figure 13-5 demonstrates, and then we brainstorm about other kinds of readings that incorporate this structure. For our pre-university students, we follow up this exercise with a similar but longer academic reading. For example, we might choose a longer excerpt from a textbook that describes a biological cycle, model the process once again, and then ask small groups of students to summarize the text graphically.

After seeing graphic responses to texts modeled in class, and after participating in group constructions of graphic summaries, students begin to develop their individual graphic response styles, either highly pictorial ones like those our students originally produced or the streamlined graphic representations that show textual structure without details, similar to Figure 13-5. We like the idea of experimenting with both and asking students to consider the advantages and disadvantages of each. For example, students have told us that the pictorial versions are "more fun," and that they make them "picture" the text more vividly, but they say that the graphics are sometimes more difficult to draw well. More linear or mathematical styles may require more thorough understanding, but they are easier to draw and look more academic. Some students may find that cartoon-like illustrations aid their memory of the text, while diagrammatic responses help clarify the structure of a text and become useful models for writing similar texts. Much of this preference for style of response varies among individuals, and we encourage our students to use what seems right for them.

We also encourage our students to consider extending visuals into their personal and academic note-taking, both as a time-saver and as a mnemonic device for recalling concepts or new vocabulary. One way to help students develop this habit is by first asking them to take notes on a passage in the way they usually do, and then to try to capture the same ideas, but in half the words, using graphics to convey ideas more simply.

Figure 13–5. Series of Events Chain

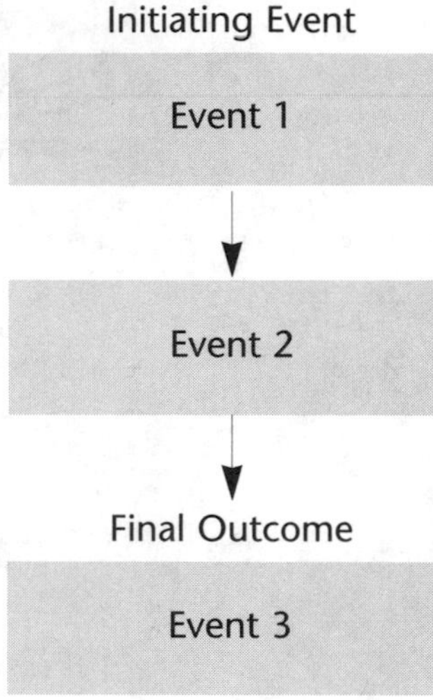

Initiating Event

Event 1

Event 2

Final Outcome

Event 3

Source: Jones, Pierce, and Hunter 1988, p. 22. Used with permission.

Conclusion

Our initial interest in teaching students to respond visually to texts was sparked by research suggesting that representing texts visually can increase reading comprehension. We also wanted to explore techniques that might favor less verbal learners. Our experiences suggest that adult students from a variety of cultures and learning styles can learn to use this strategy for responding to texts and that most enjoy doing so. This is especially true when the technique is presented as an alternative means for reflecting on the meaning of a text and sharing that view with others. Beyond functioning as a mnemonic device and an appealing technique for visual learners, visual responses help our students recognize key discourse patterns, give them practice in analyzing and interpreting texts, and improve their note-taking skills. Students themselves also noted the value of visual responses in enhancing other language skills, such as speaking, and their ability to collaborate and create meaning with other learners. Thus, this "language of visuals" (Whitin 1996) seems to empower students from a variety of backgrounds in several key ways.

One caveat is in order, however. Just as visual responses give students a variety of choices for responding to texts, we as teachers need to provide choices in strategies and classroom roles and respect the learners' right to resist change. When one of our students told us in his journal, "I dislike to draw, but I like look at other student's pictures and speech," we encouraged, but never forced, him to draw. We recognize that we as teachers need to adjust strategies to fit our students, and not vice-versa. Yet, when the teacher offers models and practice in using graphic responses and encourages students to relax and choose the strategies that work best for them, many students will find visual responses a powerful academic tool with a variety of uses.

For Further Reading

Arnheim, R. (1969). *Visual Thinking.* Berkeley: University of California Press.

   In this classic on visual learning theory, Arnheim argues that artistic activity is a form of reasoning and all productive thinking takes place in the realm of imagery. The final chapter focuses on vision in education.

Jones, B. F., Pierce, J., and Hunter, B. (1989). Teaching students to construct graphic representations. *Educational Leadership* (December/January): 20–25.

   The authors provide models and guidelines for constructing graphic representations, offering specific suggestions for teaching learners to represent text with visual summaries.

Margulies, N. (1991). *Mapping Inner Space.* Tucson: Zephyr Press.

   This text is dedicated to readers, especially students and teachers, who want to learn how to use this rather specialized method of visual note-taking. Step-by-step instructions are included. For each page of text there is an accompanying mindmap. Sections focusing on uses with the deaf and other special learners are included.

Chapter 14

Adult Learning Styles and Individual Writing Processes in the ESL/EFL Composition Classroom

Kristina Torkelson Gray

Northern Virginia Community College

This chapter is dedicated to ESL/EFL instructors who want to learn more about their students while at the same time helping the students learn about themselves and about their writing. The unit lesson plans that follow are based on two learning styles instruments: the Kolb Learning Style Indicator (LSI) (1985)[*] and Keirsey's Temperament Sorter (KTS) (1984). For seven years, my students and I have used the results of the LSI to discover and analyze their academic fields of interest, and we use the Keirsey results to investigate their preferred writing processes. Throughout this unit, the students discuss and write about the processes, the results, and their analyses of both.

Although the students in this lesson plan are in an ESL setting of immigrant adult students attending a Virginia community college, I have also successfully used these materials with university freshmen in an EFL environment in Bishkek, Kyrgyzstan; with Peace Corps trainees in Almaty, Kazakstan; and with Chinese Ph.D. students at the University of Minnesota. All of these students had one thing in common: they were interested in discovering more about themselves. It has been my experience that ESL/EFL students have not been exposed to learning styles research in their prior educational settings. Thus it is new and exciting for them to see how their "profiles" correspond to those of United States students, and to analyze individual strengths and weaknesses of their language learning. I am also convinced that using these instruments and the corresponding profiles at the beginning of my writing course helps to focus my students on how they write.

Students at Northern Virginia Community College are literally from all over the world. In a class of twenty-five students, 20 to 22 countries are often represented. The group comprises boat people, ex–political prisoners, mothers, wives of diplomats, businessmen, high school graduates, dissidents, and refugees. Some are taxi drivers, chauffeurs, maids, bank tellers, and sales clerks. Most can communicate orally with some success, but they are concerned about their written

---

[*] For a description of the Kolb instrument, see Chapter 12 in this volume by Barbara Harthill and Connie Busch.

communication skills. They range in age from 18 to 60, but they share one objective: they want to improve their lives in the United States by studying for an Associate degree.

Background

The Kolb LSI is accessible to all my adult students: it contains only 12 items and takes about ten minutes to complete. The results are not aimed at writing students directly, and I do not focus on the multitude of information that students might receive from the survey results. Rather, I use the results to discuss with the students their future goals and majors.

The Keirsey instrument is derived from the Myers–Briggs Type Indicator (MBTI). But unlike the MBTI, it is easily accessible and easy to administer; moreover, the results can be directly applied to the ESL writing classroom. Research by George Jensen and John DiTiberio (1989), which links the sixteen MBTI personality types to the composing and learning processes in the first-year composition classroom, is useful for my work in the ESL writing class at Northern Virginia Community College. Patricia Carrell and Laura Monroe (1995) applied Jensen and DiTiberio's approaches to ESL first-year university composition students, and Gladis (1993) applied the MBTI to corporate writing; their work, too, influences the unit I describe in this chapter.

The Keirsey Temperament Sorter is longer and more complex than Kolb's LSI; it contains 70 items and takes about twenty-five minutes to complete. Therefore, for lower-level classes, I have found that waiting until midway through the class is more effective for this instrument because the vocabulary and higher level of critical thinking skills involved in completing the survey may be intimidating for the students.

Framework

The lesson that follows may be adapted for any adult composition classroom, although some oral fluency is necessary for success. It requires 2 to 4 class sessions to complete. For the first class, I give alternatives (either using or not using the Keirsey Temperament Sorter in this particular class); in following lessons, I assume that the Keirsey instrument has been used.

Content:	Learning Styles and Future Academic Goals (LSI)
	Learning Styles and Individual Writing Processes (Keirsey)
Goals:	To introduce the advantages of learning styles instruments
	To complete the surveys, discuss the results, and write about them
	To allow the teacher to become familiar with the students
	To provide an extended, educational ice-breaker
Materials:	LSI, Keirsey Temperament Sorter[*]

---

[*] The LSI, the Self-Scoring Inventory and Interpretation Booklet may be obtained from McBer and Company, 116 Huntington Ave., Suite 400, Boston, MA 02116. Phone: 1-800-729-8074; Fax: 617-425-0073.

See the Reference section for *Please Understand Me: Character and Temperament Types* (5th ed.), which is available in most U.S. bookstores, or you can order it: (619) 632–1575.

Context: Administer one or both of these learning style instruments on the second and third meetings of the class. Discuss the results in the following classes.

Language Objectives:

Listening/Speaking: listening to short lectures
                          listening to directions
                          asking questions about vocabulary and idioms
                          discussing the results

Reading/Writing: completing the surveys
                          reading the interpretive charts
                          writing about the results

Thinking Skills: understanding the rank ordering for the LSI
                          selecting answers for the Keirsey

Lesson Plan

Class 1 Introduction

A. Introduce the concept and the reality of survey instruments (see Schroeder 1993 for a thorough discussion). Ask the students about their level of familiarity with questionnaires; then explain the purposes of the LSI and the Keirsey instruments that they will be completing.

B. Go over the key vocabulary of learning styles, including
   ° *inventory, survey, questionnaire, instrument*
   ° learning styles: *identifying, interpreting results, analyzing data*
   ° *ranking, rank order, profiles.*

C. Some students enter my class with a major in mind. I ask them to write about the reason(s) for that choice before we do the LSI. Others have not reflected on a major field; I ask them to do that in their pre-writing for this class.

D. Help students identify and define the most idiomatic and difficult vocabulary in the survey. Possibilities:

   ° *hunches*   ° *reserved*   ° *intuitive*
   ° *rely*   ° *open–minded*   ° *renegotiable*
   ° *"tax your reserves"*   ° *"routinized"* vs. *"whimsical"*
   ° *"head in the clouds"* vs. *"in a rut"*

E. Explain that these two inventories have been designed and used with United States subjects. Warn the students that, as a result, their profiles might not be entirely accurate. With that caveat, explain that they will not only complete the surveys but also analyze their individual results.

F. Make sure the class understands what it means to "rank order" the four items in the LSI, with "4" having the greatest value (meaning this is how they learn best).

G. Hand out the LSI; give students about 10 minutes to complete it. Then ask students to add the totals of the four columns (or the teacher can do this later), and hand in the LSI.

<u>If not using the Keirsey Temperament Sorter in this class</u>

A. Ask students to do one or more of the following, depending on class time:
   - in small groups, discuss their experiences of completing the LSI survey
   - individually write a short evaluation of the experience, then share it with the class
   - as a class, discuss what the value of discovering their preferred learning style(s) might be
   - with a partner, discuss possible major fields.

B. Homework: Write about what they learned from the class discussion.

<u>Using the Keirsey Temperament Sorter in this class</u>

A. If you are also using the Keirsey instrument at this time, help students identify and define the key vocabulary used in the survey, including
   - *extraversion* vs. *introversion*
   - *sensory perception* vs. *intuitive perception*
   - *thinking judgment* vs. *feeling judgment*
   - *judgment* vs. *perception.*

B. Briefly describe how Jensen and DiTiberio (1989) used the MBTI (which is a more complex form of the Keirsey Temperament Sorter) to describe student writing process profiles.

C. Hand out the Keirsey Temperament Sorter and give students about 25 minutes to complete the survey. Explain that it is necessary to fill in either "A" or "B." I tell them that if it is 50/50, they should go with what feels like 51 percent.

D. Collect the completed surveys.

<u>Before the Second Class:</u>

- Tabulate the survey results.
- Reflect on individual student results.
- Assign students to small groups of students with similar learning style profiles.
- Prepare questions and responses for several of the students in the class (see below).
- Make enlarged copies of the LSI interpretive chart and the MBTI/Keirsey lists (both at the end of this chapter).
- Tape the copies on the walls of the classroom.

Class 2 Discussion of LSI Results

A. Ask students to look at the LSI charts in the classroom and
   - discuss with a partner what they think their survey results will be.
   - ask questions about what the charts mean.
   - summarize in writing what they predict their results will be.

B. Put a set of individual student results from the LSI on the overhead projector.

C. Ask questions of each specific student (S); explain any problems you found about incorrectly done rank ordering.

T: Esayas, are you interested in theater?

S: No, I'm interested in electrical engineering.

T: Did you rank order the LSI with the value "4" being the MOST like you?

S: No, I thought it should be "1" as the most like my learning style.

T: Sorry—you'll have to do it over so that we can find out what your real interest is. You may even come out close to being an electrical engineer.

* * * * *

T: Feben, do you agree with the LSI that you are an Accommodator?

S: Yes. I think I am a leader and a risk-taker.

T: The results also show that you get things done, and that you learn by doing. Do you agree with those characteristics?

S: Yes, that seems like me.

* * * * *

T: Foday, are you interested in political science or home economics?

[Class chuckles because Foday is a very big man who sits in the back of the room and has a loud, booming voice.]

S: No, I want to be a politician when I go back to my country in Africa.

T: So this profile shows your interest quite closely?

S. Yes.

D. After 10 minutes of asking the students about what I have learned about them from their profiles, I hand back their LSI answer sheets. Then I ask them to study again the enlarged copies of the LSI interpretive chart on the walls of the classroom (either individually or in pairs) and to write on their answer sheets what information about their profile "fits" with their self-analysis and what doesn't.

E. Class discussion: in most cases the students in my class are still trying to figure out what they should major in, so often this discussion is a self-discovery process.

F. Homework: Students to write in their journals about
   ° what they learned about themselves in class today
   ° how their choice for a major field has been supported (or not)
   ° how their search for a major field has been helped (or not).

G. Writing assignment: "Everyone has goals. Write about the most important goal in your life right now. How does that goal relate to what you learned in your LSI?"

Class 3 Discussion of Keirsey Temperament Sorter Results

A. Follow the general lesson plan for Class #2, A–D.

B. I summarize the information about writing styles and the MBTI for the class, using overhead transparencies of the various writing processes, using information from the chart on pages 133–134.

C. Once students know whether they are an ISTJ or an ENFP (or any of the other variants), I ask them to write about specific ways in which the profiles do (or do not) match their self-perceptions.

D. Homework: In your journal, respond to the following: "Everyone has a different way to write. How does this writing profile match your writing style?"

<u>Between Class 2/3 and Class 4</u>

- Conference with each student about their survey results.
- During the conference, assign each student to a small group of "like" classmates.

Class 4 Group Work on Learning Styles

A. In small groups,* discuss written analyses of profiles.
  ° Focus on identified learning styles (to build community), and on similarities and differences of writing processes, as identified through discussion of Jensen and DiTiberio (above).

B. Class discussion: Review with the students the advantages of
  ° self-knowledge about learning styles and writing processes (empowerment, clearer sense of purpose).
  ° using information gleaned from the surveys (to focus on their goals, to determine their major fields, and to write more effectively).
  ° experimenting with lesser-used or weaker learning styles (to expand opportunities for learning, to be more effective students).

C. Collaborative writing assignment: each group must work together to draft a single paragraph about one of the following topics. Each paragraph will differ because each group represents different learning styles; each paragraph will contain specific personal experiences from the group that demonstrates what they are writing about.
  ° (one or two) of our preferred LSI results
  ° (one or two) of our preferred Temperament Sorter results
  ° (one or two) of our preferred composing processes
  ° (one or two) of our preferred drafting processes
  ° (one or two) of our preferred revision processes

D. A report to the class from each group:
  ° oral (with speaker chosen by the group)

---

* I caution against having these groups stay the same for the entire course; while some of the groups really "click," others, especially the ISTJs, just sit and look at each other. I talk with my students about these different group responses in terms of learning styles, and ask them to write analyzes about why their group worked or didn't work.

° written (paragraph written on overhead transparency).

E. Homework: "Individually evaluate in writing the experience you have had with these surveys."

Evaluation of Learning Styles Unit

Students provided very positive written feedback through their evaluation of their experiences. Most were similar to the following:

Evaluation of the LSI (and Career Choice)

After I analyzed all the information and compare with myself, I'm very surprise because everything that I read, it was true. Now, I'm sure that the career that I chose to study, it is the right one for me.

Mirael (CE/Accommodator, Bolivia)

This learning style is exactly for me. When I'm learning, I focused on people that what they say and also when I'm learning I'm so careful and interested in the topic. I value getting things done and seeing results of my influence and ingenuity. Many people who work with this kind of style they are successful.

Adem (AE/Converger, Turkey)

This kind of test really help the students to understand what kind of careers to take. For me, for example, is the true the career I really like is to be a lawyer and the way I'm developed my studies are true. I do not like put my feelings in my studies, I love to listen and watch. That is my best way to study and understand my assignments. Congratulations, your test really work on me.

Anita (AC/Assimilator, Portugal)

It's true I like to work with my hands. It's true that I depend on people's help like in engineer, I'll probably let somebody to do the graphs or sketches and I'll just do the physical work. I was interesting in scientist. But since it takes a lot of years I am going to take some other career like maintenance engineer or study for electronics.

Elmer (AE/Assimilator, Ecuador)

Learning style has many idea but some of them is matching me and some don't. For example, some that matches me is imaginative ability, approach to problems, gather information, understanding the problems, all of these will help me in majors. But there is some of them that doesn't help me like "feeling" is needed for affectiveness, adaptable to change, entertainment in other careers, effectiveness in arts.

Mohammed (CE/Diverger, Bahrain)

It is true that I rely more on my feelings than being systematic. I love being a musician, I have a guitar and right now I'm learning to play it. I enjoy group discussions because there you can express your ideas, and learning more about different things in your group.

Rosalita (CE/Diverger, the Philippines)

I am planning to study and interested in international relations, and the test suggested to me to do the same thing. My field of study is business and government and I also interested in law.

Morisato (CE/Accommodator, Japan)

I learned many things in this subject like something I don't do it, for example I don't test of ideas and make a decision very fast but I think before I make a decision. The other thing I like observe first and then join the situation before I make a decision and I would like to try to do more about it.

Rashid (AC/Converger, Somalia)

Evaluation of Keirsey Temperament Sorter (and Writing Processes)

The Temperament Sorter was perfectly correct on my thoughts on writing, I like to be a structured writer able to write facts and experience. My first draft tend to be the best just adding a few details. It may be short but I give a lot of thinking to it. The "S" section I can refer to sports, I like to be a step by step person being within the rules. I think I learned about myself and I plan to improve some wrong things to help my college education.

Jose (ISFJ, El Salvador)[*]

I think is true that my first paragraph are not clear and later my essay is getting better. Discussing with other people about the topic helps me a lot. I feel much better writing essay about something that is important to me, and having strong opinion about this (F). It is true about doing research. I want to do this fast and quickly and start my essay. It is not always the best idea. I also like to have specific direction (S).

Edyta (ESFJ, Poland)

My style of writing is true on the papers. I like to write from experience. I tend to put more ideas than necessary. When I write, I like to put everything down and then revise it.

Kidane (ESTJ, Ethiopia)

The introversion part really presents my style, I like to write alone without any sound. This is because I always have a hard time to concentrate. Also, "T" and "J" are resemble my style, I don't like to write things about myself, and I like to write something about my interest. The "N" part is the one completely resemble to me. It is true that I don't like to revise, and I like to write fast because I don't have patience to write when I write an essay for more than four hours. This is a perfect analysis.

Te-Wei (INTJ, Taiwan)

---

[*] The four pairs of categories of the Keirsey Temperament Sorter are explained in the chart on pages 133 and 134.

My habit of study fits exactly with "S" and "T." I don't think "J" effect me the most in writing. It's just "50/50" true about myself and my writing.

Loc Tran (ESTJ, Vietnam)

I agree with some of the ideas, for example, Sensory Perception, but I don't agree with Judgment, that doesn't reflect my writings at all. Usually my first draft is very good. My experience in the first six weeks showed that. About Extraversion, I think just fifty percent is true for me. In my case, I always very clear about what I'm writing.

Sole (ESTJ, Chile)

The letter "I" is the one that describes me most. It's true that I like to be quiet in class and I'm less active in the classroom. About "J" it's true that my first drafts tend to be short and undeveloped.

Alex (ESTJ, Peru)

I learn best by movement, action and talk. Group discussions help me to understand some things better and give me sureness about my ideas. "S": step by step, somehow my brain only takes in so much and the rest disappears again. "F": I need motivation by telling me I'm doing a good job or not. But then really tell me what I have to change. "P": I was like this, but I try not to wait with things to the last minute. It is usually laziness. But by the other six weeks I did pretty good. I didn't wait till the last minute to turn things in. Because it is a different language, I can set new deadlines. My brain is working differently.

Kathrin (ESFP, Germany)

Conclusion

The excitement and enthusiasm from my students' self-reports will, I hope, persuade you to try this unit on learning styles with your students. Integrating the content of learning styles with the writing assignments (and other language activities) has proved a successful way to involve students in learning how to learn and in becoming more effective writers. In addition, I hope you will use the Kolb and Keirsey instruments yourself, to gain insight into your own learning and writing processes.

Note: The categories on pages 133 and 134 are explained in greater detail in Provost and Anchors, *Applications of the Meyers-Briggs Type Indicator in Higher Education* (1987). You can take the MBTI on the World Wide Web, and hear the results analyzed by MBTI specialists.

The MBTI and Keirsey Temperament Sorter Categories and Individual Writing Processes

Extraversion (E)

Es generate ideas best by talking about the topic, interviewing people, or actively experiencing the topic. They tend to leap into writing with little anticipation and then write by trial-and-error. They tend to develop a great deal of material as they write. As a result, their in-class essays and first drafts may reflect confusion in early paragraphs and clarity in later paragraphs. If they perform traditional pre-writing strategies (such as outlining),they can often do so more easily after writing a first draft. Discussing drafts with others helps them to understand the need for revision and what needs to be revised. Some Es (especially if they are also J) may not revise at all unless they receive oral feedback.

Introversion (I)

Introverts plan before writing and want most of their ideas clarified before they put words to paper. When they begin to write, they stop frequently to anticipate the direction of the essay and where their ideas are leading them. They usually spend more time than extraverts between drafts because they like to have time to consider their revisions. Throughout the writing process, they tend to write alone, asking for advice only from closest friends or teachers who they trust.

Sensory Perception (S)

Sensing types prefer explicit, detailed, and specific directions. Their first drafts reflect their inductive thought and are often filled with facts that have not yet been related to a central idea or theme. They may feel more comfortable when following a pattern prescribed by the teacher or one that is tried and true, one that they have used in the past. Even during a first draft, they may closely attend to mechanics (grammar, spelling, etc.). They may regard revising as merely correcting or proofreading.

Intuitive Perception (N)

INtuitive types tend to write best when given general directions that allow their imagination to work. Developing a unique approach to the topic is an important part of their prewriting phase. At their best, they tend to write quickly, letting one idea trigger another and paying little attention to mechanics. They tend to innovate organizational patterns. In their first drafts, they may present generalities or concrete support.

Thinking Judgment (T)

Ts tend to select topics that can be written about with emotional distance rather than self-involvement. They tend to make organizational decisions by following a structure, such as an outline. When writing, they tend to focus on content rather than on how the message is affecting the audience. As a result, they may sometimes be overly blunt.

Feeling Judgment (F)

Feeling types prefer topics that they can care about; they often complain about topics that are dry or "boring." When writing, they tend to draw upon personal experience; for example, their introductions often begin with a personal example. They rely less on structure than Thinking types; they usually begin with a sentence and then follow the flow of their thoughts. They also tend to make organizational decisions by anticipating the audience's reaction to their text.

Judgment (J)

Js tend to limit their topics quickly and set goals that are manageable. They also tend to limit their research so that they can begin writing more quickly and complete the project. Their first drafts tend to be short and underdeveloped, with ideas stated emphatically and often without qualification.

Perception (P)

Ps tend to select broad topics and dive into research without limiting them. Topics will usually be limited only as the deadline approaches. They want to thoroughly research or analyze a topic, often with a clear focus, before beginning to write and may feel that there is always one more book or article to read. Their drafts tend to be long and thorough. Their writing may ramble because they are inclusive of ideas and data.

Concrete-abstract and active-reflective orientations of academic fields derived from Carnegie Commission study of graduate students and faculty

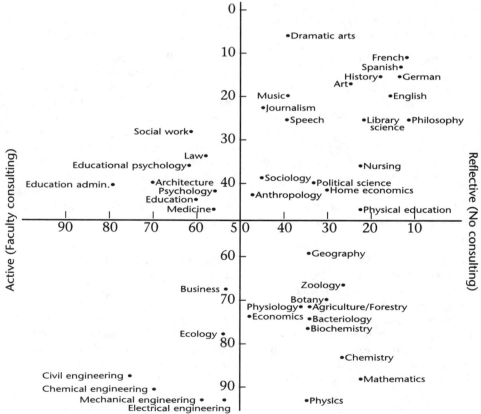

Source: Kolb, D.A. 1981. Learning styles and disciplinary differences. In *The Modern American College*, eds. A. W. Chickering and Associates. San Francisco: Jossey-Bass.

For Further Reading

Gladis, S. D. (1993). *Write Type: Personality Types and Writing Styles*. Amherst, MA: Human Resource Development Press.

> Gladis's book is practical reading, even though it is a follow-up on the complex work of the MBTI. It is intended to demonstrate to the layperson how to write within the business organization. Once one's writing style is understood, writing is easier. *Write Type* is a helpful book for managers as well because it discusses how best to utilize the strengths of those needing to write within the corporation.

Keirsey, D. and Bates, M. (1984). *Please Understand Me: Character and Temperament Styles*. Del Mar, CA: Prometheus Nemesis Books.

> This book is accessible, interesting, and available at any bookstore, or can be ordered through the Website URL http://amazon.com (with a credit card). Based on the Myers-Briggs Type Indicator (MBTI), but shorter and more easily completed, the Keirsey Temperament Sorter instrument is included in the book. In addition, Keirsey and Bates discuss the possible results of their survey, analyzing through personality examples the different temperaments represented.

Jensen, G. H. and DiTiberio, J. K (1989). *Personality and the Teaching of Composition*. Norwood, NJ: Ablex Publishing.

> This collaborative volume between psychologist DiTiberio and coordinator of academic support programs Jensen explores ways in which the MBTI sheds light on how native English speaker students in development writing classes approach writing. The book explains the Jungian theory of psychological type, summarizes MBTI previous research, and applies the theories to the composing and revising processes of college-age students.

Schroeder, C. (1993). New students and learning styles. *Change* Sept./Oct. 21–26.

> This article describes the shift that has occurred in U.S. universities where teachers have discovered that students are mismatched for the traditional university lecture format. Because many college faculty are unaware of the solution to this problem, the book offers discussion and potential remedies that include on-going needs assessment and evaluation, changes in curriculum design and course lesson plans, and extending teaching styles to include the learning styles and strategies of these "new" students.

Chapter 15

Expanding the Learning Styles of Japanese Analytic Learners

Jerry Call
Divine Word College

Rita Dunn and Shirley Griggs define learning style as "a biologically and developmentally imposed set of characteristics that make the same teaching method wonderful for some and terrible for others" (1988, p. 3). As one might predict, parallel definitions may apply to instructors and their respective teaching styles. G. J. Conti (1989, p. 3) defines teaching style as the "overall traits and qualities that a teacher displays in the classroom that are consistent for various situations." This chapter provides a means for stretching the style repertoires of analytic students—more specifically, how to approach the teaching of English to analytic Japanese learners. The ideas came about during my three years of teaching tertiary-level EFL in Tokyo. In this chapter, I give a detailed lesson that is representative of how I incorporate what I learned into the planning of lessons and the presenting of materials, especially for oral-aural classes. Although my foreign and second language teaching has been limited to university settings, this lesson's emphasis on language usage, meaning, and the stretching of learning styles should be beneficial to anyone who is striving to balance the learning styles of analytic learners.

Background

One of the first things I learned about Japanese culture when I arrived in Japan was the meaning of the Japanese saying "The nail that sticks up gets hammered down." Geert Hofstede (1986) describes these Japanese learners (from a U.S. perspective) as quiet, shy, reticent, and therefore introverted. During my four years in Japan, I also found learners to be quite willing to participate in class by listening, but to be very passive with respect to speaking. This is probably a result of two characteristics of Japanese culture: concern for precision and keeping face.[*] Students are taught culturally to value group membership, which involves a face-saving attitude, and they place little importance on individualism.

Those who teach English as a foreign language (EFL) in Japan can describe from experience how most learners are group-oriented; just as group orientation

---

[*] As teachers, we should of course keep in mind that generalizations about student populations can be useful in planning lessons, but should not be used to stereotype individuals.

and harmony are echoed throughout Japanese society, individual opinion is not valued in the EFL classroom. Therefore, two popular aspects of ESL instruction that should not be used lightly in lesson planning for Japanese students are praise and, strangely enough, group work. As Gayle Nelson (1995) warns, Japanese students do not like to be singled out from the class, and so in distributing praise, instructors should not praise any one student repeatedly. In addition, for many Japanese the ad hoc nature of small-group work, in which groups are formed and reformed continually, may be very frustrating because, as Nelson points out, the purpose of groups in the United States and Japan differs. Groups in the United States are usually task-based and exist only until their respective tasks are completed. In Japanese culture, however, groups give people identity: "They are used to groups that are constant for a much longer period of time and also to groups that define their identity (e.g., being a member of a particular group within a particular school)" (Nelson, p. 15).

Oxford, Hollaway, and Horton-Murillo (1992) summarize Harshbarger et al.'s (1986) oral description in terms of learning styles:

> Japanese ESL/EFL students like highly *structured, deductive* classes with frequent corrections of small details, indicating an *analytic* tendency. Japanese students generally desire that the teacher respect their privacy, and are not forthcoming about their personal feelings, and tend to make judgments based on *analytical* thinking. Japanese students might be classified as more *thinking-* than *feeling-oriented*. *Reflection* is a definite part of the Japanese style make-up, as shown by the concern for precision and for not *taking quick risks* in conversation [1986, p. 443, my emphasis].

Japanese Students: Analytic Learners

Reflection and focusing on facts and details are characteristic of the analytic style employed by Japanese learners.

> Reflection involves systematic, often analytic, investigation of hypotheses and is usually associated with accurate performance. [In comparison] impulsivity is the quick and uncritical acceptance of initially selected hypotheses—the fast-inaccurate style [Oxford, Erhman, and Lavine 1991, pp. 5–6].

We also know that the analytic learner is usually a left-brain learner, and that

> learners who prefer this kind of processing by the left hemisphere deal more easily with grammatical structure and contrastive analysis, while right-brain learners are more adept at learning intonation, and rhythms of language [ibid.].

Nelson (1995) suggests allowing Japanese learners time to reflect before they answer by, for example, allowing them to write responses before discussing them.

With respect to Myers–Briggs personality types, Oxford, Ehrman, and Lavine describe **thinking–type** students as analytical: a thinker "is not readily concerned with social and emotional subtleties, except possibly as data for analytically understanding a particular problem or issue" (p. 442). In contrast, a **feeling–type** student is geared toward the social and emotional aspects of learning: "His or her decision-making is likely to be globally influenced by the feelings of others, the emotional climate, and personal and interpersonal values" (ibid.).

To summarize, we might describe many Japanese students as learners who have the following style preferences:

- analytic rather than global,
- reflective rather than impulsive (that is, they are not risk-taking),
- left-brained rather than right-brained, and
- thinking-type rather than feeling-type.

Of course, we should encourage our students to expand their learning styles. While reflection and thinking-types are positive learning attributes, students who rely too strongly on the thinking-type may be counter-productive learners because reflecting on and analyzing their own language performance may have a crippling effect on their progress. In other words, too much self-criticism can be harmful. C. E. Cornett (1983) suggests that teachers encourage and actually teach style "flexing": once students learn how to learn, by learning about their learning strengths and weaknesses and by practicing extending their learning styles, they will be better able to adapt to each learning situation, all the while growing more independent of their teachers.

Planning Curriculum for Analytic Learners

I set out to teach my Japanese students in ways that would encourage them to flex their learning styles, but I knew that my attempts to stretch their style repertoires had to be conducted cautiously. First, I needed to establish an environment in which the learners could feel safe so that they would be receptive to new learning styles. Harshbarger et al. (1986) suggest that (a) giving attention to the individual and (b) creating an informal setting to alleviate formality will help to build the comfort level of Japanese students. They also indicate that, as when teaching learners from any culture, introducing topics slowly, being consistent, and avoiding learner embarrassment will help establish the classroom community so necessary for successful learning.

I found that informing the students of overall goals of the course (for example, actual listening *and* speaking in oral-aural courses) was beneficial for these analytic "planners." Asking the learners to inform me about how their previous English courses were conducted enabled me to lead directly into their expectations of our current course. It was also important for the students to see that they were to take an *active* role in the language learning process. In these ways, the students began to see that I was interested not only in right answers but in how the right answers were achieved. Using contrastive analysis, I highlighted the use of world and linguistic knowledge in making predictions, as well as the importance of mistakes.

I also established an atmosphere of informality. I was on a first-name basis with my students, and they soon realized that they had a voice with regard to content: choice of topics, chapters, activities, and schedules. Finally, I used my own experiences in learning the language of my students to demonstrate that (a) I had a sincere interest in language and (b) I was not above making mistakes when I produced that language. For instance, when defining "traditional," I used the example of *ricksha*. The students heard my accented pronunciation, and they saw that I was on their level of language learning; they graciously welcomed me. I explained that *learning* often involves *doing* and that we could learn from and help each other. If I felt really daring, I also asked them to critique the penmanship of my Japanese characters. From these techniques usually came a safe, supportive learning environment.

Similarly, when I introduced learning styles that were valued in U.S. classrooms, I began with the students' previous experiences. I pointed out that although no style is particularly better than another, in American settings the learners' existing knowledge is valued and is to be employed in the learning process. Consequently, learners in U.S. classrooms are asked to volunteer ideas and opinions as well as to justify their reasoning. I explained that the course's success would depend upon their actual participation (doing), and that it was only after participation that we could analyze our own learning. Finally, I reiterated that I expected performance mistakes.

The next step was to persuade my students that style flexing was important to the learning process; I set aside class time throughout the course for a regular weekly discussion during which students could share their individual flexing and thereby learn from one another. I kept a record of these discussions in order to develop my class's "bag of learning tricks": examples included eavesdropping in the cafeteria and meeting native speaking informants who could respond to the students' linguistic hypotheses.

Finally, I planned a lesson sequence that would allow students to identify my teaching styles, use their preferred learning styles, and practice some style flexing. In the lesson on conditionals that follows, I describe the lesson, and after each section of the lesson, I analyze the multiple learning styles I incorporated into that section. Each analysis is in italics, with the learning styles boldfaced. Usually I planned the lesson to strike a balance: to allow the students opportunities for analytic learning, but to also stretch them by requiring oral production. The lesson provides channels for many learning styles, from visual and reflective to kinesthetic and impulsive, and I included both individual and cooperative work. My other objective was to shift the focus of the lesson gradually from teacher-centered to student-centered in an environment that was safe—that is, the issue of face was not in jeopardy.

Lesson: Conditionals

<u>Sequence</u>: one two-hour session or several shorter "pieces" to be recycled over a week or more.

<u>Teacher Preparation/Trouble-shooting</u>

Conditionals rank fifth in difficulty as students struggle with the various tenses and modals (Celce-Murcia and Larsen-Freeman 1983). Yet they are typically treated too simply in textbooks. Students find it especially difficult to discern the subtle differences of meaning in some conditionals. The following readings served me as a solid background for teaching conditionals.

° *Understanding and Using English Grammar*, 2nd ed., by Betty S. Azar, pages 347–374, is a reference for "mixed time" in conditionals and implied conditions.

° *The Grammar Book: An ESL/EFL Teacher's Course* (1983), by Marianne Celce-Murcia and Diane Larsen–Freeman, pages 340–359, provides descriptions and examples of the seven most common forms of conditionals, their phrase structure rules, and obligatory rules, as well as related forms: *hope, wish, only if, unless, even though, even if,* and *whether.*

Materials: Cards with sentence halves, cards with events written on them, pictures of celebrities, overhead projector, transparencies.

Story: "The Stonecutter" is adapted from "The Quarryman" in J. Morgan and M. Rinvolucri's *Once Upon a Time: Using Stories in the Language Classroom* (1983, pp. 60–61).* Note that in my adaptation, I use the unreal/hypothetical conditional form: "If I *were* a king, I *would* be most powerful," etc.

Activities: Review the future (first) conditional in a warm-up; practice the hypothetical (second) with the story-telling, group discussion, and outside-class writing.

I. Warm-Up: Review of the future conditional

A. Distribute cards with sentence halves. Each student gets one phrase and must match with a partner.
   Example: *If it rains   I'll take an umbrella.*

B. Present two cards with events at the front of the classroom.
   Two examples: *stay in Salt Lake City   go to San Francisco*
   ° Ask students for example sentences with two conditionals for each card:
     Example: *If I stay in Salt Lake City, I will get tickets to a Jazz game.*
   ° Once successful examples have been given, tape the cards at opposite ends of the room.
   ° Explain that the students are to walk to the card they prefer. While there, they are to tell the others who have grouped with them what they will do.
     Example: *If I go to San Francisco, I will shop on Fisherman's Wharf.*
   ° Monitor the students. When they finish, introduce a new pair of cards.

*Analysis: The first task requires student **movement** and **analysis**, but not necessarily oral production. In addition, the task is completed in **pairs**, and as it is a matching activity, the process of elimination ensures that no one is left behind. The second activity demands **movement** as well. In addition, oral production is needed. However, the production is in **groups**. The analytic learners are given the opportunity to analyze (and **reflect** upon) the language of others*

---

* Morgan and Rinvolucri thank "Chris and Kathleen Sion for translating this story out of the original Dutch" (p. 62).

before speaking themselves. Moreover, more than one student may be speaking at a time, which further serves as a safety check on the issue of face.

II. Introduction of the hypothetical conditional

A. "Sometimes we use *conditionals* or *if statements* to talk about events that will probably not happen. For example, *If I were President of the United States,* I would raise the minimum wage. In other words, the events are imaginary or make-believe."

B. "Now I want to tell you a story. First, look at these vocabulary words.

conditional   crown   fairy   hypothetical   pickax

Now relax and listen."

*Analysis: Both the introduction to the hypothetical conditional and its presentation (below) are **teacher-centered**. I designed these sections of the lesson to put the students at ease: there are no demands for oral production, and the learners are permitted to **analyze** the form and usage of the L2 input.*

III. Story

I use an overhead projector to show a transparency of the properties or the characters of the story placed in a circle: a pickax, a crown, the sun (see Figure 15-1). I reveal each as it is mentioned. In this way, students can hear the story as I read it aloud the first time, and students can learn the vocabulary through pictures.

Figure 15–1. Overhead Transparency for "The Stonecutter"

Teachers might also use an overhead transparency with the story printed on it, to be used, perhaps, for the second oral reading of the story (for visual learners). However, I prefer the use of pictures and miming over the written word, with the focus on aural-oral skills rather than reading skills.

The Stonecutter

Once upon a time, stonecutter
Went to fields every day.
Didn't like work—too hard.
Wanted to be rich.
Saw the king approaching,
Golden crown, silken robes, soldiers with spears and shields, all on horseback.
Said: *If I were king,* I would be most powerful. I want to be king.
A fairy flew down and said: Okay, now you are king.

Set the pickax down.
The king took up crown and was happy, but only for a while.
Enjoyed palace and beautiful queen, delicious food and every wish.
One day on balcony saw the sun.
He said: The sun is more powerful than I.
If I were the sun, I would be most powerful.
I want to be the sun.
Fairy came again and said: Now you are the sun.
Crown was set down; sun rose in its glory.

Sun was very happy, but only for a while.
He enjoyed rising and lighting the world as well as warming it.
He caused trees, flowers, and every living thing to grow.
One day a cloud crossed in front of the sun,
Blocked the sun's rays,
Grew dark and blew a strong wind,
Rained a heavy rain and caused floods and great damage.
Sun said: This cloud is more powerful than I.
If I were a cloud, I would be most powerful. I want to be a cloud.
Fairy came and said: Okay, I now make you into a cloud.
Sunbeams faded and the sun became a cloud.

The cloud was happy, but only for a while.
Enjoyed wind and rain,
Flew around the world, flew high and low.
One day cloud noticed a stone that could not be washed away.
Said: The stone is more powerful than I.
If I were that stone, I would be most powerful. I want to be that stone.
Fairy appeared and said: You are no longer a cloud. Turn into a stone.
Cloud fell and turned to stone.

Stone was happy, but only for a while.
Withstood rain and wind.
One day man came, carrying a pickax.
Saw stones being cut.

The stone said: The man is more powerful than I.
If I were a stonecutter, I would be most powerful. I want to be a stonecutter.
Fairy came and said: You are now your former self, a stonecutter.
Stone stood up and became a stonecutter.

Stonecutter cut stones every day.
Complained that his work was too hard.[*]

IV. *Practice/Evaluation*

A. The learners re-tell the story as the teacher guides them through with questions (such as "How does the story begin?"). Point to the pickax, the fairy, etc.; mime "happy," etc. Monitor the learners' use of the conditional as they re-tell the story.

B. The learners form groups of three or four. They talk about which characters in the story they would like to be and why (what they could do), using the hypothetical (second) conditional. For instance, one student wished to be the cloud. She said that **if she were a cloud,** she would climb high into the atmosphere with other clouds. Then she would strike out on her own and fly fast and low over the ocean.

C. Additional activity: Explain that in the United States a wife may share her husband's family name or she may keep her own family name. Ask the students how new couples share (or do not share) names in their countries, eliciting use of the hypothetical conditional. For example, a Korean student explained that **if he were to marry,** his wife would not share his surname. However, **if he were to have children,** they would take his name rather than his wife's.

D. Additional activity: Using pictures of celebrities (such as Yoko Ono, Sonny Bono, Ella Fitzgerald, Darth Vader), ask students to hypothesize about marriages, using the hypothetical (second) conditional. For instance, "If Yoko Ono were to marry Sonny Bono, she would be called Yoko Ono Bono." Or "If Ella Fitzgerald were to marry Darth Vader, she would be Ms. Ella Vader." NOTE: Be sure that students understand that these "marriages" are hypothetical and that each result is amusing.

Analysis: *The* **oral production** *required in the first activity is guided by the teacher with prompts, and the issue of face is protected as learners tell the story in one voice. Then the* **group** *discussion of the characters (the second activity) makes oral demands upon the learners, but again the learners are speaking in front of only a fraction of the class. In addition, I designed this* **cooperative group work** *to be easier for my Japanese learners by having the groups remain*

---

[*] Morgan and Rinvolucri suggest using "skeletons" for telling stories They believe each telling should be a natural and enthusiastic piece of language. Therefore, they recommend having just the "gist" of the story in mind. Articles, pronouns, and even potential detail have therefore been deleted in the "skeleton" story of "The Stonecutter."

*intact throughout the term (see Eliason 1995). Finally, the **analytic** learners could take heart because the content of the discussions centers on the **analysis** of the characters.*

*The section continues with a cultural point on marital names (the third and fourth activities). This point serves to reinforce the language, to work with the **analytic** "puzzle" of making up names, and to move away from the content of "The Stonecutter" toward real-world application. In addition, learners enjoy giving input and learning about the customs of their classmates.*

V. Worksheet Activity

<u>Directions</u>: Change each of the statements below to either a future conditional or a present unreal conditional. The first one has been done for you.

NOTE: Students should analyze the fact that the form of their answers depends upon their meaning (that is, future or hypothetical). Students may work alone, in pairs, or in small groups.

1. I don't have a car. I want to drive to Washington, D.C.
    If I had a car, I would drive to Washington, D.C.
2. I don't have enough money to buy lunch at the Mandarin Garden.
3. It rains. I take an umbrella.
4. The weather is too cold for us to play soccer.
5. There is not enough snow for us to go skiing.
6. I don't have enough time. I want to study English.
7. I have the time and the money. I want to study in Sydney this winter.
8. I don't have a boy(girl)friend to go out with this Saturday.
9. The weather is good. We want to have a picnic.
10. I can't remember her name, so I have to ask her to tell me again.

Analysis: *The worksheet brings the Practice/Evaluation component to a class, as learners work **individually** or in **groups** to **analyze** the conditionals further. This exercise puts the **analytic** learners at ease and allows students to choose to work independently or with others. Of course, this task can take place at home just as easily as it can in the classroom.*

VI. Application

Students prepare to give individual speeches to the class about their "dream vacations." They begin with the hypothetical conditional ***"If money were not an issue, and if I had enough time,"*** . . . (possible conclusion: "I would cruise the Mediterranean").

Students must include details which answer such questions as

- When would be the best time to make the trip?
- With whom would you go?
- What would you see and do?
- How would you travel?
- How much would it cost?

Analysis: *The hypothetical conditional is applied by the learners in their 5–8 minute "dream vacation" speeches. This task, more than any other, demands that the students perform in the area of oral production. Further, it may be an issue of face, but it was designed as a culminating activity for just those reasons. By now, students feel comfortable within the classroom environment; they have had adequate time to reflect upon and plan their speeches. Such analysis involved in the preparation of the speech should ensure successful performances.*

In addition, I discuss with the students (during our weekly class discussion about learning styles) the fact that the more familiar they are with oral performances (such as speeches in learner-safe classroom communities), the more they will be able to stretch their styles. For example, they may be able to participate more freely in classroom discussions without relying too greatly on reflection or other components of their strongly analytic styles.

Conclusion

Despite the potential danger of stereotyping, learning about the major styles of most of my analytic Japanese students allowed me to make some generalizations that were beneficial in (a) predicting classroom behavior and (b) planning lessons. That is, once I was aware of the needs of the learners, and of my own teaching style preferences, it seemed pedagogically sound to

- help my students identify and discuss their major learning styles
- inform the students about the advantages of flexing their styles
- establish a safe class environment in which students could experiment
- plan lessons that offered a variety of teaching and learning styles
- initiate the process of meshing learning and teaching styles.

By learning about their styles and expanding their repertoires, my students developed more resources. One consequence of the process described in the lesson above is that my students grew to be more autonomous learners. As they experimented with styles that balanced their use of analysis, they began to take risks, develop compensatory skills, and improve their overall oral-aural communication skills. In short, I found that helping learners to meet their newly established communicative goals required my helping them to view alternative styles in their learning to reach their goals.

For Further Reading

Eliason, P. (1995). Difficulties with cross-cultural learning-styles assessment.
In J. Reid (Ed.), *Learning Styles in the ESL/EFL Classroom* (pp. 19–33). Boston: Heinle & Heinle.

Dilemmas regarding students' background (length of stay in the U.S. and English language proficiency) as well as translations of style-assessment instruments are explored in this chapter. In addition, cultural considerations such as face-saving characteristics and suggestions for style assessment (e.g., student participation in analyzing assessment results) are described.

Morgan, J. and Rinvolucri, M. (1983). *Once Upon a Time: Using Stories in the Language Classroom.* Cambridge: Cambridge University Press.

Activities such as Greek choruses and role play engage learners in communicative alternatives to traditional activities. An outline of 70 stories, ranging from South American fairy tales to modern African stories, is arranged for activities designed to recycle new language, discuss themes and characters, promote problem-solving, and explore students' feelings.

Chapter 16

Encouraging Learner Independence

David Nunan

The English Centre, University of Hong Kong

In this chapter I describe a program I developed for my students at the University of Hong Kong. The program was designed to sensitize students to their own learning styles and to help them develop strategies for coping with university-level study through the medium of English. Although the sample tasks described in the body of the chapter were designed for self-study, they are equally applicable as classroom tasks and were, in fact, initially developed for the classroom.

Background

A program that introduces students to their learning strengths is necessary because students come into my classroom fresh from high school. The educational system they have come from is based on a "transmission" approach to learning. In other words, the teachers transmit knowledge to the students, who are expected to absorb this knowledge and regurgitate it in examinations. Such a system breeds students who are passive in their orientation and who expect teachers to deliver the education "goods" to them. They expect their university teachers to tell them what to learn and how to learn. Most find it unsettling (and some even find it distressing) to enter an institution in which they have most of the responsibility for their own learning.

Further, when it comes to studying English, their motivation is generally low. While most of them have had many years of English instruction in school, the instruction itself is often poor, and the resulting competence of the students is not as high as might be expected. This is particularly true in the productive skills of writing and speaking. With the handover of Hong Kong to Chinese rule, many students also feel pressure to develop competence in Putonghua, which is now the official language in Hong Kong.

An additional complication is the fact that the University of Hong Kong is an international, English-medium institution. Students therefore receive the bulk of their instruction in a language that is not their native tongue, very often from faculty who are themselves second language speakers of English. Many therefore have a double struggle: coming to grips with highly challenging intellectual content, and at the same time struggling with a language in which their proficiency may not be particularly high.

Developing the Course

Originally, I developed a course for integrating styles and strategies training with content-based instruction (a description of this course can be found in Nunan 1996). But there was little time in the regular content courses to achieve language-content objectives. Therefore, I modified some of the materials into a self-study course that students could complete in their own time, either at home or in the university's Independent Learning Centre, which is operated by the English Centre. The Centre contains audio, video, computer, and print materials that students can use for independent language study. In the Centre they can work alone, with other learners, or with the guidance and support of a teacher/consultant. The self-study materials that were placed in the Centre were aimed at encouraging students to develop independence and responsibility.

The program comprises four task-based modules, each focusing on a different dimension in the learning process.

Module A: Your Approach to Learning   (learning styles)

Module B: Developing Listening and Note-Taking Skills

Module C: Developing Reading and Note-Taking Strategies

Module D: Strategies for Improving Language Skills

Motivation for undertaking the modules comes in the form of credit for the work students complete. All students are required to complete one third of their course in independent study, and the work they complete during this time is assessed and forms part of their grade. Students undertaking the modules, which come in self-study booklets, are required to complete self-reports on the tasks they complete, and these self-reports are graded.

Module A consists of a bank of tasks designed to encourage learners to start thinking about some of the general processes underlying the learning process. It is a good starter activity for students who are making the rather dramatic transition from high school to university. The tasks are also designed to encourage students to think about the "how" and the "where" of the learning process. Students are involved in thinking about and discussing such questions as

- What makes a good teacher?
- What are the characteristics of an effective learner?
- How can one make use of resources beyond the classroom itself for learning?

Modules B and C are designed to teach learners direct strategies for developing listening, speaking, reading, and writing for university purposes. Learners are introduced to, and given practice in, techniques and strategies such as skimming, scanning, selective listening, and so on.

The final bank of tasks introduces strategies for working directly on language. The tasks are designed to help learners improve their vocabulary, grammar, pronunciation, and discourse. Students are shown how to use context to work out the meaning of unknown words, how to monitor their pronunciation, and how to develop their grammatical knowledge through inductive and deductive learning experiences.

Preparing the Students

Students are introduced to the self-study component of their course in a classroom orientation session.[*] The rationale for the component is explained to them, they are given the self-study packet, and then they participate in a guided tour of the Independent Learning Centre. The following is the written introduction to the self-study packet.

To the student:

The aim of this course is to give you an opportunity to practice some of the study skills and learning strategies that will help you to be a more effective university student. The tasks in the course should take you between 12 and 15 hours to complete.

While most of the work can be done wherever you choose, it is recommended that you do the work in the self-access centre. Here you will find listening and reading materials that can be used to practice the skills and strategies introduced during the course. More important, English Centre consultants will also be available in the Centre to help you if you encounter problems, to give you advice, and to check your progress as you complete each module.

You will notice that some of the modules have tasks entitled "Pair Work" option. While this course can be completed on your own, I strongly urge you to find another student who can complete the course with you. You will then be able to learn cooperatively, to check each other's work, to discuss the strategies you have developed, and to compare your responses to the material with another person.

For the first three sessions of the self-study component, I set a time for my students to attend the Independent Learning Centre, and I make sure that I am available in the Centre at that time to act as an advisor and guide. I also introduce the students to the Centre's consultants, and tell them that the consultants, all of whom are trained teachers, are available to help them as and when they need it. Each student also has a record card that the consultants fill in after each consultation.

The Learning Style Materials

Near the beginning of Module A, students are asked to discuss or write about the kinds of tasks that they enjoy, to compare their choices with several other students', and, on the basis of these comparisons, to decide what it is that makes an effective classroom task. Table 16-1 shows one of the exercises students are asked to complete.

---

[*] See Ramburuth, this volume, for an in-class application.

Table 16–1. The "Good" Classroom Task

I

Directions: Study the following descriptions of small group tasks and evaluate them according to the following key:
1. I don't like this type of task at all.
2. I don't like this type of task very much.
3. I don't mind this type of task.
4. I like this type of task very much.

Task A: Information Sharing
The class is split into two groups, A and B. You listen to a discussion between three people talking about these aspects of their lifestyle: where they go on vacation, what they like to do on the weekend, and their favorite hobby. The other half of the class listens to a discussion between three people talking about these aspects of their lifestyle: their favourite forms of entertainment, their favourite kinds of food, and the kinds of sports they play. You then work in pairs with a student from the other group to complete the following form:

	Person 1	*Person 2*	*Person 3*
Vacations			
Weekends			
Hobbies			
Entertainment			
Food			
Sports			

TASK RATING: _____

Task B: Decision-Making/Problem-Solving
You work in pairs. You are given a job description and three completed job applications. You decide which person should get the job.

TASK RATING: _____

Task C: Grammar Practice
You read a short passage containing a number of grammatical errors. You correct the errors and say what rules have been broken.

TASK RATING: _____

Task D: Dialog Practice
You listen to a conversation and then practice it with another student.

TASK RATING: _____

Task E: Authentic Reading
You bring an English language newspaper to class. You work with three or four other students to select an article, then prepare a set of reading comprehension questions to accompany the article. You exchange the article and questions with

another group. They read your article and answer your questions. You read their article and answer their questions.

TASK RATING: _____

Task F: Gap Filling
You read a passage in which every fifth word has been deleted. Work out which words were deleted and replace them.

TASK RATING: _____

Task G: Small Group Discussion
Working with several other students, you carry out a discussion task. You record the discussion. At the conclusion, you listen to the tape and identify your errors.

TASK RATING: _____

Task H: Role Play
You take part in a role play with three or four other students. One of you pretends to be someone who is being interviewed for a job. The other students pretend to be the interview panel.

TASK RATING: _____

II

Directions: Compare your responses with three or four other students' responses. Note the similarities and differences. Rank the tasks from most to least popular. You will need to negotiate with your classmates to arrive at a group decision on the popularity of these tasks.

Most popular _____ _____ _____ _____ _____ _____ *Least popular*

III

Directions: Discuss with the other students the reasons you chose the three "most popular" learning tasks. What was similar about the tasks? What made them "good" tasks? List up to five of the characteristics of a "good" classroom task.

1. _____

2. _____

3. _____

4. _____

5. _____

IV

Directions: Compare your list with another group of students. Discuss the similarities and the differences.

The last time I conducted this task with a group of students, they came up with statements such as the following to characterize the "good" task:

- ° "Gets all students to participate actively."
- ° "Doesn't make students feel embarrass."
- ° "Doesn't make students feel very stressful."
- ° "The task can be done outside the classroom."
- ° "Students can acquire sense of successfulness through the task."
- ° "Practical to daily life."
- ° "Students have the opportunity to give a response, an opinion."
- ° "Students are able to work in groups."

In general, my students like tasks that are fun, low-risk, practical, involve cooperative group interaction, and are carried out in a friendly atmosphere.[*]

Other items in this bank of tasks include exercises that allow students to explore self-access learning facilities and to evaluate the advantages and disadvantages of small group learning, as well as several simulations in which students explore the various role relationships inherent in different tasks.

Using Learning Styles to Develop Study Skills

The exercises set out in Table 16–2 are from Module D, the macro-skill module that focuses on speaking in general and on taking part in tutorials in particular. Actively contributing to tutorials is one area in which most first-year students have problems because the tutorial is an unfamiliar learning mode for them; nevertheless, in many departments students receive part of their final grade from such contributions.

The exercises comprise multiple tasks that tap into a variety of learning styles. First, students consider a range of language functions, which they can do individually or collaboratively, and which allows each student time for reflection. Then the students watch a videotaped tutorial in which all of the language functions can be observed. Using both visual and auditory stimuli, and asking students to check off the functions as they see them (tactile), provides a multimedia, multistyle approach to learning.

Finally, students can discuss the language functions that they have seen and reflected upon and that they need in order to contribute successfully to a tutorial. I encourage my students to work with one another when possible. Hong Kong students enjoy working together, and they are good at it. The value of such collaboration, of course, is that the students can actively practice their speaking while working on the tasks. Table 16–2 shows the progression of this exercise.

---

[*] See Call, this volume, for learning style similarities between Hong Kong and Japanese EFL students.

Table 16–2. Contributing to Tutorials

I

Directions: The following is a list of those things you would expect to do/hear others do in a small group/tutorial discussion. Can you add 3 or 4 items to the list? Reflect on your own participation in tutorial/seminar discussions. Which of these things do you do? Check off the spaces provided in the column marked **YOU**.

	YOU	OTHER STUDENTS
provide information	____	_____
make a suggestion	____	_____
add information to previous speaker	____	_____
disagree with previous speaker	____	_____
agree with previous speaker	____	_____
make comparisons	____	_____
give opinions	____	_____
express preferences	____	_____
give explanations	____	_____
ask for clarification	____	_____
check understanding	____	_____
invite contribution from others	____	_____
_____	____	_____
_____	____	_____
_____	____	_____
_____	____	_____

II

Directions: Observe a small group discussion, and put a tally mark under the column marked **OTHER STUDENTS** (above) each time you hear one of these functions. You can get a videotape of a tutorial discussion from the self-access consultant.

III

Directions: Discuss your language function checklist with 3 or 4 other students. What similarities and differences do you have? Then discuss what you think the most important language functions are in an effective tutorial. Write those functions below.

1. _____
2. _____
3. _____
4. _____
5. _____

IV

Directions: Write a short evaluation of this exercise. How did you benefit from it? How well did you do? What did you learn about taking part in tutorial discussions that you were not aware of beforehand? How would you modify this task for other students? What would you do differently next time?

Conclusion

This sequence of self-study modules allows students to select according to their needs, to focus on those areas where they feel they need the most help. For those students who lack confidence, support is available from the independent learning centre consultants, who can help them select tasks appropriate to their needs, who can guide them through the tasks, and who can assist them in the evaluation of the tasks.

In the final analysis, we need to ask, "Does this approach lead to change?" I pursued this question in follow-up interviews with a group of students who had used the modules. They all drew comparisons between the restrictive and, in their view, ineffective ways that they had been taught in school, and the freedom, flexibility, and effectiveness of the self-study modules. Here is a short extract from one of the students.

> I think in University, we don't do much exercises with our English because it's not a test, but we have to concern about how we can use English effectively in our studying. For example, learn more vocabulary or read more quickly, or oral skill in tutorial, so the approach is different. . . . I think interest is most important. I did very bad in my A Level English exam [the final English examination in high school], I don't like to write those formal and informal letters, memos, I hate that very much. But now I can choose whatever I am interested in and I think I have progress.

For Further Reading

Benson, P. and Voller, P. (Eds.). (1997). *Autonomy and Independence in Language Learning.* London: Longman.

This edited collection offers important theoretical and practical insights into principles of autonomy and independence in language learning.

Gardner, D. and Miller, L. (Eds.). (1996). *Tasks for Independent Language Learning.* Washington, DC: TESOL.

This practical book provides dozens of ideas for learner training in the areas of reading, writing, listening, speaking, vocabulary, grammar, paralinguistics, and self-assessment.

Nunan, D. (1995). *ATLAS: Learning-Centered Communication.* Boston: Heinle & Heinle.

This four-level textbook series provides many practical illustrations of ways in which a learning-centered philosophy can be integrated into teaching materials.

Nunan, D. (1996). Learner strategy training in the classroom: An action research study. *TESOL Journal 6* (1), 35–41.

This study describes a classroom-based action research study that used the materials described in this chapter to investigate the effect of learner strategy training on student learning, motivation, and attitudes.

 # Appendix 1

Multiple Intelligence Inventory for Teachers

Mary Ann Christison

<u>Directions</u>: Rank each statement below as **0**, **1**, or **2**. Write **0** in the blank if the statement is not true. Write **2** in the blank if you strongly agree with the statement. A score of **1** places you somewhere in between. Compare your scores in different intelligences. What is your multiple intelligence profile? Where did you score highest? lowest?

Linguistic Intelligence

_____ 1. I like to write articles and have them published.

_____ 2. I read something almost every day that isn't related to my work.

_____ 3. I often listen to the radio, cassette tapes of lectures, and books

_____ 4. I always read billboards and advertisements.

_____ 5. I enjoy doing crossword puzzles.

_____ 6. I use an overhead projector, posters, quotations, etc., in my teaching.

_____ 7. I am a good letter writer.

_____ 8. If I hear a song a few times, I can usually remember the words.

_____ 9. I ask my students to read and write most of the time in my classes.

_____ 10. I have written something that I like.

Musical Intelligence

_____ 1. I have a very expressive voice in front of my class, varying in intensity, pitch, and emphasis.

_____ 2. I often use music and chants in my lesson plans.

_____ 3. I can tell if someone is singing off-key.

_____ 4. I know the tunes to many different songs.

_____ 5. I play a musical instrument and play it frequently.

_____ 6. If I hear a new song once or twice, I can usually remember the tune.

_____ 7. I often sing in the shower.

_____ 8. Listening to music I like and am in the mood for makes me feel good.

_____ 9. When I hear a piece of music, I can easily harmonize with it.

_____ 10. I have no trouble identifying or following a beat.

Logical Mathematical Intelligence

_____ 1. I feel more comfortable believing an answer is correct if it has been measured or calculated in some way.

_____ 2. I can calculate numbers easily in my head.

_____ 3. I like playing card games such as hearts, gin rummy, and bridge.

_____ 4. I liked math classes in school.

_____ 5. I believe that most things have a logical and rational explanation.

_____ 6. I like brain-teaser games.

_____ 7. I am interested in new developments in science.

_____ 8. When I cook, I measure things exactly.

_____ 9. I use problem-solving activities in my classes.

_____ 10. My classes are consistent; my students know what to expect in terms of rules and routines.

Spatial Intelligence

_____ 1. I pay attention to the colors I wear and colors other people wear.

_____ 2. I take lots of photographs on trips and vacations.

_____ 3. I like to use video in my lessons.

_____ 4. It is easy for me to find my way around in unfamiliar cities.

_____ 5. I like to draw.

_____ 6. I like to read articles with many pictures.

_____ 7. I am partial to textbooks with illustrations, graphs, charts, and pictures.

_____ 8. I like doing puzzles and mazes.

_____ 9. I was good at geometry in school.

_____ 10. When I enter a classroom, I notice whether the positioning of the students and teacher supports the learning that is to take place.

Bodily/Kinesthetic Intelligence

_____ 1. I like to go on rides at amusement parks.

_____ 2. I like to dance.

_____ 3. I engage in at least one sport.

_____ 4. I like to do things with my hands, such as knit, weave, sew, carve, or build models.

_____ 5. I find it most helpful to practice a new skill rather than to read about it or to watch a video.

_____ 6. I often get my best ideas when I am jogging, walking, vacuuming, or doing something physical.

_____ 7. I love being in the outdoors.

_____ 8. I find it very hard to sit for long periods of time.

_____ 9. I do activities in my classes that require that my students get out of their seats and move around.

_____ 10. Most of my hobbies involve physical activity of some sort.

Intrapersonal Intelligence

_____ 1. I regularly spend time meditating.

_____ 2. I consider myself independent.

_____ 3. I keep a journal and record my thoughts.

_____ 4. I would rather adapt lessons or create my own than use lessons directly from a book.

_____ 5. I frequently create new activities and materials for my classes.

_____ 6. When I get hurt or disappointed, I bounce back quickly.

_____ 7. I can articulate the main values that govern my life and describe the activities that I regularly participate in that are consistent with these values.

_____ 8. I have hobbies or interests that I enjoy doing on my own.

_____ 9. I frequently choose activities in the classroom so my students can work alone or independently.

_____ 10. I give my students quiet time, thinking time, time to reflect on what they are doing.

Interpersonal Intelligence

_____ 1. I would prefer going to a party rather than spending the evening home alone.

_____ 2. When I have problems, I like to discuss them with my friends.

_____ 3. People often come to me with their problems.

_____ 4. I am involved in social activities several nights a week.

_____ 5. I like to entertain friends and have parties.

_____ 6. I consider myself a leader and often assume leadership roles.

_____ 7. I have more than one close friend.

_____ 8. I love to teach or show someone how to do something.

_____ 9. I am comfortable in a crowd or at a party with many people I don't know.

_____ 10. My students have input into the choice of content and the learning process in my classrooms.

Scoring: Add your total scores in each area. The higher your total score, the stronger that intelligence.[*]

[*] For permission to use this questionnaire, contact the author by e-mail (see e-mail address in the "Contributors" section of this volume) or at Snow College, International Center/ESL Dept., Ephraim, Utah 84627.

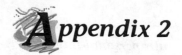

Appendix 2

Student-Generated Inventory for Secondary Level and Young Adult Learners

Mary Ann Christison

<u>Directions</u>: Rank each statement as 0, 1, or 2. Write 0 if you disagree with the statement. Write 2 if you strongly agree. Write 1 if you are somewhere in between.

Verbal/Linguistic Intelligence

_____ 1. I like to read books, magazines, and newspapers.

_____ 2. I consider myself a good writer.

_____ 3. I like to tell jokes and stories.

_____ 4. I can remember people's names easily.

_____ 5. I like to recite tongue twisters.

_____ 6. I have a good vocabulary in my native language.

Musical Intelligence

_____ 1. I can hum the tunes of many songs.

_____ 2. I am a good singer.

_____ 3. I play a musical instrument or sing in a choir.

_____ 4. I can tell when music sounds off-key.

_____ 5. I often tap rhythmically on the table or desk.

_____ 6. I often sing songs.

Logical/Mathematical Intelligence

_____ 1. I often do arithmetic in my head.

_____ 2. I am good at chess and/or checkers.

_____ 3. I like to put things into categories.

_____ 4. I like to play number games.

_____ 5. I love to figure out how computers work.

_____ 6. I ask many questions about how things work.

Spatial/Visual Intelligence

_____ 1. I can read maps easily.

_____ 2. I enjoy art activities.

_____ 3. I draw well.

_____ 4. Movies and slides really help me learn new information.

_____ 5. I love books with pictures.

_____ 6. I enjoy putting puzzles together.

160

Bodily/Kinesthetic Intelligence

_____ 1. It is hard for me to sit quietly for a long time.
_____ 2. It is easy for me to follow exactly what other people do.
_____ 3. I am good at sewing, woodworking, building, or mechanics.
_____ 4. I am good at sports.
_____ 5. I enjoy working with clay.
_____ 6. I enjoy running and jumping.

Interpersonal Intelligence

_____ 1. I am often the leader in activities.
_____ 2. I enjoy talking to my friends.
_____ 3. I often help my friends.
_____ 4. My friends often talk to me about their problems.
_____ 5. I have many friends.
_____ 6. I am a member of several clubs.

Intrapersonal Intelligence

_____ 1. I go to the movies alone.
_____ 2. I go to the library alone to study.
_____ 3. I can tell you some things I am good at doing.
_____ 4. I like to spend time alone.
_____ 5. My friends find some of my actions strange sometimes.
_____ 6. I learn from my mistakes.

Scoring: Add your total scores in each area. The higher your total score, the stronger that intelligence.[*]

---

[*] Reprinted from Christison, M. A. (1996). *TESOL Journal 6* (1): 10-14. For permission to use this questionnaire, contact the author by e-mail (see e-mail address in the "Contributors" section of this volume) or at Snow College, International Center/ESL Dept., Ephraim, Utah 84627.

Appendix 3

Perceptual Learning Style Preference Survey

Joy Reid

Directions: People learn in many different ways. For example, some people learn primarily with their eyes (visual learners) or with their ears (auditory learners); some people prefer to learn by experience and/or by "hands-on" tasks (kinesthetic or tactile learners); some people learn better when they work alone, and others prefer to learn in groups. This questionnaire has been designed to help you identify the way(s) you learn best—the way(s) you *prefer* to learn.

Read each statement on the following pages. Please respond to the statements **as they apply to your study of English.** Decide whether you agree or disagree with each statement. For example, if you *strongly agree* (SA), mark:

strongly agree (SA)	agree (A)	undecided (U)	disagree (D)	strongly disagree (SD)
X				

Please respond to each statement quickly, without too much thought. Try not to change your responses after you choose them. Please answer all the questions. Then use the materials that follow the questionnaire to score your responses.

	SA	A	U	D	SD
1. When the teacher tells me the instructions, I understand better.					
2. I prefer to learn by doing something in class.					
3. I get more work done when I work with others.					
4. I learn more when I study with a group.					
5. In class, I learn best when I work with others.					
6. I learn better by reading what the teacher writes on the chalkboard.					
7. When someone tells me how to do something in class, I learn it better.					
8. When I do things in class, I learn better.					
9. I remember things I have heard in class better than things I have read.					
10. When I read instructions, I remember them better.					

	SA	A	U	D	SD
11. I learn more when I can make a model of something.					
12. I understand better when I read instructions.					
13. When I study alone, I remember things better.					
14. I learn more when I make something for a class project.					
15. I enjoy learning in class by doing experiments.					
16. I learn better when I make drawings as I study.					
17. I learn better in class when the teacher gives a lecture.					
18. When I work alone, I learn better.					
19. I understand things better in class when I participate in role-playing.					
20. I learn better in class when I listen to someone.					
21. I enjoy working on an assignment with two or three classmates.					
22. When I build something, I remember what I have learned better.					
23. I prefer to study with others.					
24. I learn better by reading than by listening to someone.					
25. I enjoy making something for a class project.					
26. I learn best in class when I can participate in related activities.					
27. In class, I work better when I work alone.					
28. I prefer working on projects by myself.					
29. I learn more by reading textbooks than by listening to a lecture.					
30. I prefer to work by myself.					

Self-Scoring Sheet for Perceptual Learning Style Preference Survey

<u>Directions</u>: There are 5 statements for each learning category in this questionnaire. The questions are grouped below according to each learning style. Each question you answer has a numerical value:

strongly agree (SA)	*agree* (A)	*undecided* (U)	*disagree* (D)	*strongly disagree* (SD)
5	4	3	2	1

Fill in the blanks below with the numerical value of each answer. For example, if you answered *strongly agree* for statement 6 (a visual question), write the number 5 (*SA*) on the blank next to question 6.

Visual

6— __5__

When you have completed all the numerical values for **Visual**, add the numbers together. Multiply the answer by **2**, and put the total in the appropriate blank.

Follow this process for each of the learning style categories. When you are finished, look at the scale that follows. It will help you determine your

        major learning style preference(s):   score: 38–50
        minor learning style preference(s)   score: 25–37
        negligible learning styles: score: 0–24

If you need help, please ask your teacher.

Scoring Sheet

Visual

6 _____
10 _____
12 _____
24 _____
29 _____

Total _____ x 2 = _____
                   Score)

Tactile

11 _____
14 _____
16 _____
22 _____
25 _____

Total _____ x 2 = _____
                   (Score)

Auditory

1 _____
7 _____
9 _____
17 _____
20 _____

Total _____ x 2 = _____
                   Score)

Group

3 _____
4 _____
5 _____
21 _____
23 _____

Total _____ x 2 = _____
                   (Score)

Kinesthetic	*Individual*
2 _____	13 _____
8 _____	18 _____
15 _____	27 _____
19 _____	28 _____
26 _____	30 _____

Total _____ x 2 = _____   Total _____ x 2 = _____
            Score)   (Score)

Major learning style preference(s)   score: 38–50

_____

Minor learning style preference(s)   score: 25–37

_____

Negligible learning styles   score: 0–24

_____

Explanation of Perceptual Learning Style Preferences[*]

Students learn in many different ways. The results of the Perceptual Learning Style Preference Questionnaire show which ways you prefer to learn English. In many cases, students' learning style preferences show how well students learn material in different situations.

The explanations of major learning style preferences below describe the characteristics of those learners. The descriptions will give you some information about ways in which you learn best.

Visual Major Learning Style Preference

You learn well from *seeing words* in books, on the chalkboard, and in workbooks. You remember and understand information and instructions better if you *read* them. You don't need as much oral explanation as an auditory learner, and you can often learn alone with a book. You should take notes of lectures and oral directions if you want to remember the information.

Auditory Major Learning Style Preference

You learn from *hearing words* spoken and from oral explanation. You may remember information by *reading aloud* or by moving your lips as you read, especially when you are learning new material. You benefit from hearing audiotapes, lectures, and class discussion. You benefit from making tapes to listen to, by teaching other students, and by conversing with your teacher.

_____

[*] The explanation of learning styles has been adapted from the C. I. T. E. Learning Styles Instrument, Murdoch Teacher Center, Wichita, Kansas 67208. Used with permission.

Kinesthetic Major Learning Style Preference

You learn best by experience, by being involved physically in classroom experiences. You remember information well when you actively participate in activities, field trips, and role-playing in the classroom. A combination of stimuli— for example, an audio tape combined with an activity—will help you understand new material.

Tactile Major Learning Style Preference

You learn best when you have the opportunity to do *"hands-on" experiences* with materials. That is, working on experiments in a laboratory, handling and building models, and touching and working with materials provide you with the most successful learning situations. *Writing notes or instructions* can help you remember information, and *physical involvement* in class-related activities may help you understand new information.

Group Major Learning Style Preference

You learn more easily when you study with at least one other student, and you will be more successful completing work well when you *work with others*. You value group interaction and class work with other students, and you remember information better when you work with two or three classmates. The stimulation you receive from group work helps you learn and understand new information.

Individual Major Learning Style Preference

You learn best when you work *alone*. You think better when you study alone, and you remember information you learn by yourself. You understand material best when you learn it alone, and you make better progress in learning when you work by yourself.

Minor Learning Styles

In most cases, minor learning styles indicate areas where you can function well as a learner. Usually, a very successful learner can learn in several different ways, and so you might want to experiment with ways to practice and strengthen your minor learning styles.

Negligible Learning Styles

Often, a negligible score indicates that you may have difficulty learning in that way. One solution may be to direct your learning to your stronger styles. Another solution may be to try to work on some of the skills to strengthen your learning style(s) in the negligible area(s).[*]

---

[*] For permission to use this survey, contact the author by e-mail (see e-mail address in the "Contributors" section of this volume) or at Department of English, University of Wyoming, Hoyt 201, Laramie, WY 82071-3355.

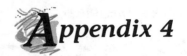

Appendix 4

The Tyacke Profile

Marian Tyacke

Name: _____   Language: _____

Class/Level: _____

I. What kind of learning situation do you like best? Circle *one* letter (ABCD) only.

   A) A class with an expert teacher who gives you exercises, tests, and rules in a clear order.

   B) A class where you are allowed to work independently, developing your own rules and consulting the teacher when necessary.

   C) A class where you interact frequently with other students, exploring possibilities and practicing the language rather than learning the rules.

   D) A class where you are allowed to sit quietly, watching and listening, rather than actively practicing or learning rules.

II. How do you find learning a new language?   (Please <u>underline</u> one only.)

   i) very easy   ii) fairly easy   iii) fairly difficult   iv) very difficult

III. Which skill (reading, writing, speaking, listening) do you find easiest to learn?

   _____

IV. Which skill is the most difficult for you? _____

V. What kind of person are you? Put an X in the box that describes you.

	very	fairly	a little	a little	fairly	very	
<u>cautious</u> (careful, considers consequences)							<u>impulsive</u> (jumps in, takes chances)
<u>convergent</u> (goes along with group or authority)							<u>divergent</u> (goes own way, decides independently)
<u>practical</u> (understands how things work)							<u>artistic</u> (creates art, music, literature)
<u>analytical</u> (takes ideas apart and examines each one)							<u>holistic</u> (puts ideas together, sees things as a whole)
<u>serious</u> (thoughtful, sober)							<u>playful</u> (jokes, plays games)

	very	fairly	a little	a little	fairly	very	
logical (decides based on reason, rational thinking)							intuitive (able to "feel" or know without evidence)
plans (works things out ahead of time)							spontaneous (does things on spur of the moment)
realistic (deals with facts, things as they are)							imaginative (likes fantasy, unusual ideas)
intellectual (relies on reason and knowledge)							emotional (relies on feelings and instincts)
reflective (lets things sink in before acting)							active (likes to get on with things) *

* For permission to use this survey, contact the author by e-mail (see e-mail address in the "Contributors" section of this volume) or at 24 Millbrook Crescent, Toronto, Ontario, Canada M4K 1H3.

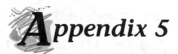

Appendix 5

Motivation and Strategies Questionnaire (MSQ)

Madeline E. Ehrman[*]

Name: _____   Date: _____

Language: _____

MSQ Part I: Aptitude and Motivation

1. How do you rate your own ability to learn foreign languages relative to others in general? _____
   1. poor
   2. below average
   3. average
   4. above average
   5. superior

2. How well do you think you will do in this language course? _____
   1. poor
   2. below average
   3. average
   4. above average
   5. superior

3. How motivated are you to learn this language? _____
   1. not at all motivated
   2. not motivated
   3. sufficiently motivated
   4. very motivated
   5. highly motivated

4. Why are you taking this language? _____
   _____

5. How much do you want to do what you described in Item 4 above?
   1. not at all
   2. not very much
   3. sufficiently
   4. very much
   5. really looking forward to it

6. Students have indicated that they are motivated to learn languages by one or more of the following. Please check (✓) those that apply to you now. (TL = Target Language, the language you are studying now.)

   ____ meeting a program requirement.   ____ language learning is fun.
   ____ getting a payment for proficiency.   ____ like country where the TL is used.
   ____ need it to do my job.   ____ this is a real challenge.
   ____ want to be top in my class.   ____ enjoy talking with TL people.
   ____ hope to get an award.   ____ love to learn something new.
   Other motivations: _____

[*] Adapted from Ehrman and Christensen (1994); originally published in *Understanding Second Language Learning Difficulties* by Madeline E. Ehrman, Sage Publications, 1996, pp. 306–319. Used with permission. For permission to use this survey, contact the author at School of Language Studies, Foreign Service Institute, National Foreign Affairs Training Center, 4000 Arlington Blvd., Arlington, VA 22204-1500.

7. I would say my anxiety about learning this language is _____
    1. none at all
    2. not very much
    3. a fair amount
    4. a lot
    5. really nervous about it

8. My anxiety about speaking in class (answering questions, giving reports, asking questions, etc.) is about this level: _____
    1. none at all
    2. not very much
    3. a fair amount
    4. a lot
    5. really nervous about it

MSQ Part IIa: Learning and Teaching Techniques

A variety of techniques may be used to help you learn, by you and by your teachers. How helpful do you think you will find these ways of teaching/learning? Please use the following scale to rate each item. Language X is the "target language" that you are studying.

1. waste of time
2. not very helpful
3. neither/nor
4. helpful
5. nearly indispensable

1. _____ The instructor systematically follows a textbook or syllabus.

2. _____ A written in-class exercise in which students fill in the correct forms of verbs in sentences, for example:

    (walk)   Martha _____ to school every day.

3. _____ The class breaks up into smaller groups to talk.

4. _____ Students ask each other questions in pairs.

5. _____ Students interview language X speakers and report on the interviews.

6. _____ Teacher explains grammar in English, with examples and a handout.

7. _____ Teacher reads new material in the textbook aloud, followed by students reading it aloud, one by one.

8. _____ Each student finds and reports on an interesting news or magazine article in language X.

9. _____ Students are given a list of words that will appear in an article they will read later. They look up the words in the dictionary and copy out the translations.

10. _____ Students select an article of interest to them to read in class, guessing the meanings of unknown words from context, without a dictionary.

11. _____ Teacher speaks in language X while explaining grammar.

12. _____ Teacher gives a sentence, to which entire group responds orally, changing the sentences in some way indicated by the teacher, for example, making it negative:

    Teacher: *John walks to school.*
    Class: *John doesn't walk to school.*

> **Teacher:** *John is walking to school.*
> **Class:** *John isn't walking to school.*

13. _____ Students have a classroom discussion of some topic such as the economy or social problems. The emphasis is on exchanging personal opinions.

14. _____ Students read a number of sentences, finding and correcting the mistakes.

15. _____ The teacher calls on each student in turn to make a change in a target sentence in some specified way, for example:

> **Teacher:** *John walks to school.* (Teacher calls on *Monica*.)
> **Monica:** *John doesn't walk to school.*
> **Teacher:** *Good. John is walking to school.* (Teacher calls on *Victor*.)
> **Victor:** *John isn't walking to school.*

16. _____ Teacher corrects all mistakes in students' writing.

17. _____ The teacher pays attention to the ideas and feelings in students' writings.

18. _____ There are chances to get up and move around the classroom.

19. _____ The class takes field trips to places where they can use the language outside the classroom.

20. _____ The teacher corrects all mistakes when students speak.

21. _____ Students help design the program as it goes along.

22. _____ Students learn dialogues by heart.

23. _____ The class goes away for several days or more for an "immersion" learning experience.

24. _____ Sometimes students are forced to use what they know to communicate, however little, even though it isn't exact.

25. _____ Each student discovers grammar patterns for himself/herself.

26. _____ Students do role plays, simulations, and skits in class.

27. _____ The students listen to material that is "over their head."

28. _____ The students read material that is "over their head."

29. _____ There is plenty of early pronunciation drill, so it will be perfect early.

30. _____ The class masters one thing before going on to more material or a new grammar point.

31. _____ Group study with classmates is part of the lesson.

32. _____ The program is step-by-step so the students won't be confused.

33. _____ The teacher has the main responsibility to see that students get what they need.

34. _____ Students use language X at the training site as much as they can.

35. _____ Students use language X outside the training site as much as they can.

36. _____ Students study alone.
37. _____ Students study with others outside class.
38. _____ Classroom exercises involve use of hands [drawing, pointing, construction, etc.].
39. _____ Students use audiotapes in the language lab or at home.
40. _____ Students use videotapes at school or outside.
41. _____ Students use computer-assisted instruction.

MSQ Part IIb: Personal Learning Techniques

You may do various things to help yourself learn. How often do you think you are likely to do the following? Use the following scale to rate each item.

1. almost never	3. sometimes	5. most of the time
2. rarely	4. often	

1. _____ I usually plan out what I will cover and how I will study when I start to study.
2. _____ I need to take study breaks.
3. _____ I remember better if I have a chance to talk about something.
4. _____ I have a number of projects going on, in varying states of completion.
5. _____ Mental images help me remember.
6. _____ I like to know how the "system" works and what the rules are, then apply what I know.
7. _____ I like to work with some background music.
8. _____ I try to keep my mistakes and reverses in perspective.
9. _____ If I write things down, I can remember them better.
10. _____ I like to be able to move around when I work or study.
11. _____ I don't mind when the teacher tells us to close our books for a lesson.
12. _____ I can trust my "gut feeling" about the answer to a question.
13. _____ I take a lot of notes in class or lectures.
14. _____ I find ways to fill in when I can't think of a word or phrase, such as pointing, using my hands, or finding a "filler" word (such as *whatchamacallit* or equivalent in the target language).
15. _____ I hear words in my mind when I read.
16. _____ I work better when it's quiet.
17. _____ I look at the ending when I start a book or story.
18. _____ If I use a computer to learn, I like programs with color and movement.
19. _____ My mind wanders in class.
20. _____ Figuring out the system and the rules for myself contributes a lot to my learning.

21. _____ It's useful to talk myself through a task.
22. _____ I feel the need to check my answers to questions in my head before giving them.
23. _____ I forget things if I don't write them down quickly.
24. _____ I consider myself a "horizontal filer" (e.g., my desk has piles of papers and books all over it),
25. _____ but I can find what I need quickly. (Answer only if #24 is 3, 4, or 5.)
26. _____ When I need to remember something from a book, I can imagine how it looks on the page.
27. _____ I can do more than one thing at once.
28. _____ I prefer to jump right into a task without taking a lot of time for directions.
29. _____ I am comfortable using charts, graphs, maps, and the like.
30. _____ I try to be realistic about my strengths and weaknesses without dwelling on the weaknesses.
31. _____ I like to complete one task before starting another.
32. _____ I prefer to demonstrate what I've learned by doing something "real" with it rather than taking a test or writing a paper.
33. _____ I have trouble remembering conversational exchanges word for word.
34. _____ Hearing directions for a task is better for me than reading them.
35. _____ I like to be introduced to new material by reading about it.

Interpreting the answers: [*] Responses to the MSQ are associated with other learning style dimensions. Following are interpretations based on low to moderate correlations with other instruments as well as experience.

Statements in **Part I** ask respondents to determine

1. previous success; self-efficacy
2. previous success; self-efficacy
3. motivation
4. the nature of the motivation
5. weight for students of end goal
6. Column 1 = extrinsic motivators
   Column 2 = intrinsic motivators
7. overall learning anxiety
8. anxiety about oral performance

---

[*] It is essential for users of the MSG to understand that for all of the responses to the MSG, the interpretations are tentative and should be treated as hypotheses to be explored with the person who filled out the questionnaire. For more complete interpretations, see Ehrman's detailed discussion in her *Understanding Second Language Learning Difficulties* (1996) and/or communicate directly with the author (see the "Contributors" section in this volume for her address).

Responses to statements in **Part IIa** and **Part IIb** indicate strong student learning preferences in the following areas:*

Need for External Structure	*Field Independent*	*Sequential*	*Analytic*	*Field Sensitive*	*Field Dependent*
Part IIa 1, 6, 7, 9, 12, 15, 22, 29, 30, 32, 33	14, 25	1, 7, 22, 30, 32	2, 14, 16, 20, 25, 36	11	6
Part IIb			31		

Random	*Open-ended Learning*	*Global*	*Kinesthetic*	*Auditory*	*Visual*
Part IIa 5, 10, 13, 17	5, 8, 10, 19, 21, 23, 24, 26, 27, 28	13, 19, 24, 26, 27, 28, 31	18, 19, 23, 38	39	
Part IIb 4, 24, 25, 33	12	33	2, 3, 10, 18, 19, 28, 33	3, 11, 15 21, 34	5, 9, 13, 23, 26, 30, 35

Inductive	*Deductive*	*Reflective*	*Impulsive*	*Interpersonal*	*Multi-tasking*
Part IIa 25				3, 4, 31	
Part IIb	6, 20	1, 22	12, 28		4, 7, 19, 27*

* Note that not every statement is strongly correlated with instruments used in this volume. However, in each case, the statements are clear and unambiguous, and that means that students and teachers can discuss what each means and what the student answer means in terms of learning preferences.

** For permission to use this survey, contact the author at Director, Research, Evaluation and Development, School of Language Services, Foreign language Institute, National Foreign Affairs Language Center, 4000 Arlington Boulevard, Arlington, Virginia 22204-7254.

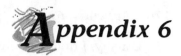

Appendix 6

Academic Work Style Survey

Kate Kinsella

<u>Directions</u>: This survey has been designed to help you and your teacher better understand **the way you usually prefer to work on assignments in class.**

Please read each statement; then, taking into consideration your past and present educational experiences, decide whether you **mostly** agree or **mostly disagree** with each statement.

	Agree	Disagree
1. When I work on assignments by myself, I often feel frustrated or bored.	_____	_____
2. When I work by myself on assignments (instead of with a partner or a small group), I usually do a better job.	_____	_____
3. I enjoy having opportunities to share opinions and experiences, compare answers, and solve problems with a group of classmates.	_____	_____
4. When I work by myself on assignments, I usually concentrate better and learn more.	_____	_____
5. I prefer working on assignments in class with a single partner rather than with a group of classmates.	_____	_____
6. Most of the time, I prefer to work by myself in class rather than with a partner or a small group.	_____	_____
7 I enjoy having opportunities to share opinions and experiences, compare answers, and solve problems with a single partner more than with a group.	_____	_____
8 When I work with a partner or a small group in class instead of by myself, I often feel frustrated or like I am wasting time.	_____	_____
9. When I work with a small group in class, I usually learn more and do a better job on the assignment.	_____	_____
10. Most of the time, I prefer to work in class with a single partner rather than by myself.	_____	_____
11. Most of the time, I prefer to work with a group rather than with a single partner or by myself.	_____	_____
12. When I work with a partner in class, I usually learn more and do a better job on the assignment.	_____	_____
13. I am more comfortable working with classmates when I can select the partner or group with whom I will be working.	_____	_____
14. Usually, I prefer that the instructor select the partner or the group of classmates with whom I will be working.	_____	_____

15. Usually, I find working with a partner to be more interesting and productive than working alone in class.   _____   _____

16. I prefer working in groups when there is a mixture of students from different backgrounds.   _____   _____

17. I hope we will have regular opportunities in this class to work in groups.   _____   _____

18. I generally accomplish more when I work with a partner on a task in class.   _____   _____

19. I hope we will not do too much group work in this class.   _____   _____

20. I prefer working with classmates from my same background.   _____   _____

21. I hope we will have regular opportunities in this class to work with a partner.   _____   _____

22. I mainly want my teacher to give us classroom assignments that we can work on by ourselves.   _____   _____

23. Usually, I find working in a group to be more interesting and productive than working alone in class.   _____   _____

24. Usually, I find working in a group to be a waste of time.   _____   _____

25. I generally accomplish more when I work with a group on a task in class.   _____   _____

Directions: Give yourself **1 point** if you **agree** with the following survey items and **0 points** if you **disagree**. Next, add the points under each heading. The greatest total indicates the way you usually prefer to work in class.

Independently	With a partner	With a group
2. __	5. __	1. __
4. __	7. __	3. __
6. __	10. __	9. __
8. __	12. __	11. __
19. __	15. __	17. __
22. __	18. __	23. __
24. __	21. __	25. __
TOTAL _____	TOTAL _____	TOTAL _____*

* For permission to use this survey, contact the author by e-mail (see e-mail address in the "Contributors" section of this volume) or at Dept. of Secondary Education, San Francisco State University, 1600 Holloway Ave., San Francisco, CA 94132.

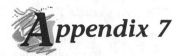

Appendix 7

Instructor Self-Assessment Form: Group Work Design and Implementation

Kate Kinsella

Instructor: _____   Class: _____

Date:_____

<u>Directions</u>: Rate yourself for each instructional behavior using the following scale:

   3 – Always   **2** – Usually   **1** – Sometimes   **0** – Never

_____   1. I establish consistent routines and procedures for group work: e.g., roles, physical arrangement, grouping formations, reporting, processing, and assessment.

_____   2. I prepare my students with vocabulary and language strategies necessary for the activity.

_____   3. I select or design activities which lend themselves to group process, those which clearly necessitate task-based, active collaboration and invite multiple contributions.

_____   4. I select or design activities with multiple parts, which allow students with diverse learning and work styles to draw upon their strengths.

_____   5. I make explicit the purpose, procedures, and expected outcome of the group activity.

_____   6. I select or design activities which require that students produce some form of meaningful and tangible final product.

_____   7. I include, when possible, group work assignments which help to personalize the curriculum by relating it to the students' cultures, communities, daily lives, and interests.

_____   8. I build in considerable context before presenting the assignment, using techniques which accommodate a variety of sensory modalities and information-processing strengths.

_____   9. I relate the assignment to previous lessons and previous group activities.

_____ 10. I break a more complicated and challenging task into manageable, clearly delineated steps.

_____ 11. I give clear oral instructions for the assignment, accompanied by some form of visual aid; I write the assignment goals, time frame, and procedures on a handout, on the chalkboard, or on an overhead transparency.

_____ 12. I model the task or a part of the task, and check to see if all students understand the instructions before placing them in groups.

_____ 13. I establish a clear and adequate time frame for students to complete all parts of the task.

_____ 14. I explain the various group member roles with behaviors necessary for completion of the task.

_____ 15. If I assign students to groups or if I allow them to form their own groups, I have a clear rationale for the group formations.

_____ 16. When I form groups, I am sensitive to cultural and affective variables.

_____ 17. I encourage cooperation, mutual support, and development of group accomplishment.

_____ 18. I take a noticeably active, facilitative role while groups are in progress by providing feedback and guidance, and when necessary getting students back on track.

_____ 19. I save adequate time to process the completed small-group activity as a unified class, clarifying what was learned and validating what was accomplished.

_____ 20. I incorporate listening and responding tasks for students to complete during individual small-group reports, to facilitate task processing and ensure active learning and accountability: e.g., note-taking, oral summarizing, question formation.

_____ 21. I provide feedback to individuals and groups on their prosocial skills and academic accomplishments during and/or after completion of the small-group activity.

_____ 22. I ask students to assess their individual and/or small group performance by means of a manageable form, quickwrite, or journal entry.

_____ 23. I make sure that students see the connection between what was generated, practiced, or accomplished during a small-group activity and any follow-up individual assignment.

_____ 24. I incorporate regular and balanced opportunities for my students to work in class in varied groupings: independent, partner, small group, and unified class.[*]

---

[*] For permission to use this form, contact the author by e-mail (see e-mail address in the "Contributors" section of this volume) or at Dept. of Secondary Education, San Francisco State University, 1600 Holloway Ave., San Francisco, CA 94132.

Appendix 8

Style Analysis Survey (SAS):
Assessing Your Own Learning and Working Styles
Rebecca L. Oxford

<u>Purpose</u>: The SAS is designed to assess your general approach to learning and working. It does not predict your behavior in every instance, but it is a clear indication of your overall style preferences.

<u>Timing</u>: It usually takes about 30 minutes to complete the SAS. Do not spend too much time on any one item. Indicate your immediate response and move on to the next item.

<u>Instructions</u>: For each item *circle* the response that represents your approach:

    0 – Never   1 – Sometimes   2 – Very Often   3 – Always

Complete all items. There are five major activities representing five different aspects of your learning and working style. At the end you will find a self-scoring key and an interpretation of the results.

Activity 1: How I Use My Physical Senses to Study or Work

	SCORE
1. I remember something better if I write it down.	0 1 2 3
2. I take lots of notes.	0 1 2 3
3. I can visualize pictures, numbers, or words in my head.	0 1 2 3
4. I prefer to learn with video or TV more than any other media.	0 1 2 3
5. I underline or highlight the important parts as I read.	0 1 2 3
6. I use color-coding to help me as I learn or work.	0 1 2 3
7. I need written directions for tasks.	0 1 2 3
8. I get distracted by background noises.	0 1 2 3
9. I have to look at people to understand what they say.	0 1 2 3
10. I am more comfortable when the walls where I study or work have posters and pictures.	0 1 2 3
11. I remember things better if I discuss them out loud.	0 1 2 3
12. I prefer to learn by listening to a lecture or a tape, rather than by reading.	0 1 2 3
13. I need oral directions for tasks.	0 1 2 3

179

14. Background sounds help me think.   0 1 2 3

15. I like to listen to music when I study or work.   0 1 2 3

16. I can easily understand what people say even if I can't see them.   0 1 2 3

17. I remember better what people say than what they look like.   0 1 2 3

18. I easily remember jokes that I hear.   0 1 2 3

19. I can identify people by their voices.   0 1 2 3

20. When I turn on the TV, I listen to the sound more than watching the screen.   0 1 2 3

21. I'd rather just start doing things rather than pay attention to directions.   0 1 2 3

22. I need frequent breaks when I work or study.   0 1 2 3

23. I move my lips when I read silently.   0 1 2 3

24. I avoid sitting at a desk when I don't have to.   0 1 2 3

25. I get nervous when I sit still too long.   0 1 2 3

26. I think better when I can move around.   0 1 2 3

27. Manipulating objects helps me to remember.   0 1 2 3

28. I enjoy building or making things.   0 1 2 3

29. I like a lot of physical activities.   0 1 2 3

30. I enjoy collecting cards, stamps, coins, or other things.   0 1 2 3

Activity 2: How I Deal with Other People

For each item *circle* the response that represents your approach:

0 – Never   **1 – Sometimes**   **2 – Very Often**   **3 – Always**

1. I prefer to work or study with others.   0 1 2 3

2. I make new friends easily.   0 1 2 3

3. I like to be in groups of people.   0 1 2 3

4. It is easy for me to talk to strangers.   0 1 2 3

5. I keep up with personal news about other people.   0 1 2 3

6. I like to stay late at parties.   0 1 2 3

7. Interactions with new people give me energy.   0 1 2 3

8. I remember people's names easily.   0 1 2 3

9. I have many friends and acquaintances.	0 1 2 3	
10. Wherever I go, I develop personal contacts.	0 1 2 3	

11. I prefer to work or study alone.	0 1 2 3
12. I am rather shy.	0 1 2 3
13. I prefer individual hobbies and sports.	0 1 2 3
14. It is hard for most people to get to know me.	0 1 2 3
15. People view me as more detached than sociable.	0 1 2 3
16. In a large group, I tend to keep silent.	0 1 2 3
17. Gatherings with lots of people tend to stress me.	0 1 2 3
18. I get nervous when dealing with new people.	0 1 2 3
19. I avoid parties if I can.	0 1 2 3
20. Remembering names is difficult for me.	0 1 2 3

Activity 3: How I Handle Possibilities

For each item *circle* the response that represents your approach:

0 – Never	1 – Sometimes	2 – Very Often	3 – Always

1. I have a vivid imagination.	0 1 2 3
2. I like to think of lots of new ideas.	0 1 2 3
3. I can think of many different solutions to a problem.	0 1 2 3
4. I like multiple possibilities and options.	0 1 2 3
5. I enjoy considering future events.	0 1 2 3
6. Following a step-by-step procedure bores me.	0 1 2 3
7. I like to discover things rather than have everything explained.	0 1 2 3
8. I consider myself original.	0 1 2 3
9. I am an ingenious person.	0 1 2 3
10. It doesn't bother me if the teacher or boss changes a plan.	0 1 2 3

11. I am proud of being practical.	0 1 2 3
12. I behave in a down-to-earth way.	0 1 2 3
13. I am attracted to sensible people.	0 1 2 3
14. I prefer realism to new, untested ideas.	0 1 2 3

15. I prefer things presented in a step-by-step way.	0 1 2 3
16. I want a class or work session to follow a clear plan.	0 1 2 3
17. I like concrete facts, not speculation.	0 1 2 3
18. Finding hidden meanings is frustrating or irrelevant to me.	0 1 2 3
19. I prefer to avoid too many options.	0 1 2 3
20. I feel it is useless for me to think about the future.	0 1 2 3

Activity 4: How I Approach Tasks

For each item *circle* the response that represents your approach:

    0 – Never   1 – Sometimes   2 – Very Often   3 – Always

1. I reach decisions quickly.	0 1 2 3
2. I am an organized person.	0 1 2 3
3. I make lists of things I need to do.	0 1 2 3
4. I consult my lists in order to get things done.	0 1 2 3
5. Messy, unorganized environments make me nervous.	0 1 2 3
6. I start tasks on time or early.	0 1 2 3
7. I get places on time.	0 1 2 3
8. Deadlines help me organize work.	0 1 2 3
9. I enjoy a sense of structure	0 1 2 3
10. I follow through with what I have planned.	0 1 2 3
11. I am a spontaneous person.	0 1 2 3
12. I like to just let things happen, not plan them.	0 1 2 3
13. I feel uncomfortable with a lot of structure.	0 1 2 3
14. I put off decisions as long as I can.	0 1 2 3
15. I have a messy desk or room.	0 1 2 3
16. I believe that deadlines are artificial or useless.	0 1 2 3
17. I keep an open mind about things.	0 1 2 3
18. I believe that enjoying myself is the most important thing.	0 1 2 3
19. Lists of tasks make me feel tired or upset.	0 1 2 3
20. I feel fine about changing my mind.	0 1 2 3

Activity 5: How I Deal with Ideas

For each item *circle* the response that represents your approach:

0 – Never	1 – Sometimes	2 – Very Often	3 – Always

1. I prefer simple answers rather than a lot of explanations.   0 1 2 3
2. Too many details tend to confuse me.   0 1 2 3
3. I ignore details that do not seem relevant.   0 1 2 3
4. It is easy for me to see the overall plan or big picture.   0 1 2 3
5. I can summarize information rather easily.   0 1 2 3
6. It is easy for me to paraphrase what other people say.   0 1 2 3
7. I see the main point very quickly.   0 1 2 3
8. I am satisfied with knowing the major ideas without the details.   0 1 2 3
9. I can pull together (synthesize) things easily.   0 1 2 3
10. When I make an outline, I write down only the key points.   0 1 2 3

---

11. I prefer detailed answers instead of short answers.   0 1 2 3
12. It is difficult for me to summarize detailed information.   0 1 2 3
13. I focus on specific facts or information.   0 1 2 3
14. I enjoy breaking general ideas down into smaller pieces.   0 1 2 3
15. I prefer looking for differences rather than similarities.   0 1 2 3
16. I use logical analysis to solve problems.   0 1 2 3
17. My written outlines contain many details.   0 1 2 3
18. I become nervous when only the main ideas are presented.   0 1 2 3
19. I focus on the details rather than the big picture.   0 1 2 3
20. When I tell a story or explain something, it takes a long time.   0 1 2 3

SCORING SHEET

Activity 1: How I Use My Physical Senses to Study or Work

Add your score for items   1–10.   _____ (visual)

Add your score for items 11–20.   _____ (auditory)

Add your score for items 21–40.   _____ (hands-on)

Circle the score that is the largest. If two scores are within 2 points of each other, circle both of them. If all three scores are within 2 points of each other, circle all three. The circle(s) represent(s) your preferred sense(s) for learning and working.

Activity 2: How I Deal with Other People

Add your score for items 1–10.   _____ (extroverted)
Add your score for items 11–20.   _____ (introverted)

Circle the score that is the largest. If two scores are within 2 points of each other, circle both of them. The preferred circle(s) represent(s) your preferred way(s) of dealing with other people.

Activity 3: How I Handle Possibilities

Add your score for items 1–10.   _____ (intuitive)
Add your score for items 11–20.   _____ (concrete-sequential)

Circle the score that is the largest. If two scores are within 2 points of each other, circle both of them. The preferred circle(s) represent(s) your preferred way(s) of handling possibilities.

Activity 4: How I Approach Tasks

Add your score for items 1–10.   _____ (closure-oriented)
Add your score for items 11–20.   _____ (open)

Circle the score that is the largest. If two scores are within 2 points of each other, circle both of them. The preferred circle(s) represent(s) your preferred way(s) of approaching tasks.

Activity 5: How I Deal with Ideas

Add your score for items 1–10.   _____ (global)
Add your score for items 11–20.   _____ (analytic)

Circle the score that is the largest. If two scores are within 2 points of each other, circle both of them. The preferred circle(s) represent(s) your preferred way(s) of dealing with ideas.

HOW TO UNDERSTAND AND USE THE RESULTS

Activity 1: How I Use My Physical Senses to Study or Work

In class: If you are a visual person, you rely on the sense of sight, and you learn best through visual means (books, videos). If you are an auditory person, you prefer listening and speaking activities (discussions, debates, audiotapes, role-plays, lectures). If you are a hands-on person, you benefit from doing projects, working with objects, and moving around the room (games, building models, conducting experiments).

On the job: If you are a visual person, you rely most on your sense of sight to gain knowledge or understanding (manuals, graphics). If you are an auditory person, you prefer to listen to information (meetings, tapes) rather than read it. If you are a hands-on person, you benefit most from getting involved in the information-gathering process (computers, research) or from doing projects, building things, and working with objects.

Anywhere: If two or all three of these senses are strong, you are flexible enough to enjoy a wide variety of activities.

Activity 2: How I Deal with Other People

In class: If you are extroverted, you enjoy a wide range of social, interactive learning tasks (games, conversations, discussions, debates, role-plays, simulations). If you are more introverted, you like to do more independent work (studying or reading by yourself or learning with the computer) or enjoy working with one other person you know well.

On the job: If you are extroverted, you enjoy a wide range of social and interactive tasks (meetings, discussions, teamwork). If you are introverted, you like to work independently (computers, individual projects) or enjoy working with one other person you know well.

Anywhere: If your scores are close, then you are balanced in the sense that you work easily with others and by yourself.

Activity 3: How I Handle Possibilities

In class: If you are intuitive, you are future-oriented, able to seek out the major principles of the topic, like to speculate about possibilities, enjoy abstract thinking, and avoid step-by-step instruction. If your preference is concrete-sequential, you are present-oriented and prefer one-step-at-a-time activities and want to know where you are going in your learning at every moment.

On the job: If you are intuitive, you like to plan ahead for creative, new directions (designing, overall planning) in a non-linear, flexible way. If you prefer a concrete-sequential approach, you want people to be able to depend on your abilities, are highly organized, prefer step-by-step work procedures, and like control.

Anywhere: If the two scores are close, then you can switch modes easily from intuitive to concrete-sequential.

Activity 4: How I Approach Tasks

In class: If your score is higher for closure, you focus carefully on all learning tasks, meet deadlines, plan ahead for assignments, and want explicit directions. If openness has a high score, you enjoy discovery learning (in which you pick up information in an unstructured way) and prefer to relax and enjoy your learning without concern for deadlines or rules.

<u>On the job</u>: If your higher score is closure, this means your work habits are very structured and serious, and you are oriented toward getting the job done on time or early. If your score is higher for openness, you are more relaxed and unstructured in your approach to work, and you don't care much about deadlines or regulations.

<u>Anywhere</u>: If the two scores are close, you have a balance between closure and openness; you enjoy the freedom of limited structure and can still get the task done before the deadline without stress.

Activity 5: How I Deal with Ideas

<u>In class</u>: If you are global, you enjoy getting the main idea, guessing meanings, and communicating even if you don't know all the words or concepts. If you are analytic, you focus more on details, logical analysis, and contrasts.

<u>On the job</u>: If you are global, you focus at work on the key points and are not as concerned about details. If you are analytic, you are a "detail person" who is known for being logical, and you are not as skilled with seeing the big picture right away.

<u>Anywhere</u>: If the two scores are close, you easily move from global thinking to analytic thinking and back again.

TIPS

Each style preference (within a given activity above) offers significant strengths in learning and working. Recognize your strengths and apply them often. Also, enhance your learning and working power by being aware of the style areas that you do <u>not</u> use and by developing them. Tasks that do not seem quite as suited to your style preferences will help you stretch beyond your ordinary "comfort zone" and expand your learning and working potential.

For example, if you are a highly global person, you might need to learn to use analysis and logic in order to work or learn more effectively. If you are an extremely analytic person, you might be missing out on some useful global characteristics, like getting the main idea quickly, and you can develop such qualities in yourself through practice. You won't lose your basic strengths by trying something new; you will simply develop another side of yourself that is likely to be very helpful.

If you aren't sure how to attempt new behaviors that go <u>beyond</u> your favored style, then ask your colleagues, friends, or teachers to give you a hand. Talk with someone who has a different style from yours, and see how that person does it.

Improve your learning or working situation by stretching your style!*

---

* For permission to use this survey, contact the author at Department of Curriculum/Instruction, 207 Graves Hall, University of Alabama, Tuscaloosa, AL 35487.

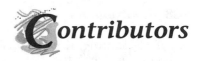

Contributors

Banya, Kingsley
Professor Banya is associate professor and chairperson of the Department of Educational Leadership and Policy Studies, College of Education, at Florida International University. He was born in Sierra Leone and was awarded his Ph.D. in the Ontario Institute of Studies in Education, University of Toronto. His research focus has been on curriculum theory and comparative education.
e-mail: Banyak@servms.fiu.edu

Busch, Connie
Connie Stultz Busch is an international educator who has taught ESL/EFL in the United States and the Republic of Korea. She also has worked as the International Student Advisor at the University of Denver, designed and presented numerous cross-cultural training workshops for international and U.S. students, and designed and taught the undergraduate course "Workshop in Cross-Cultural Adjustment" for the School of Communication at the University of Denver. She holds a Master's degree in English and is currently enrolled in a doctoral program in intercultural communication.
e-mail: buschcs@aol.com

Call, Jerry
Jerry Call taught EFL at the tertiary level in Tokyo from 1990 to 1993. From 1993 to 1995 he taught ESL at Ohio University while earning a Master's degree in Applied Linguistics. He completed a two-year position in in the Intensive English Language Institute at Utah State University. Currently Jerry is an IEP instructor at Divine Word College, Epworth, Iowa. His interests include learning styles, intercultural communication, and ITA training.
e-mail: jcall@mwci.net

Cheng, Maria Hsueh-Yu
Maria Cheng is an associate professor in the Department of Languages at the Chinese Military Academy in Fengsan, Taiwan. Her twenty years of teaching experience include junior high school and vocational education in Taiwan. She received her MA in TESOL at Oklahoma City University and her Ph.D. at Florida International University. She has given presentations concerning learning styles, strategies, attitudes, and motivation in Australia, the United States, Singapore, and Taiwan.
e-mail: hycheng@cc.cma.edu.tw

Christison, Mary Ann
Mary Ann Christison is a professor and the director of the International Center at Snow College in Ephraim, Utah, and is currently a visiting professor at the University of Utah. She is 1997–98 President of the International TESOL association, and she was Convention Chair of the 1995 TESOL Convention in Long Beach, California. Dr. Christison is the author of more than 60 published articles and such popular resource books as *Look Who's Talking, Drawing Out, Community Spirit, Purple Cows and Potato Chips,* the *TREAT* series, *A Handbook for Language Program Administrators, Becoming a Language Teacher,* and the *Star Series: Content and Learning Strategies.* Her current research interests include teacher beliefs, reflective teaching, and Multiple Intelligences. She consults widely both within and outside the United States.
e-mail: maryann.christison@snow.edu

Ehrman, Madeline E.
Madeline Ehrman is the director of Research Evaluation and Development in the School of Language Studies of the Foreign Service Institute, U.S. Department of State. She combines a background in both linguistics and clinical psychology and now specializes in diagnosing learning difficulties that classroom teachers refer to her as especially troublesome. She has recently authored a book on understanding second language learning difficulties; both that book and Dr. Ehrman's many articles and book chapters address individual differences in

language learning, from language aptitude through personality dispositions and learning styles to affective factors.

address: Director, Research, Evaluation, and Development
          School of Language Services, Foreign Language Institute
          National Foreign Affairs Training Center
          4000 Arlington Blvd
          Arlington, VA 22204-7254

Gedeon, Éva

Éva Gedeon has taught in the English Department in the ELTE Center for English Teacher Training in Budapest, Hungary. After taking part in a USIS summer symposium in Veszprém, Hungary, she worked with **Katalin Takacs** to gather data from their students concerning their perceptual learning styles. Éva taught Hungarian in the Central Eurasian Studies Department at Indiana University, and she plans to pursue doctoral work. Katia is in the United States, pursuing an alternate lifestyle.

address: Lorand Eotovos University
          Unw of Budapest
          Center for English Teacher Training
          H-1146 Budapest
          Adtosi Dorer SOR 19   HUNGARY

Gray, Kristina

Being from Minnesota with Viking blood helped Kristina Torkelson Gray to know that many cultures existed outside her own roots. She has lived overseas for six years, teaching EFL in the Philippines, China, Kazakstan, and Kyrgyzstan. Her last overseas stint was as a Fulbright lecturer in Bishkek, Kyrgyzstan. At present she is an adjunct faculty member at Northern Virginia Community College, where she teaches intermediate writing to students from more than 50 countries, principally from Asia, South America, and Africa.

e-mail: 76501.2312@compuserve.com

Harthill, Barbara

Barbara V. Harthill is an award-winning ESL teacher at the University of Denver's English Language Center, and an adjunct professor of German in the Department of Languages and Literature at the University of Denver. She has taught ESL/EFL for 26 years, both in the United States and in Germany, and has also taught Spanish at the college level.

e-mail: bharthil@du.edu

Kinsella, Kate

Kate Kinsella is a teacher-educator at San Francisco State University, where she conducts seminars for interdisciplinary university colleagues as well as pre-service K–12 teachers in curricula and instruction. She has given seminars as a TESOL Fulbright lecturer in Italy, and she has worked extensively with secondary schools and colleges throughout the United States that are striving to craft more effective programs for linguistically and culturally diverse student populations.

e-mail: katek@sfsu.edu

Koebke, Ken

Ken Keobke is a lecturer at City University of Hong Kong and a Ph.D. candidate at the University of Hong Kong with Professor David Nunan and Dr. Amy Tsui. He has taught in China and Hong Kong for nine years and is the author of a listening series published by Oxford University Press. His most recent publications include a CD-ROM based on *Frankenstein.*

e-mail: LSKEOBKE@CITYU.EDU.HK

Korotikikh, Zhanna

Zhanna Korotikikh was born in Russia. In 1954 her family moved to Barnaul, Siberia. In 1974 she graduated from the Barnaul State Pedagogical Institute Foreign Languages Department.

Later she took a two-year course at Moscow State Pedagogical Institute, majoring in Linguistics and Methods of Teaching. In 1979 she defended her dissertation in Lexicology, and she has been teaching EFL at Barnaul State Pedagogical Institute ever since. She also supervises evening courses for adult learners of English. Her current research is centered around cross-cultural aspects in language teaching.

address: Barnaul State Pedagogical Institute
Foreign Languages Dept.
Kruyskara, 108
656015   RUSSIA

Mata, Manuel

Manuel Mata teaches English at a secondary school in Castellón, Spain. As part of his work toward a graduate degree, he administered the Perceptual Learning Styles Preference survey to first- and second-year classes, and in third- and fourth-year humanities and science specializations at the Instituto de BUP, Villarreal de los Infantes secondary school.

address: Avda. Pio XII, 30 7oH
Villarreal (Castellón)
12540   SPAIN

Nam, Christine

Christine Nam majored in English in her undergraduate studies at Brandeis University and is now working on her Master's degree in the field of learning disabilities at Teacher's College, Columbia University. She has recently traveled to Korea, where she studied Korean and worked in English language teaching. She is concerned mainly with language and culture. Her current specializations are learning disabilities, learning styles, and anxiety in learning.

address: Department of Special Education
Teachers College
Columbia University
New York, NY 10027

Nunan, David

David Nunan has worked as a TESOL teacher in Thailand, Singapore, Hong Kong, Japan, Britain, Australia, and the Middle East. He is Professor of Applied Linguistics and Director of the English Centre at the University of Hong Kong, where his current research interests include learning styles and strategies, academic writing, teaching listening comprehension, and discourse in the multilingual workplace.

e-mail: dcnunan@hkucc.hku.hk

Oxford, Rebecca

Rebecca Oxford is Associate Dean of the College of Education, University of Alabama. She has authored books on language learning strategies and culture, has co-authored a book on the tapestry of language learning, has edited books on motivation and cross-cultural learning strategies, and has co-edited a book on simulation and gaming for language learning. Several of these are published in multiple languages. In addition, she co-edited the Heinle & Heinle ESL/EFL Tapestry Program (approximately 40 volumes). She is internationally known as a speaker.

address: Dept. of Curriculum/Instruction
207 Graves Hall
University of Alabama
Tuscaloosa, AL 35487

Ramburuth, Prem

Ms. Prem Ramburuth is currently the Senior Learning Adviser at The Learning Centre at the University of New South Wales in Australia. She has studied and taught in South Africa, the United Kingdom, and Australia over a period of 25 years in the areas of Education, Drama, English, and ESL. Her M.Ed. is from the University of Sydney, and she holds a Licentiate from the Royal Academy of Music, London, in Speech and Drama. She has recently completed her doctoral studies on the learning style preferences of international students studying in Australia.

e-mail: P.Ramburuth@unsw.edu.au

Reid, Joy

Joy Reid is an associate professor of English at the University of Wyoming. She has published an ESL composition textbook series (Prentice Hall Regents), a teacher-reference book titled *Teaching ESL Writing* (Prentice Hall Regents), and another learning styles anthology (Heinle & Heinle). Her research interests also include discourse analysis, the change process in the classroom, and intercultural communication. She consults worldwide in the areas of writing and learning styles.

e-mail: jreid@uwyo.edu

Sauer, Chris

Christopher Sauer has taught ESL/EFL in Botswana, the Navajo Nation, and at Ohio University. Currently he is the director of the Intensive English Institute of Divine Word College, a Catholic seminary college in Epworth, Iowa.

e-mail: sauer@mwci.net

Sherak, Kathy

Kathy Sherak is academic coordinator at the American Language Institute at San Francisco State University, where she supervises novice teachers and develops curriculum to meet the needs of university-bound students. A Fulbright teacher trainer in Italy in 1990, she has made numerous professional presentations on promoting active student behavior, honoring diverse learning styles in the composition class, teaching pre-listening schema-building strategies, and developing effective strategies for teacher observation and feedback.

e-mail: ksherak@sfsu.edu

Tyacke, Marian

Marian Tyacke has coordinated and taught courses in English for Professional and Academic Purposes, trained TESL teachers, and developed language proficiency tests at the University of Toronto. She helped develop the Ontario Test of ESL, and was part of the original team that developed the (TOEFL) Test of Written English. She was also involved in designing curricula for Chengdu Medical College (PRC) and the Sultanate of Oman. Her interest in learning styles and strategies is based on classroom research carried out since the 1970s, which culminated in a Ph.D. in Applied Linguistics from the University of Lancaster in the United Kingdom.

e-mail: tyacke@ecf.utoronto.ca

Vann, Roberta

Roberta Vann is a professor in the Department of English and the Program of Linguistics at Iowa State University, where she teaches TESL methods in the MA program and coordinates the TESL certification program. Her most recent research has focused on learner strategies, and she is especially interested in the impact of visual strategies on the reading process.

e-mail: rvann@iastate.edu

Violand-Sánchez, Emma

Emma Violand-Sánchez is the supervisor of the English for Speakers of Other Languages/High Intensity Language Training (ESOL/HILT) program for the Arlington Public Schools in Arlington County, Virginia. She coordinates curriculum and staff development, family education, bilingual counseling services, and placement and registration for students. Dr. Violand received a senior Fulbright Award to assist in the education reform in Bolivia and to research the learning styles of Bolivian teachers and university professors. She also serves as a consultant to the Ministry of Education in El Salvador regarding training in Multiple Intelligences and implications of brain research in learning. Dr. Violand is an adjunct professor at George Washington University and George Mason University.

e-mail: evioland@osf1.gmu.edu

References

Abraham, R. (1985). Field dependence/independence in the teaching of grammar. *TESOL Quarterly 19* (4), 689–702.

Alderson, J. C. (1991). Language testing in the 1990s: How far have we come? How much farther do we have to go? In S. Anivan, Ed., *Current Developments in Language Testing* (pp. 1–27). Anthology Series 25, Seameo/RELC.

Alderson, J. C. and Lukmani, Y. (1989). Cognition and reading: Cognitive levels as embodied in test questions. *Reading in a Foreign Language 5* (2), 253–270.

Allen, A. (1992). Reading test validation: Investigating aspects of process appraisal. Unpublished doctoral thesis. Department of Linguistics and Modern English Language, University of Lancaster.

Amer, A.A. (1994). The effect of knowledge-map and underlining training on the reading comprehension of scientific texts. *English for Specific Purposes 13* (1), 35–45.

Anderson, J. (1988). Cognitive styles and multicultural populations. *Journal of Teacher Education 39*, 2–9.

Anderson, J.A. (1995). Toward a framework for matching teaching and learning styles for diverse populations. In R. S. Sims and S. J. Sims, Eds., *The Importance of Learning Styles: Understanding the Implications for Learning, Course Design, and Education* (pp. 69–78). Westport, CT: Greenwood Press.

Armstrong, T. (1994). *Multiple Intelligences in the Classroom.* Alexandria, VA: Association for Supervision and Curriculum Development (ASCD).

Arnheim, R. (1969). *Visual Thinking.* Berkeley: University of California Press.

Azar, B. S. (1989). *Understanding and Using English Grammar*, 2nd Ed. Englewood Cliffs, NJ: Prentice Hall Regents.

Backes, J. (1993). The American Indian high school dropout rate: A matter of style? *Journal of American Indian Education* (May): 16–29.

Ballard, B. and Clanchy, J. (1991). *Teaching Students from Overseas: A Brief Guide to Lecturers and Supervisors.* Melbourne: Longman Cheshire.

Barlund, D. C. (1975). *Communicative Styles of Two Cultures.* Tokyo: Kinseido.

Bassano S.K. and Christison, M.A. (1995a). *Look Who's Talking.* Burlingame, CA: Alta Book Center Publishers.

Bassano, S. K. and Christison, M. A. (1995b). Drawing out communication: Student-created visuals as a means for promoting language development in adult ESL classrooms. In J. Reid, Ed., *Learning Styles in the ESL/EFL Classroom* (pp. 63–73). Boston: Heinle & Heinle.

Bejarano, Y. (1987). A cooperative small-group methodology in the language classroom. *TESOL Quarterly 21*, 483–504.

Benson, P. and Voller, P. (Eds.). (1997). *Autonomy and Independence in Language Learning.* London: Longman.

Bickley, V. (1989). *Language Teaching and Learning Styles Within and Across Cultures.* Hong Kong: Education Department, Institute of Language in Education.

Biggs, J. B. (1987) *Student Approaches to Learning and Studying.* Melbourne: Australian Council for Educational Research.

Binet, A. and Simon, T. (1908). Le développement de l'intelligence chez les enfants. *Anné Psychologie 14*, 1–94.

Black, S. (1993). They do it their way. *Executive Educator* (November): 21–24.

Bonham, L. (1989). Using learning style information, too. In E. Hayes, Ed., *Effective Teaching Styles.* New Directions for Continuing Education, 45. San Francisco: Jossey-Bass.

Boyd, G. M. and Mitchell, D. P. (1992). How can intelligent CAL better adapt to learners? *Computers Education 18* (1–3), 23–28.

Bradbury, R. (1958). *The Martian Chronicles.* Garden City, NY: Doubleday.

Brown, H. D. (1994). *Principles of Language Learning and Teaching*, 3rd Ed. Englewood Cliffs, NJ: Prentice Hall Regents.

Brown, J. I., Bennett, J. M., and Hanna, G. (1981). *Nelson-Denny Reading Test Manual* (Forms E and F). Boston: Riverside.

Bruner, C.E. and Majewski, W.S. (1990). Mildly handicapped students can succeed with learning styles. *Educational Leadership 48*, 15–19.

Caine, G. and Caine, R. (1991). *Making Connections: Teaching and the Brain.* Alexandria, VA: Association of Supervision and Curriculum Development.

Campbell, L., Campbell, B., and Dickenson, E. (1996). *Teaching and Learning Through Multiple Intelligences.* Needham Heights, MA: Allyn & Bacon.

Carrell, P. L. and Monroe, L. (1995). ESL composition and learning styles. In J. Reid, Ed., *Learning Styles in the ESL/EFL Classroom* (pp. 148–157). Boston: Heinle & Heinle.

Carroll, J. and Sapon, S. M. (1959). *Modern Language Aptitude Test.* New York: Psychological Corporation.

Cattell, R. B. (1963). Theory of fluid and crystallized intelligence: A critical experiment. *Journal of Educational Psychology 54*, 1–22.

Celce-Murcia, M. and Larsen–Freeman, D. (1983). *The Grammar Book: An ESL/EFL Teacher's Course.* Boston: Heinle & Heinle.

Chapelle, C. (1983). The relationship between ambiguity tolerance and success in acquiring English as a second language with adult learners. Unpublished doctoral thesis, University of Illinois, Urbana-Champagne.

Chapelle, C. (1992). Disembedding "Disembedded figures in the landscape": An appraisal of Griffiths and Sheen's "Reappraisal of L2 research on field dependence/independence." *Applied Linguistics 13* (3), 375–384.

Chapelle, C. (1995). Field dependence/Field independence in the L2 classroom. In J. Reid, Ed., *Learning Styles in the ESL/EFL Classroom* (pp. 158–168). Boston: Heinle & Heinle.

Chapelle, C. and Green, P. (1992). Field independence/dependence in second language acquisition research. *Language Learning 42*, 47–83.

Cheng, Hsueh-Yu. (1995). Motivation, attitude, and achievement in English learning. A case study at the Chinese Military Academy. Doctoral thesis, Florida International University.

Cherry, C. (1978). *On Human Communication*, 3rd Ed. Boston: MIT Press.

Christison, M.A. (1990). Cooperative learning in the ESL classroom. *English Teaching Forum 28*, 6–9.

Christison, M.A. (1996a). Teaching and learning languages through multiple intelligences. *TESOL Journal 6 (1)*, 10–14.

Christison, M.A. (1996b). Multiple intelligences and second language learners. *The Journal of the Imagination in Language Teaching 3*, 8–13.

Christison, M.A. (1998). *Teaching and Learning ESL Through Multiple Intelligences.* Burlingame, CA: Alta Book Center Publishers.

Christison, M. A. and Bassano, S. (1995). Expanding student learning styles through poetry. In J. Reid, Ed., *Learning Styles in the ESL/EFL Classroom* (pp. 96–107). Boston: Heinle & Heinle.

Claxton, C. and Murrell, P. (1987). Learning styles: Implications for improving educational practices. *ASHE-ERIC Higher Education Reports 4.* Washington, DC: Association for the Study of Higher Education.

Coe, M. (1996). *Human Factors for Technical Communicators.* New York: John Wiley and Sons.

Coehlo, E. (1994). *Learning Together in the Multicultural Classroom.* Markham, Ontario: Pippin Publishing Limited.

Cohen, A. (1990). *Language Learning: Insights for Learners, Teachers, and Researchers.* Boston: Heinle & Heinle.

Cohen, A. (1994). *Assessing Language Ability in the Classroom.* Boston: Heinle & Heinle.

Cohen, E. G. (1994). *Designing Groupwork: Strategies for the Heterogeneous Classroom.* New York: Teacher's College Press, Columbia University.

Cohen, R. (1968). The relation between socio-conceptual styles and orientation to school requirements. *Sociology of Education 41*, 201–220.

Cohen, R. (1969). Conceptual styles, culture conflict, and nonverbal tests of intelligence. *American Anthropologist 71*, 828–856.

Condon, J. S. (1984). *With Respect to Japanese.* Yarmouth, ME: Intercultural Press.

Conti, G. J. (1989). Assessing teaching style in continuing education. In E. Hayes, Ed., *Effective Teaching Styles* (pp. 3–16). San Francisco: Jossey-Bass.

Cornett, C.E. (1983). *What You Should Know About Teaching and Learning Styles.* Bloomington, IN: Phi Delta Kappa Education Foundation.

Costa, A. (1984). Mediating the metacognitive. *Educational Leadership 42* (3), 57–62.

Cummins, J. (1989). *Empowering Language Minority Students.* Sacramento: California Association for Bilingual Education.

Dennison, P. and Dennison, G. (1989). *Brain Gym* (Rev. ed.) (Teacher's Ed.). Ventura, CA: Edu-Kinesthetics, Inc.

Derycke, A. C., Smith, C., and Hemery, L. (1995). Metaphors and interactions in virtual environments for open and distant education. In H. Maurer, Ed., *Educational Multimedia and Hypermedia* (pp. 181–186). Proceedings of ED-MEDIA 95 World Conference on Educational Multimedia and Hypermedia (June). Charlottesville, VA: Association for the Advancement of Computing in Education.

Dowling, W.J. (1982). Melodic information processing and its development. In D. Deutsch, Ed., *The Psychology of Music* (pp. 82–101). New York: Academic Press.

Dunkel, P. (1991). The effectiveness research on computer-assisted instruction and computer-assisted language learning. In P. Dunkel, Ed., *Computer-Assisted Language Learning and Testing: Research Issues and Practice* (pp. 5–36). New York: Newbury House/HarperCollins.

Dunn, R. S. (1991). Do students from different cultures have different learning styles? *InterEd 15,* 12–16.

Dunn, R. S. and Dunn, K. J. (1979). Learning styles/teaching styles: Should they . . . can they . . . be matched? *Educational Leadership 36,* 238–244.

Dunn, R. S. and Griggs, S. (1988). *Learning Styles: Quiet Revolution in American Secondary Schools.* Reston, VA: National Association of Secondary School Principals.

Dunn, R. S. and Griggs, S. (1990). Research on the learning style characteristics of selected racial and ethnic groups. *Journal of Reading, Writing, and Learning Disabilities International 6,* 261–280.

Dunn, R. S. and Griggs, S. A. (1995). *Multiculturalism and Learning Style: Teaching and Counseling Adolescents.* Westport, CT: Praeger.

Dunn, R. S., Beaudry, J. S., and Klavas, A. (1989). Survey of research on learning styles. *Education Leadership 46* (6), 50–58.

Dunn, R. S., Dunn, K., and Price, G. E. (1989). *Learning Styles Inventory (LSI): An inventory for the identification of how individuals in grades 3 through 12 prefer to learn.* Lawrence, KS: Price Systems.

Dunn, R. S.; Gemake, J.; Jalali, F.; and Zenhausern, R. (1990). Cross-cultural differences in learning styles of elementary-age students from four ethnic backgrounds. *Journal of Multicultural Counseling and Development 18,* 68–93.

Ehrman, M. E. (1993). Ego boundaries revisited: Toward a model of personality and learning. In J. E. Alatis, Ed., *Strategic Interaction and Language Acquisition: Theory, Practice and Research* (pp. 331–362). Washington, DC: Georgetown University.

Ehrman, M. E. (1996). *Understanding Second Language Learning Difficulties: Looking Beneath the Surface.* Thousand Oaks, CA: Sage Publications.

Ehrman, M. E. and Christensen, L. (1994). Language learner motivation and learning strategies questionnaire. Unpublished manuscript.

Ehrman, M. E. and Leaver, B. L. (1997). Sorting our global and analytic functions in second language learning. Paper presented at the annual meeting of the American Association for Applied Linguistics, Orlando (March).

Ehrman, M. E. and Oxford, R. (1995). Cognition plus: Correlates of language learning success. *Modern Language Journal 79* (1), 67–89.

Eliason, P. (1995). Difficulties with cross-cultural learning styles assessment. In J. Reid, Ed., *Learning Styles in the ESL/EFL Classroom* (pp. 19–33). Boston: Heinle & Heinle.

Elliott, A. R. (1995). Foreign language phonology: Field independence, attitude, and the success of formal instruction in Spanish pronunciation. *Modern Language Journal 79* (4), 530–542.

Ellis, R. (1989). Classroom learning styles and their effect on second language acquisition: A study of two learners. *System 17* (2), 249–262.

Ellison, L. (1993). *Seeing with Magic Glasses: A Teacher's View from the Front Line of the Learning Revolution.* Arlington, VA: Great Ocean Publishers.

Ely, C.M. (1989). Tolerance of ambiguity and use of second language learning strategies. *Modern Language Journal 73*, 97–116.

Ely, C.M. (1995). Second language tolerance of ambiguity scale. In J. Reid, Ed., *Learning Styles in the ESL/EFL Classroom* (pp. 216–217). Boston: Heinle & Heinle.

Ely, C. M. and Pease-Alvarez, C. (1996). Learning styles and strategies in ESOL: Introduction to the special issue. *TESOL Journal 6* (1), 5.

Felder, R.M. and Henriques, E.R. (1995). Learning and teaching styles in foreign and second language acquisition. *Foreign Language Annals 28* (1), 21-31.

Feldman, D.H. (1980). *Beyond Universals in Cognitive Development.* Norwood, NJ: Ablex.

Feurstein, R. (1980). *Instrumental Enrichment.* Baltimore: University Park Press.

Fiechtner, S., and Davis, E. (1992). Why some groups fail: A survey of students' experiences with learning groups. In A. Goodsell, M. Maher, and V. Tinto, Eds., *Collaborative Learning: A Sourcebook for Higher Education.* University Park: Pennsylvania State University, National Center on Postsecondary Teaching, Learning, and Assessment.

Fuchs, M. and Bonner, M. (1995). *Focus on Grammar: A High Intermediate Course of Reference and Practice.* New York: Addison-Wesley.

Gardner, D. and Miller, L. (Eds.). (1996). *Tasks for Independent Language Learning.* Washington, DC: TESOL.

Gardner, H. (1982). Artistry following damage to the human brain. In A.W. Ellis, Ed., *Normality and Pathology in Cognitive Functions* (pp. 299–323). London: Academic Press.

Gardner, H. (1983). *Frames of Mind: The Theory of Multiple Intelligences*. New York: Basic Books.

Gardner, H. (1993). *Multiple Intelligences: The Theory in Practice*. New York: Basic Books.

Gardner, H. (1995). Reflections on multiple intelligences: Myths and messages. *Phi Delta Kappa 77*, 200–209.

Geisert, G. and Dunn, R. (1991). Effective use of computers: Assignments based on individual learning style. *Clearing House 64*, 219–224.

Gladis, S. D. (1993). *Write Type: Personality Types and Writing Styles*. Amherst, MA: Human Resource Development Press.

Golebiowska, A. (1984). Motivating those who know it all. *ELT Journal 38* (4), 274–278.

Goodman, K. S. (1967). Reading: A psycholinguistic guessing game. *Journal of the Reading Specialist 6*, 13–26.

Goodson, T. (1993). Learning style preferences of East Asian ESL students. Unpublished doctoral thesis, University of Tennessee.

Gray, K. (1990). Syllabus design for the general class: What happens to theory when you apply it. *ELT Journal 44* (4), 261–269.

Griffiths, R. and Sheen, R. (1992). Disembedded figures in the landscape: A reappraisal of L2 research on field dependence/independence. *Applied Linguistics 13*, 133–148.

Griggs, S. A. (1982). Counseling middle school students for their individual learning styles. In J. Keefe, Ed., *Student Learning Styles and Brain Behavior: Programs, Instrumentation, Research* (pp. 63–64). Reston, VA: National Association of Secondary School Principals.

Griggs, S. A. (1991). *Learning Styles Counseling*. Washington, DC: ERIC Clearinghouse on Counseling and Personnel Services.

Griggs, S. A. and Dunn, R. (1984). Selected case studies of the learning style preferences of gifted students. *Gifted Child Quarterly 28* (3), 115–119.

Guild, P. (1994). The culture/learning style connection. *Educational Leadership 52*, 16–21.

Guilford, J.P. (1982). Cognitive psychology's ambiguities: Some suggested remedies. *Psychological Review 89*, 48–59.

Hale-Benson, J. (1986). *Black Children: Their Roots, Culture, and Learning Styles*. Baltimore: Johns Hopkins University Press.

Hall, E. and Hall, M. R. (1990). *Understanding Cultural Differences: German, French, and American*. Yarmouth, ME: Intercultural Press.

Hannaford, C. (1995). *Smart Moves: Why Learning Is Not All in Your Head.* Arlington, VA: Great Ocean Publishers.

Hansen, J. and Stansfield, C. (1991). The relationship of field dependent-independent cognitive styles to foreign language achievement. *Language Learning 31* (3) 349–367.

Hansen-Strain, L. (1989). Student and teacher cognitive styles in second language classrooms. In V. Bickley, Ed., *Language Teaching and Learning Styles Within and Across Cultures* (pp. 218–233). Hong Kong: Education Department, Institute of Language in Education.

Harshbarger, B.; Ross, T.; Tafoya, S.; and Via, J. (1986). Dealing with multiple learning styles in the ESL classroom. Symposium presented at the annual international meeting of Teachers of English to Speakers of Other Languages (TESOL), San Francisco (March).

Hartmann, E. (1991). *Boundaries in the Mind: A New Psychology of Personality.* New York: Basic Books.

Hill, A.L. (1978). Savants: Mentally retarded individuals with special skills. In N.R. Ellis, Ed., *International Review of Research in Mental Retardation,* vol. 9. New York: Academic Press.

Hofstede, G. (1986). Cultural differences in teaching and learning. *International Journal of Intercultural Relations 10,* 301–320.

Holt, D. (Ed.). (1993). *Cooperative Learning: A Response to Linguistic and Cultural Diversity.* McHenry, IL: Delta Systems.

Horwitz, E. (1988). The beliefs about language learning of beginning university students. *Modern Language Journal 72* (3), 182–193.

Horwitz, E. K., Horwitz, M. B., and Cope, J. (1986). Foreign language classroom anxiety. *Modern Language Journal 70* (1), 125–132.

Hosenfeld, C. (1977). A preliminary investigation of the reading strategies of successful and nonsuccessful second language learners. *System 5* (2), 11–12.

Jacobs, R. L. S. (1990). Learning styles of Black high, average, and low achievers. *Clearing House 63,* 253–262.

Jensen, G. H. and DiTiberio, J. K. (1984). Personality and individual writing processes. *College Composition and Communication 35,* 285–300.

Jensen, G. H. and DiTiberio, J. K. (1989). *Personality and the Teaching of Composition.* Norwood, NJ: Ablex.

Johnson, W., Johnson, R., and Holubec, E. (1994). *The New Circles of Learning: Cooperation in the Classroom and School.* Alexandria, VA: Association for Supervision and Curriculum Development.

Jones, B.F., Pierce, J., and Hunter, B. (1988). Teaching students to construct graphic representations. *Educational Leadership 46,* 20–25.

Jonnassen, D. H.; Wilson, B. G.; Wang, S.; and Grabinger, R.S. (1993). Constructivist uses of expert systems to support learning. *Journal of Computer-based Instruction 20* (3), 86–94.

Kagan, J., Moss, H., and Siegel, I. (1963). Psychological significance of styles of conceptualization. *Monographs of Society for Research in Child Development 28*, 73–112.

Kagan, S. (1986). Cooperative learning and sociocultural factors in schooling. In *Beyond Language: Social and Cultural Factors in Schooling Language Minority Students.* Los Angeles: Evaluation, Dissemination and Assessment Center, California State University.

Kail, R. and Pellegrino, J. W. (1985). *Human Intelligence: Perspectives and Prospects.* New York: W.H. Freeman and Company.

Keirsey, D. and Bates, M. (1984). *Please Understand Me: Character and Temperament Types.* DelMar, CA: Prometheus Nemesis Book Company.

Keller, E. and Warner, S. T. (1988). *Conversation Gambits.* Hove, UK: Language Teaching Publications.

Keobke, K. (1996). *Writing the Electronic Textbook.* Hong Kong: City University of Hong Kong Press.

Kessler, C. (Ed.). (1992). *Cooperative Language Learning: A Teacher's Resource Book.* Englewood Cliffs, NJ: Prentice Hall Regents.

Kinsella, K. (1995). Understanding and empowering diverse learners in the ESL classroom. In J. Reid, Ed., *Learning Styles in the ESL/EFL Classroom* (pp. 170–194). Boston: Heinle & Heinle.

Kinsella, K. (1996). Designing group work that supports and enhances diverse classroom work styles. *TESOL Journal 6* (1), 24–30.

Kinsella, K. and Sherak, K. (1994). *Making groupwork really work: More than meets the eye.* Pre-conference institute conducted at the Annual CATESOL Conference, San Diego, CA (March).

Kline, Peter. (1988). *The Everyday Genius: Restoring Children's Natural Joy of Learning.* Arlington, VA: Great Ocean Publishers.

Kolb, D. A. (1984). *Experiential Learning.* Englewood Cliffs, NJ: Prentice Hall.

Kolb, D. A. (1985). Learning Style Inventory Booklet.

Krashen, S. (1981). *Second Language Acquisition and Second Language Learning.* Oxford: Pergamon Press.

Kroonenberg, N. (1995). Meeting language learners' sensory-learning-style preferences. In J. Reid, Ed., *Learning Styles in the ESL/EFL Classroom* (pp. 74–86). Boston: Heinle & Heinle.

Kumaravadivelu, B. (1991). Language-learning tasks: Teacher intention and learner interpretation. *ELT Journal 45* (2), 98–107.

Landau, O.; Gutman, H.; Ganor, A.; Nudelman, I.; Rivlin, E.; and Reiss, R. (1992). Post-pepper pain, perforation, and peritonitis. *Journal of the American Medical Association 268* (13), 1686.

Lazear, D. (1991). *Seven Ways of Teaching.* Palatine, IL: IRI/Skylight Training and Publishing.

Lazear, D. (1994). *Seven Ways of Learning*. Tucson, AZ: Zephyr Press.

Lewis, J. (1991). Nursery schools: The transition from home to school. In B. Finkelstein, A. E. Imamura, and J. J. Tobin, Eds., *Transcending Stereotypes: Discovering Japanese Culture and Education* (pp. 81–95). Yarmouth, ME: Intercultural Press.

Logan, R. K. (1995). *The Fifth Language*. Toronto: Stoddart Publishing.

Long, M. and Porter, P. (1985). Group work, interlanguage talk, and second language acquisition. *TESOL Quarterly 19*, 207–228.

MacLean, P. D. (1978). A mind of three minds: Educating the Triune Brain. In *The 1977 Yearbook of the National Society for the Study of Education*. Chicago: University of Chicago Press.

Margulies, N. (1991). *Mapping Inner Space*. Tucson, AZ: Zephyr Press.

Marshall, C. (1991). Teachers' learning styles: How they affect student learning. *The Clearing House 64* (1), 225–226.

Marzano, R.J.; Brandt, R. S.; Hughes, C.S.; Jones, B.F.; Presselsen, B.Z.; and Rankin, S.C. (1988). *Dimensions of Thinking: A Framework for Curriculum and Instruction*. Alexandria, VA: ASCD.

McGroarty, M. (1992). Cooperative learning: The benefits for content-area teaching. In P.A. Richard-Amato and M.A. Snow, Eds., *The Multicultural Classroom: Readings for Content-Area Teachers*. New York: Longman.

Messick, S. (1976). Personality consistencies in cognition and creativity. In S. Messick, Ed., *Individuality in Learning: Implications of Cognitive Styles and Creativity for Human Development* (pp. 4–37). San Francisco: Jossey-Bass.

Miller, G.A. (1983). Varieties of intelligence. Review of H. Gardner's *Frames of Mind*. *New York Times Book Review*, December 25, pg. 5.

Morgan, G. (1989). *Creative Organization Theory: A Resource Book*. Newbury Park, CA: Sage Publications.

Morgan, J. and Rinvolucri, M. (1983). *Once Upon a Time: Using Stories in the Language Classroom*. Cambridge: Cambridge University Press.

Myers, I. B. and McCaulley, M. (1985). *Manual: A Guide to the Development and Use of the Myers-Briggs Type Indicator*. Palo Alto, CA: Consulting Psychologists.

Neely, R. O. and Alm, D. (1992). Meeting individual needs: A learning styles success story. *The Clearing House 66*, 109–113.

Nelson, G.L. (1995). Cultural differences in learning styles. In J. Reid, Ed., *Learning Styles in the ESL/EFL Classroom* (pp. 3–18). Boston: Heinle & Heinle.

Norman, D. A. & Rumelhart, D. E. (Eds.) (1975). *Explorations in Cognition*. San Francisco: W. H. Freeman and Co.

Nunan, D. (1989). *Understanding Language Classrooms*. Englewood Cliffs, NJ: Prentice-Hall.

Nunan, D. (1990). The questions teachers ask. *JALT Journal 12* (2), 187–202.

Nunan, D. (1994). *The Learner Centred Curriculum*. Melbourne: Cambridge University Press.

Nunan, D. (1995). *Learning Matters*. Hong Kong: The English Centre, University of Hong Kong.

Nunan, D. (1996). Learner strategy training in the classroom: An action research study. *TESOL Journal 6* (1), 35–41.

O'Brien, L. (1989). Learning styles: Make the student aware. *National Association of Secondary School Principals' Bulletin 73*, 85–89.

O'Malley, J. M. and Chamot, A. U. (1990). *Learning Strategies in Second Language Acquisition*. Cambridge: Cambridge University Press.

O'Neil, H. F., Jr. (1994). Measurement of teamwork processes using computer simulation. Los Angeles: National Center for Research on Evaluation Standards and Student Testing. ERIC Research Report, EDRS Number ED 381 578.

Ornstein, R. and Thompson, R.F. (1984). *The Amazing Brain*. Boston: Houghton–Mifflin.

Oxford, R. (1989). Strategy Inventory for Language Learning (SILL). In R. Oxford, *Language Learning Strategies: What Every Teacher Should Know* (pp. 293–300). Boston: Heinle & Heinle.

Oxford, R. (1990a). *Language Learning Strategies: What Every Teacher Should Know*. Boston: Heinle & Heinle.

Oxford, R. (1990b). Styles, strategies, and aptitude: Connections for language learning. In T. S. Parry and C. W. Stansfield, Eds., *Language Aptitude Reconsidered* (pp. 67–125). Englewood Cliffs, NJ: Prentice Hall.

Oxford, R. (1992). Who are our students?: Synthesis of foreign and second language research on individual differences with implications for instructional practice. *TESL Canada Journal/Revue TESL du Canada 9* (2), 30–48.

Oxford, R. (1993). *Style Analysis Survey (SAS)*. Tuscaloosa, AL: University of Alabama.

Oxford, R. (1995). Gender differences in language learning styles: What do they mean? In J. Reid, Ed., *Learning Styles in the ESL/EFL Classroom* (pp. 34–46). Boston: Heinle & Heinle.

Oxford, R. (1996). *Language Learning Strategies Around the World: Crosscultural Perspectives*. Manoa: University of Hawaii Press.

Oxford, R. and Erhman, M. E. (1995). Adults' language learning strategies in an intensive foreign language program in the United States. *System 23* (3), 359–386.

Oxford, R. and Green, J. M. (1996). Language learning histories: Learners and teachers helping each other understand learning styles and strategies. *TESOL Journal 6* (1), 22–24.

Oxford, R., Ehrman, M. E., and Lavine, R. Z. (1991). Style wars: Teacher-student style conflicts in the language classroom. In S. Magnan, Ed., *Challenges in the 1990s for College Foreign Language Programs* (pp. 1–25). Boston: Heinle & Heinle.

Oxford, R., Holloway, M.E., and Horton-Murillo, D. (1992). Language learning styles: Research and practical considerations for teaching in the multi-century tertiary ESL/EFL classroom. *System 20,* 439–456.

Papert, S. (1980). *The Children's Machine.* New York: HarperCollins.

Park, C. C. (1995). Teaching Korean-American students in U.S. public schools. In *Educating Americans in a Multiethnic Society.* New York: McGraw-Hill.

Peak, L. (1991). Training learning skills and attitudes in Japanese early education settings. In B. Finkelstein, A. E. Imamura, and J. J. Tobin, Eds., *Transcending Stereotypes: Discovering Japanese Culture and Education* (pp. 96–108). Yarmouth, ME: Intercultural Press.

Piaget, J. (1926). *The Language and Thought of the Child.* London: Kegan Paul.

Piaget, J. (1950). *The Psychology of Intelligence.* New York: International Universities Press.

Piaget, J. (1952). *The Origins of Intelligence in Children.* New York: International Universities Press.

Pica, T. (1987). Second-language acquisition, social interaction, and the classroom. *Applied Linguistics 8,* 3–21.

Pica, T. and Doughty, C. (1985). The role of group work in classroom second language acquisition. *Studies in Second Language Acquisition 7,* 233–248.

Pica, T., Young, R., and Doughty, C. (1987). The impact of interaction on comprehension. *TESOL Quarterly 21,* 737–758.

Pressley, M.; John, C.; Symons, S.; McGoldrick, J.; and Kurita, J. (1989). Strategies that improve children's memory and comprehension of text. *Elementary School Journal 90* (1), 3–32.

Provost, J. and Anchors, S. (1987). *Applications of the Myers-Briggs Type Indicator in Higher Education.* Gainesville, FL: Consulting Psychologists Press.

Ramasamy, R. (1996). Cultural implications of Navajo students' learning styles and effective teaching methods. *Journal of Educational Issues of Language Minority Students 17,* 139–152.

Ramírez, M., III and Castañeda, A. (1974). *Cultural Democracy: Bicognitive Development and Education.* New York: Academic Press.

Reed, S. K. (1992). *Cognition: Theory and Applications,* 3rd Ed. Pacific Groves, CA: Brooks/Cole.

Reid, J. (1987). The perceptual learning style preferences of ESL students. *TESOL Quarterly 21* (1), 87–111.

Reid, J. (1993). *Teaching ESL Writing.* Englewood Cliffs, NJ: Prentice Hall Regents.

Reid, J. (1995a). Perceptual Learning Style Preference Survey. In J. Reid, Ed., *Learning Styles in the ESL/EFL Classroom* (pp. 202–204). Boston: Heinle & Heinle.

Reid, J. (1995b). Preface. In J. Reid, Ed., *Learning Styles in the ESL/EFL Classroom* (pp. ix–xvii). Boston: Heinle & Heinle.

Reid, J. (Ed.). (1995c). *Learning Styles in the ESL/EFL Classroom*. Boston: Heinle & Heinle.

Reid, J. (1996). A learning styles unit for the intermediate ESL/EFL writing classroom. *TESOL Journal 6* (1), 42–47.

Richards, J. (1996). Teachers' maxims in language teaching. *TESOL Quarterly 30* (2), 281–296.

Richards, J. and Lockhart, C. (1994). *Reflective Teaching in Second Language Classrooms*. Cambridge: Cambridge University Press.

Rossi-Le, L. (1995). Learning styles and strategies in adult immigrant ESL students. In J. Reid, Ed., *Learning Styles in the ESL/EFL Classroom* (pp. 118–125). Boston: Heinle & Heinle.

Rubin, J. and Thompson, I. (1983). *How to Be a More Successful Language Learner*. Boston: Heinle & Heinle.

Russell, P. (1979). *The Brain Book*. New York: E. P. Dutton.

Sauer, C. *Multiple Intelligences*. [On-line] (1996). Available URL: http://oak.cats.ohiou.edu/~cs882288.

Schroeder, C. (1993). New students and learning styles. *Change* (September/October): 21–26.

Scott, M. R. (1990). Demystifying the Jabberwocky: A research narrative. Unpublished doctoral thesis, Department of Linguistics and Modern English Language, University of Lancaster.

Seaton, W. J. (1993). Computer-mediated communication and students' self-directed learning. *Open Learning 8* (2), 49–54.

Shade, B. (Ed.). (1989). *Culture, Style, and the Educative Process*. Springfield, IL: Charles Thomas Pub. Ltd.

Sheen, R. (1993). A rebuttal to Chapelle's response to Griffiths and Sheen. *Applied Linguistics 14* (1), 98–100.

Shuter-Dyson, R. (1982). Musical ability. In D. Deutsch, Ed., *The Psychology of Music*. New York: Academic Press.

Silvester, R. A. (1995). *A Celebration of Neurons: An Educator's Guide to the Human Brain*. Alexandria, VA: Association of Supervision and Curriculum Development.

Sims, R.S. and Sims, S. J. (Eds.). (1995). *The Importance of Learning Styles: Understanding the Implications for Learning, Course Design, and Education*. Westport, CT: Greenwood Press.

Smalley, R.L. and Hank, M.R. (1992). College teachers. In A. K. Koshi, Ed., *Discoveries: Reading, Thinking, Writing* (pp. 125–127). Boston: Heinle & Heinle.

Smith, L. H. and and Renzuli, J. S. (1984). Learning style preferences: A practical approach for classroom teachers. *Theory into Practice 23* (1), 44–50.

Smith, S. L. (1986). The cognitive learning styles of international students. Unpublished Master's thesis, Portland State University.

Sparks, R. L. and Ganchow, L. (1995). A strong inference approach to causal factors in foreign language learning: A response to MacIntyre. *Modern Language Journal 79*, 235–244.

Stansfield, C. and Hansen, J. (1983). Field dependence-independence as a variable in second language cloze test performance. *TESOL Quarterly 17*, 29–38.

Sternberg, R. J. (1977). *Intelligence, Information Processing and Analogical Reasoning.* Hillsdale, NJ: Lawrence Erlbaum Associates.

Sternberg, R. J. (1984). Toward a triarchic theory of human intelligence. *Behavioral and Brain Sciences 7*, 269–287.

Swisher, K. and Deyhle, D. (1987). Styles of learning and learning of styles: Educational conflicts for American/Alaskan native youth. *Journal of Multilingual and Multicultural Development 8*, 345–360.

Tang, G. M. (1992/1993). Teaching content knowledge and ESOL in multicultural classrooms. *TESOL Journal* (Winter), 8–12.

Tudor, I. (1993). Teacher roles in the learner-centered classroom. *ELT Journal 47* (1), 22–31.

Turkle, S. (1995). *Life on the Screen: Identity in the Age of the Internet.* New York: Simon & Schuster.

Tyacke, M. (1996). Exploring cognitive diversity in language teaching and testing: A three-phase investigation of the relationships between learning style, learner behaviour and reading task performance. Unpublished doctoral thesis, Department of Linguistics and Modern Languages, University of Lancaster.

van Dijk, T. A. and Kintsch, W. (1983). *Strategies of Discourse Comprehension.* New York: Academic Press.

Vann, R. and Abraham, R. (1990). Strategies of unsuccessful language learners. *TESOL Quarterly 24*, 177–192.

Vincent, S. (1990). Motivating the advanced learner in developing writing skills: A Project. *ELT Journal 44* (4), 272–278.

Violand-Sánchez, E. (1995). Cognitive and learning styles of high school students: Implications for ESL curriculum development. In J. Reid, Ed., *Learning Styles in the ESL/EFL Classroom* (pp. 48–62). Boston: Heinle & Heinle.

Violand, E. and Esterman, M. (forthcoming). Learning styles, multiple intelligences, and a learner-friendly environment in the ESL classroom. In B. Bliss, *Side by Side Management System for Classmates.* Englewood Cliffs, NJ: Prentice Hall Regents.

Von Daeniken, E. (1972). *Chariots of the Gods.* New York: Bantam.

Vos Savant, M. (1996). Ask Marilyn. *Parade.* May 21, p. 20.

Wallace, B. and Oxford, R. (1992). Disparity in learning styles and teaching styles in the ESL classroom: Does this mean war? *AMTESOL Journal 1*, 45–68.

Walters, J. and Gardner, H. (1986). The crystallizing experience: Discovery of an intellectual gift. In R. Sternberg and J. Davidson, Eds., *Conception of Giftedness* (pp. 342–377). New York: Cambridge University Press.

Wegerif, R. (1996). Collaborative learning and directive software. *Journal of Computer Assisted Learning 12*, 22–32.

Whitin, P.E. (1996). Exploring visual responses to literature. *Research in the Teaching of English 30* (1), 114–140.

Wild, M. (1996). Mental models and computer modeling. *Journal of Computer Assisted Learning 12*, 10–21.

Willing, K. (1988). *Learning Styles in Adult Migration Education*. Adelaide, Australia: National Curriculum Resource Centre.

Wink, J. and Towell, J. (1993). Teacher research in a linguistically diverse classroom. *ERIC/CLL News Bulletin 17* (19), 6–7.

Witkin, H. A. (1969). *Embedded Figures Test*. Palo Alto, CA: Consulting Psychologists Press.

Witkin, H. A. and Goodenough, D. R. (1981). *Cognitive Styles: Essence and Origins: Field Dependence and Field Independence*. New York: International Universities.

Witkin, H. and Moore, C. (1975). *Field-Dependent and Field-Independent Cognitive Styles and Their Educational Implications*. Princeton, NJ: Educational Testing Service.

Witkin, H.; Moore, C.; Goodenough, D.; and Cox, P. (1977). Field dependent and field independent cognitive styles and their educational implications. *Review of Education Research 47*, 1–64.

Witkin, H.A.; Oltman, P.K.; Raskin, E.; and Karp, S.A. (1971). Manual: Embedded Figures Test. Palo Alto, CA: Consulting Psychologists Press.

Wolfe, P. (1996). *Translating Brain Research into Classroom Practice*. Alexandria, VA: Satellite Broadcast, Session 1 (January 11). Available through ASCD Satellite Broadcast, Association of Supervision and Curriculum Development, Alexandria, VA.